Haunted Liverpool 25

Tom Slemen

The Tom Slemen Press

Copyright © 2013 Tom Slemen

All rights reserved.

ISBN-10: 1500172448
ISBN-13: **978- 1500172442**

DEDICATION

For
Tim Farnworth
A very patient man.

CONTENTS

Introduction	1
The Ultraterrestrials	6
Strange Mannequins	17
True Faith	24
The Hand	31
Love and Teleportation	45
Sefton's Haunted Punchbowl Hotel	49
Anfield Apparitions	54
A Cult of Bloodlust?	73
Paradise Found	90
A Crisis Apparition	98
Whispering Jack	101
The Sheil Road Ghost	104

One Lucky Child	108
A Woolton Succubus	113
The Devil's Tip	127
The Necromancers	134
Back to the Eighties	149
Garston Ghosts	157
Coming Through the Rye	179
Haunted People	190
The Karma Gang Mystery	206
Strange Warnings	210
Liverpool Ley Lines	221
John Goodwill of Huyton	230
Brought to Book	236
Gateacre's Ghostly Coach	242
More Shadow Entities	248
The Hanging Brides and Grooms	258
The Amnesiac	267

Not Yet	275
The Great Morse Code Mystery	279
Speke's Spectres	283
Timeslips Galore	306
Will Proudlove	323
Love Beyond Death	328
Broomsticks Over Birkenhead	334
The Body in the Oven	340
Who's Been Down Your Ear?	343
Mum in the Mirror	347
Looking Glass Alice	350
A Real Zombie Plague	354
Patriotic Ghosts	370
The Wheel of Death	378

INTRODUCTION

A few years ago I was holding a vigil at a bus station where the suspected ghost of a former bus driver had been seen turning up for work, the day after his cremation. I unfortunately witnessed no paranormal activity (although typically, the ghost became active again once I had gone) but I did get talking to a certain bus engineer, and he told me a fascinating story about his brother-in-law which I subsequently checked out, and found to be pretty accurate. The story is as follows. On the afternoon of Monday 8 December 1980, a 39-year-old cabby named Mike dropped off a mother and child on Whitechapel. He refused the sizeable tip from the mum, as she reminded him of his wife, Heidi, who was seriously ill in Clatterbridge Hospital. Mike glanced in the window of the white goods store Rumbelows and noticed that the programme *Pebble Mill At One* was just starting on the screen of one of the store's display TVs, and that meant it was lunchtime already, so he went to Brian's, a café on nearby Stanley Street. At the café Mike studied the racing page of the newspaper and picked a few horses running in the Nottingham programme, and as he did this, he happened to look up to see a mugger, aged about 22, trying to wrench a handbag from a young lady. Mike hared it out of the café and laid into the mugger, delivering an upper-cut, followed by a blow to the cowardly thief's solar plexus. The mugger fell to his knees and dropped the handbag, and the shocked lady held her hands to her mouth in horror as Mike took a step back, intending to kick the mugger in the face – but suddenly a huge shaven-headed man appeared on the scene and threw his long muscular tattooed arms around Mike, who was literally foaming at the mouth like a man possessed.

'Stop it Mike!' yelled the man, named Terry – a fellow cabby - and as Mike swore and shouted: 'Let me kill him! Let me have the bastard!' the mugger got to his feet and ran off in terror.

'Go on, love, I'll deal with this,' Terry said, nodding to the wide-eyed woman, who picked up her handbag and backed away. Terry lifted Mike up and carried him to the doorway of the café and threw him inside the place. 'You're going worse, you are, Charles Bronson!' Terry bawled at his colleague. Ever since Mike's wife Heidi had been hospitalised, Mike had gone out looking for trouble, and had recently told Terry and a few other taxi drivers he couldn't care less if he lived or died now that his wife was dying. Mike had a coffee and a smoke and when Terry thought he had calmed down, the loose cannon cabby was back on the streets, trying to curb the cauldron of anger bubbling within him. He rolled the window down at the lights on London Road, and a workman's pneumatic drill startled him. The acoustic pollution of the city centre closed in on him, and he began blasting his horn at the old driver in front. 'Green!' he screamed, 'Go! Go! Green!' but the driver had stalled - and the lights cycled back to red. A policeman stormed over and cautioned Mike about his language. 'Any more of that foul language from you and I'll nick you, mate! Now keep your vile trap shut!' the copper berated the inflamed cab-driver, who mouthed an f-word back at the lawman.

Mike went home but couldn't sleep, because a group of teenagers three doors down were having a party, and a few of the songs they were blasting out on the record player happened to be favourites of Heidi, and Mike's heart was breaking in two. And so he got up out of bed with bags under his eyes and a ringing in his ears (which he always got when he was deprived of sleep) and he ended up driving round till nearly 6am – when something life-changing took place. As he drove up Menlove Avenue, he swore loudly with shock when he suddenly noticed someone sitting behind him; a very familiar person it was too; the white suit, long hair and wire-frame NHS specs – the very double of John Lennon.

'Your wife will be alright, man,' he said in his distinctive Scouse accent. 'Stop being so damn angry, okay? I was like that once. Peace.'

And he vanished in an instant.

Mike pulled over, turned around, and looked at the space where the Beatle had sat. 'Mike,' he said to his eyes reflected in the rear-view mirror, 'you are definitely losing it, lad.' And he knew he had not seen that ghost because of some lack of sleep or because he was in such an unstable and suicidal state because of his wife's terminal condition. Mike knew he had seen a real ghost, but could not understand why.

He drove to an all-night café, ready to tell a lone cabby what had just happened but before he could even find a way to phrase the words, that cabby said: 'Hey Mike, have you heard the news? Some nut has shot John Lennon in New York. He's dead.'

Mike felt dizzy. He said nothing about his experience. He felt very confused and a sense of nausea came over him. He went home and lay on his bed, and a strange sense of peace came over him, and somehow, he fell fast asleep. Several days later there was a call from the hospital. A doctor wanted to have a word with Mike – not over the phone though – but in person. Mike thought the worst: that Heidi had died, and he got in his cab and cried like a baby. He eventually told another cabby what had happened and this driver said, 'Mike, you don't know for sure what they're going to tell you, it could be good news mate.'

Mike swore at him but then apologised. The cabby said, 'Come on lad, I'll take you over, you're in no fit state to drive.'

And so the cabby took Mike over to Clatterbridge Hospital, where a doctor told him some very unexpected news. That Heidi, for some unaccountable reason, had started to make a recovery. It was too soon to say how things would turn out, but she was apparently getting better, and within almost six months, Heidi made a complete miraculous recovery. She's still alive today.

That day when Mike received the good news, he recalled what the ghost of the former Beatle had promised him in his cab, and he also later learned that the ghost of John Lennon had appeared in his cab as he passed Lennon's old home at 251 Menlove Avenue, and Mike left a bunch of roses there at the gate of the house with a little note on saying, 'Thankyou John, rest in peace mate.'

When John Lennon's beloved mother Julia was knocked down by a speeding off-duty policeman on Menlove Avenue on 15 July 1958, the teenaged Lennon was left so shattered, he turned to heavy drinking and deliberately picked fights with anyone just to vent his anger at losing his mum. Eventually John came to terms with the loss but it took a long time. Perhaps there is some twisted joker up there because the man who mowed down Julia subsequently left the police force to become a postman, and, believe it or not, in the early days of Beatlemania he used to deliver fan mail to Paul McCartney's house on Forthlin Road…

Tom Slemen
Liverpool

THE ULTRATERRESTRIALS

Lurking just beyond the edge of our known world, just outside the rim of our everyday experience, there are denizens of the downright strange; beings, forms, phantasms that are probably better left unseen, and over the centuries, I believe these entities have been interpreted as aliens, angels, demons, doppelgängers, djinn, apparitions of the Devil, and visions of the dearly departed, and here are just a few local incidents concerning these "ultraterrestrials" as I personally call them.

In the late 1990s during a wintry January lunchtime, four people – a lady in her thirties, a youth of eighteen, a man of about forty, and a man in his sixties, entered the Littlewoods store on Church Street. The youth, David, normally used the escalator but decided to take the elevator because he was on crutches with a foot set in a plaster cast. The four looked at the floor and averted their gaze from one another as the elevator climbed, when suddenly there was a jolt – and the lift came to a halt. David muttered a complaint and 32-year-old Karen leaned past him and repeatedly stabbed the second-floor button – but the lift refused to budge. Karen was already late for work, she explained to the three males, and a man in his sixties named Ray, advised her to press the alarm button. Karen did and a faint but somewhat reassuring electric bell sounded. A man in a blue, well-cut suit, white shirt and black tie, began to make wheezing sounds, as if he was hyperventilating, and he clutched at his throat and made abhorrent attempts to cough up phlegm. 'I've got to get out of here! Get me out!' he yelled. He pushed David out the way and tried to open the door, prising at the vertical groove with his fingertips, but it was no use. He staggered backwards – and grabbed at his face – and muttered: 'Bastard…come on!' And suddenly the man's face began to change before the eyes of the three other passengers in that lift. Karen backed into a corner of the elevator with a look of horror, and David swore and lifted one of his crutches up in a defensive gesture, while Ray looked on with a mixture of trepidation and fascination – he didn't scare easily, having served in the King's Regiment in his younger days.

The man shrieked and his face began to develop patches of a greenish and purple colour, and his eyes bulged. David turned away from the surreal, terrifying metamorphosis and frantically pressed the alarm button again, and a few moments later a female voice crackled from the intercom speaker of a grille below the elevator buttons. 'Someone's on their way,' she said twice, then added in a mock cheerful voice: 'We'll have you out of there soon! Don't worry.'

Karen held her hands over her ears as the stranger with the morphing face emitted a deafening howl, and by now his head looked longer, his forehead had noticeably protruded, and he had hunched over. His hands rested on the floor of the elevator, and he made choking sounds. Throughout this phase of the nightmare there was a strong aroma of ammonia present in the lift. When the 'thing' looked up, its face was grinning, and had changed completely, looking now like some grotesque multicoloured reflection in a distorted fairground mirror. The face now bore no resemblance whatsoever to the face of the unknown man who had suffered a panic attack moments ago, and the face did not look human.

In a classical example of what is known in psychology as a 'fight or flight reaction', David, feeling cornered, panicked and struck the monster on the head with a crutch, and it fell on the floor, shrieking with laughter as Karen screamed and got behind Ray. David tried to press the rubber tip of the crutch against the neck of the bizarre-looking humanoid, but the creature wouldn't stop moving, and David kept making stabbing movements with the crutch but kept missing. Then the lift jolted, stopped again, then continued, and the lights went out for a heart-stopping moment, and Karen recalls a clammy cold hand grasping at her knee for a few seconds, but when the lights came on again, the door of the elevator grated open – revealing that the lift had stopped about five feet short of the second floor. With amazing agility the weird unearthly man leapt upwards and fled through the two-foot tall opening, startling the rescuers kneeling outside on the upper floor. He ran on all fours, laughing like a hyena through screaming shoppers and he fell and rolled down a flight of stairs, then left the store via the Church Alley door. Karen later called me at Radio Merseyside to tell me of her strange encounter, and the two other lift passengers also got in touch to confirm the weird but unexplained incident. Just who or what that entity was which underwent a physical change like a real life Dr Jekyll, is anybody's guess, but I have heard of similar occurrences before.

Back in the blistering summer of 1982, a 21-year-old Liverpool University student named Will went into the Midland Hotel public house on Ranelagh Street to slake his thirst with a lager or two, and he met the girl of his dreams. She was an absolutely beautiful and petite 19-year-old blonde named Gemma, and she was deep in conversation as she sat at a table with her stunning red-headed friend Hannah, who was also 19. Gemma had a camera slung over her shoulder, and Will could plainly see it was not your usual Kodak Instamatic; it was bigger than a standard camera of that type, and being intrigued by this unusual piece of hardware, he listened in to the conversation between the very attractive girls. He soon discovered that that old proverb about appearances being deceptive was quite true, for there was obviously more to these girls than pretty faces. The attractive teens were discussing polarising filters, Kerr cells, and the quadratic electro-optic effect. Will, who was studying organic chemistry at the university's Robert Robinson Laboratories on Oxford Street, was greatly impressed by the techno-speak, and he smiled at Gemma and Hannah, and enquired about the oversized camera. Gemma said it was a 'home-made kind of rapatronic' model – for taking high-speed pictures with exposures as brief as nanoseconds and milliseconds, and it was loaded with Polaroid instant film. 'Ah, I see,' Will nodded, and then Gemma told him she and Hannah were 'accidental ghost-hunters' and to Will's puzzled reaction Gemma explained that she and Hannah had made an intriguing discovery. They'd been taking high-speed photographs of Liverpool street life for their photography course at Mabel Fletcher Technical College, and in one picture, which showed pigeons frozen in mid-air during take-off in Williamson Square, a weird man in a strange black tight-fitting costume could be seen in the centre of the scene, even though Gemma and Hannah had not seen anyone in the square when the shot was taken. Gemma showed Will this photo and because of its sharp pinpoint focus he could clearly see the peculiar man in some sort of black balaclava and one-piece black tight-fitting suit – reminiscent of the wet suits worn by divers and canoeists. 'There are more of them,' Gemma handed Will several 8 by 10-inch photographs of Church Street, and amongst the people frozen in the millisecond-instant snaps, three of the mysterious and oddly-attired men in black could be plainly seen, each of them gazing close-up at passers-by who were obviously unaware of the eerie figures scrutinising them. In one photograph, taken by Hannah, one of these sinister observers is looking at Gemma so closely, his long pointed nose is almost touching her face. Will could see that the uncanny spectator had a Vandyke beard and moustache, and creepy bulging eyes. 'I can assure you this is no hoax, either,' Hannah told Will, and within days, Will tried out the high-speed camera for himself, and managed to capture the image of one of the baffling scrutinizers gazing into a woman's face outside Greenwoods store on the corner of Whitechapel and Church Street.

'Who the hell are they?' Will mused out loud, 'They've got to be moving at a phenomenal speed – too fast for the human eye to register.'

'Yes, definitely quicker than the eye,' Hannah concurred, 'but how? It's scientifically impossible to move so fast.'

'Its like the blades of a fan, or a bullet for that matter,' Will hypothesised, 'pieces of plastic or metal that are clearly opaque, but when they move at a certain velocity, the eye can't follow them and our vision just gives up.'

'They could be around us right now, watching and eavesdropping on us,' Gemma added, looking around at the myriad shoppers on Church Street.

Will had an idea. He had the photograph featuring the unseen trio enlarged and printed and he blu-tacked it to a wall on Church Street to see if the 'watchers' reacted to it. That poster vanished into thin air, minutes after it went up, and after that, the unearthly spies were never captured by Gemma's camera again. Gemma later turned her ultra-high-speed camera to the skies of the North West and captured some very odd objects that cannot be perceived by normal human vision. These aerial anomalies included globes of light, discs, cigars and cone-shaped craft of some sort. Birds and flying insects were ruled out. A few years ago the so-called "Rod phenomenon" was reported across the globe and it caused quite a controversy which still hasn't died down. A number of people claimed they had captured some unidentified life-form flying around the skies which resembled a rod with spiralling wings of some sort. Videos of these rods can still be seen on the world-wide web, and while some sceptics have stated that the rods are just winged insects and faults within the video cameras that film them, just as many believe the rods are truly an unknown phenomenon. Unknown airborne creatures are one thing to contend with, but what are we to make of the weird trio of figures in tight-fitting black costumes photographed by a student's high-speed camera? Could there be invisible beings prowling about as you read these worlds? On 23 May 1964, an off-duty Carlisle fireman named Jim Templeton took three photographs of his five-year-old daughter Elizabeth as she crouched on the grass holding a posy of flowers. The backdrop to this photograph was Burgh Marsh, overlooking Solway Firth. Besides little Elizabeth Templeton and her father and mother, the only other people in the remote but picturesque area where the photographs were taken were two old ladies sitting in a car at the far end of the marsh, and yet, when the photographs Jim Templeton took were subsequently developed at the chemist, the middle one showed a sinister humanoid figure in white, just visible over the right side of Elizabeth's head. The figure looked as if it had been within about twenty feet of Elizabeth when the child's picture was taken. Jim Templeton was naturally baffled by the presence of this figure, because he and his wife saw no one else on the marshes while the photographs were being taken, and so Jim submitted the photograph to be analysed by photographic experts to see if there had been some fault in the film. No such fault was found with the film and a similar thorough examination of Jim's camera – a Zeiss Contax Pentacon SLR model – also established that there was no mechanical fault in the camera to account for the figure which the Press later dubbed "The Solway Spaceman". If you have never seen this figure, I advise you to Google it and see it for yourself. There have been half-baked suggestions that the figure is Jim's wife, but she was behind her husband when the pictures were taken and the figure seems to be wearing some sort of headgear, and Mrs Templeton was not wearing a hat that day.

The mystery deepened when Jim Templeton was later visited by two shady "Men-in-Black" type of characters who claimed to be working for the Government. They identified themselves as "9" and "11" and asked Jim to recall just what he had seen on Burgh Marsh that day when he unwittingly captured the figure in white. Jim said he had seen no one, and had not noticed the figure until he saw it on one of the three photographs of his daughter, but the mysterious duo took the fireman to Burgh Marsh, where they asked him again to give an account of what he had seen. When Jim insisted he had seen no one, the two men became irritated, stormed off to their vehicle, and left Jim to make his own way home.

A few years ago I gave a talk on the supernatural at a library in Liverpool, and afterwards a soldier approached me and said that his younger brother, who was currently serving in Afghanistan, had told him a very strange story during his leave. The alleged incident happened in the notorious Helmand Province in the south of Afghanistan in the hellish summer of 2009 – during Operation Panther's Claw – a British-led five-week-long military offensive against Taliban insurgents. The operation to secure an area of land the size of the Isle of Wight was a success, and it involved the legendary Black Watch, the Welsh Guards, the Danish Battle Group, the Mercian Regiment, the Light Dragoons, and of course, the Afghan National Army. According to the soldier I met that day in the library, he said that as his brother was taking time out to rest with the other troops during the offensive, he and a few others saw something very strange. A sandstorm had blown up and reduced the visibility to about thirty feet, and a figure of a semi-transparent soldier – apparently an American marine, judging by his battledress, came out of the clouds of sand. He was see-through except for his helmet and his legs below his knees. He looked at the dumbfounded battle-weary British soldiers, then vanished completely. This same "invisible soldier" was seen days later when a Chinook supply chopper landed and kicked up a man-made sandstorm during its descent. A figure materialised in the midst of the clouds of sand, and this time, when one of the British soldiers pointed at the eerie figure and drew the attention of the troops to it, the partially-visible figure put a gloved hand to its face and placed its index finger to its mouth, as if to gesture to the alarmed soldier to say nothing – and then the American combatant vanished into thin air. Combat boot prints of the type made by footwear worn by US troops were found at the spot where the vanishing soldier had stood. When the Scottish mathematical physicist James Clerk Maxwell formulated the equations which revealed the secret workings of light in 1861, the road to practical invisibility was opened up, although most scientists of the 19th century (and some in the 20th century too with the exception of

Einstein) were not aware of the full significance of Maxwell's findings, namely that light, being an electromagnetic wave, could be manipulated and bent by magnetic fields. Stealth technology, by which the military can make warplanes almost invisible to radar beams, was only achieved through an understanding of the behaviour of electromagnetic waves and a manipulation of Maxwell's equations, and now it seems as if the race is on to make objects invisible in the visible-light range. In recent times a range of exotic artificially-created substances known as metamaterials are providing scientists with ingenious ways to make objects invisible. Metamaterials violate the laws of optics and the first of these materials made objects invisible to microwave radiation, but now we have metamaterials that have a cell-sized matrix which makes up their unique structure, and this matrix, created by nanotechnology, consists of gaps that are smaller than the wavelength of the light they are designed to manipulate. Metamaterials have been used as a type of invisibility cloaking device, and they were first developed at Duke University, Virginia, and also at London's Imperial College. DARPA, the Pentagon's Defence Advanced Research Projects Agency, funded the research into this invisibility technology, and for an obvious reason too – because the nation which develops invisibility will have an enormous military advantage over the rest of the world; invisible intercontinental ballistic missiles could bypass radar and destroy cities without any threat of immediate retaliation, and invisible planes, tanks, battleships, nuclear subs and soldiers would naturally wreak havoc against any nation with a traditional programme of defence. Its possible that the 'invisible soldier' seen in the Helmand Province was a Marine trying out some sort of stealth-suit technology involving metamaterials or perhaps an electronic form of active camouflage, whereby tiny electronic cameras embedded in the soldier's body armour feed the image of the scene behind him onto LCD-type of pixel-size cells on the front of his suit, creating a sort of pseudo invisibility, or "illusory transparency" as scientists call the effect. Electronics enthusiasts have actually made crude but fairly effective versions of these suits using webcam imaging chips and interlocking LCD screens. The military are, by their very nature, highly secretive about their research into invisibility, so no one knows just how far they have progressed, but I can imagine their hardware will generate a lot of ghost sightings in the near future if the technology is tested out in the civilian sector. Such an electronic cloak of invisibility would also provide the law enforcement agencies with a real headache if the technology is ever disclosed on something like Wikileaks.

From the realm of the invisible, we move on to something much more sinister and inexplicable in the next chapter – mannequin-like beings.

STRANGE MANNEQUINS

A few rather strange things happened in the year 1960. In March of that year it was reported in newspapers throughout the land that trawler skipper Fred Ireland had caught a "whopper" to end all exaggerated fishing stories: a dead elephant. To this day, no one has explained how the body of an elephant ended up in the net of the fishing trawler *Ampulla* off the coast of Flamborough Head, near Bridlington. Then came the record sightings of the Loch Ness Monster, both on land and in the water up in the Highland Region. Dozens of people saw the possible surviving dinosaur, but as soon as a methodical investigation got into full swing, Nessie disappeared back into her loch. Then a peculiar mystery visited our neck of the woods. Around April 1960, a 32-year-old man named Angus Beard was driving his new Morris Oxford down Mount Pleasant when he saw a woman who seemed to be in her early twenties dash out in front of his car. Mr Beard braked but the bonnet struck the woman and the impact sent her into the path of an oncoming bus facing the Shaftesbury Hotel, near to the Mardi Gras nightclub. Mr Beard then gazed in stunned horror as the woman went under the front wheel of the bus. She lay there, motionless, face up, with the wheel of the double-decker bus on her mid-section. The driver of the bus got out of his vehicle in a frantic state and shouted to bystanders to get a doctor, and a few ran off to a telephone box near Roscoe Gardens to summon an ambulance. 'You hit her and knocked her into me!' the bus driver yelled at Mr Beard, who was still speechless. 'I can't see any blood there, mate,' an elderly man said, and he was kneeling down by the woman's body. 'Reverse the thing off her!' another man advised the traumatised bus driver, and the driver actually got back into the bus to take the dangerous advice. 'Don't! Don't, you'll crush her!' a woman shouted into the bus, but the driver reversed the vehicle off the victim, and then a crowd encircled the body. There wasn't a sign of blood, but some thick milk-white liquid instead, and it was steadily seeping out the mouth of the body onto the road. 'She's not real! It's a bloody dummy!' said the old man kneeling over the "victim", and it seemed as if he was right. Several people touched the woman's wrist and found the skin hard and plastic-like, and one female bystander said the figure in the road looked like a mannequin. The ambulance men were furious when they arrived at the scene, for they soon established that the body was indeed a dummy of the sort used to display clothes in a store window. The face of the mannequin was, however, quite life-like except for the eyes, which seemed lifeless. The head of curly hair seemed to be synthetic, and Mr Beard said it definitely looked like a wig. It was conjectured that students or some irresponsible pranksters had thrown the clothed figure into the path of Mr Beard's car, but nothing could be proved. Twenty years after this, during one afternoon in early April 1980, an identical incident took place at the busy junction of Fazakerley's Longmoor Lane, Copple House Lane, Valley Road and Aintree Lane, only on this occasion several motorists swore that a real living woman had dashed out into the road near the Copplehouse pub, and had been knocked down by a lorry. Traffic came to a standstill, but when the 'body' was examined by medics, it was found to be a clothed and wigged mannequin with 'oddly jointed limbs'. One of the medics saw that some gelatinous substance was coming out of the mouth of the dummy, and when he inspected the mouth, he was surprised to see it was fitted with realistic dentures and a foam tongue. This mannequin was examined further and was found to have a lifelike vagina and anus, and so some wondered if the thing was some life-size sex toy, but there were no stamped serial numbers or any identifying marks on the "doll" and no labels on the clothes it wore – which included underwear. One of the ambulance men who examined the mysterious mannequin later contacted me at Radio Merseyside and told me that he sensed something very sinister about the dummy. Its insides made sounds just like human wind in a real stomach, and the medic was almost sure the breasts of the simulacrum moved faintly up and down at one point. There were strange globes of liquid inside the torso of the glorified shop-window dummy but no recognisable internal organs resembling any found in the human body. Again, pranksters were said to be behind the bizarre mock traffic accident, especially with it being early April, it seemed possible that the whole thing had been some April Fool's stunt, but so many people reported seeing a woman running from the direction of the Copplehouse pub, and the van driver who ran down the dummy even made a statement to the police. How then, can we explain these two incidents? Were the so-called mannequins some sort of aliens walking about disguised as humans? Or were they artificial man-made androids? Robotic technology today is making quantum leaps of progress, and in Japan and the US there are two-legged robots that can dance and run up stairs, but no such technology existed on this earth in 1960 and 1980 which could account for the automated mannequins which unsuccessfully negotiated the crossing of a busy road – unless it was alien technology of course, but we are piling on a lot of ifs and maybes.

In 1997, a former prostitute named Monica called in to Radio Merseyside to tell me of a very strange experience she'd had in 1979 – the year before the report of the mannequin being knocked down on Longmoor Lane. One wintry morning around 1.45am in January 1979, Monica – who was then aged just eighteen – was 'on the game' as she described her occupation, and her procurer had dropped her off on that lonely stretch of Smithdown Road which runs past the eerie expanses of Toxteth Park Cemetery. The pimp drove off and left Monica to linger on the kerbside in a short skirt, calf-length white pvc boots and a flimsy top which she wore under a leather jacket. She took a woollen scarf out of her handbag as soon as the pimp had driven into the distance, and she coiled it around her neck. Around two that morning, a car cruised past Monica and two youths of about 17 or 18 hurled insults at her. They drove up and down the road and so, Monica, fearing the young men might go too far and attack her, decided to walk up Smithdown Road to an area where there were a few people still about at that time in the morning. Sleet began to fall, and around twenty minutes past two, Smithdown Road fell silent and not even a car or taxi passed Monica. She stood by the Number 60 bus stop outside of a Fish and Chip shop that had long closed for the night, and she waited, and waited, for a customer to approach. She stamped her boots and was so cold she actually wanted the police to pick her up and take her into custody, where she would at least be warm. Instead, a Ford Cortina came up Smithdown Road from the eastern end, from the direction of the cemetery, and the car slowed down in the vicinity of the prostitute. Monica walked to the vehicle and saw that the driver had a very peculiar face. He looked handsome, but when Monica leaned forward and spoke to him through the side window, she saw that he was just *too* good-looking – as if he was wearing make-up. She estimated his age as being no more than 25 years of age. He wore a finely-tailored pinstriped suit, a pale blue shirt and a royal blue tie kept in place with a jewelled tiepin. The man's hair was a reddish brown in colour and closely cropped.

'Would you like to do a bit of business, love?' Monica asked automatically, as she'd done so on many previous occasions.

The driver looked at her without an ounce of feeling or emotion in his eyes, and in a flat monotonous-sounding voice he answered: 'Yeah.'

Monica got in the car and asked him where they were going, but the man started to grin. He turned to Monica and started to talk gibberish which she could not understand. He just kept saying random words, and Monica noticed that the sound of his voice did not come from his mouth – but much lower down by his chest, and she found this unnerving. Her left hand felt for the door handle and she tried to open it but found the door locked. The strange young man put his left hand on Monica's knee – and she could see that the hand was not real, but looked plastic and felt ice-cold. She began to scream at the surreal nightmare she found herself in, and all of a sudden, the man seated next to her began to laugh, and like his voice, the laughter did not originate in his mouth or throat, but his lower chest. Monica tried to turn the handle of the door again and again, and then she noticed a horrible burning smell inside the Cortina, and she turned to see smoke rising from the laughing man's chest. Flames ignited from the lapels of the man's jacket as well as his tie, and Monica could feel the heat on her face and legs. She somehow squeezed through the open window in the car door and fell onto the pavement. She got to her feet and saw that the man in the car was now engulfed in flames. She ran off and didn't stop until she reached the Boundary public house at the top of Smithdown Road. By this time another car had come to a halt near to the blazing vehicle and the driver was watching the blaze. Residents in the area must have then called the fire brigade, because within minutes, a fire engine was on the scene, and the Ford Cortina was being hosed by jets of high-pressured water. Monica made her way back to the Number 60 bus stop but a fireman and a policeman told her to stay back. She asked if the man in the car was dead, but the policeman told her there was no one in the car.

Monica saw no one run from that car when it burst into flame, so perhaps we must deduce that the 'man' who caused the blaze burnt with such ferocity, no *human* remains were left – but what was the thing in that car which burned itself to a crisp and, according to Monica, looked and sounded artificial? The entity sounds to me as if it's of the same genus as the life-size dummies encountered in 1960 and 1980. Just what are these things and is there some sinister agenda behind their bizarre activities? Perhaps time will tell.

TRUE FAITH

All of this really happened, many years ago. The place was Walton Prison, stronghold of eleven hundred souls, and one night in one of the cells of the jail, two men, poles apart in every conceivable way, were arguing in subdued voices in the dark. I have to withhold their real names, but we will call them Brian and Tony. Brian was a habitual criminal – a recidivist is the official label of such a person – and at the age of fifty-five he had become so bitter at the world and even at himself. Tony, on the other hand, was in his twenties, and for as long as he could remember, he had strived – in the face of constant temptation – to believe in God, and since his teens he had undertaken an in-depth study of mysticism and the occult. In recent weeks, Tony had obtained a book called *Clairvoyance and Occult Powers* by William Walker Atkinson, and among the arcane lessons found in this mysterious book, Tony found the teachings regarding healing, telepathy and the amplification of willpower the most fascinating. Brian lay on the bottom bunk in the cell with a migraine one night, after all the lights had been switched off, and Tony asked him if he could attempt to cure his agonising vascular headache with his faith-healing technique, but Brian swore at him and said his faith was delusional, and they argued so much that a guard visited the cell and rapped a warning on the door. Brian later let Tony try the laying-on of hands, and the headache stopped after a minute or so. Something bizarre then took place over that week. Hairs began to sprout on the area of Brian's bald pate where Tony had stroked him with his hands, and Brian reported a tingling sensation during the miraculous growth. This regrowth of hair on a scalp that was previously devoid of hair has been noted many times as a side-effect in the healing of headaches with the hands, and while a rational scientist or trichologist would say the hair had sprouted up as a side-effect of increased circulation to dormant follicles through the rubbing of the scalp, the faith healer would say a more divine force was at work. Just after the miracle regrowth, Tony began to recite some sort of mantra over and over as he lay on the top bunk at night, and Brian would tell him to shut up, but Tony then merely whispered the unintelligible sacred utterance. One night Brian awoke in the dark cell to the rich smell of tobacco, an aroma that was immediately evocative of happier times when smoking was not even thought of as a luxury. Tony was smoking a woodbine cigarette on his bunk. Brian got up and watched the orange tip glowing in the darkness, then whispered: 'Where did you get that? It's barley that, smoking and not sharing!'

'I asked and it was given to me by the Higher

Power,' said Tony, cryptic as usual. 'Here, take it,' he said, and he thumbed the wheel of a lighter he had somehow come into possession of. 'I am leaving here now, Brian, and you can come with me if you believe.'

'What do you mean, leaving?' Brian asked, greedily puffing on the ciggy.

'Watch this! It's all in the mind; we can do anything if we believe!' Tony said, and recited that accursed mantra for some time. Just when Brian had had quite enough of the mantra mumbo-jumbo, something resembling a glowing Venetian blind dropped from the ceiling and unfolded into steps as it descended; a staircase that went from the cell floor to the ceiling - and beyond, for at the top of this unearthly staircase, Brian could see what looked like billowing grey clouds where the off-white ceiling would normally be.

Tony stepped on the staircase and lit the way ahead with the lighter as he carefully walked up the flimsy steps. 'Come on!' Tony whispered, and held his friend's hand, but halfway up, Brian became afraid and he swore then said, 'I don't believe it's even there! It *can't* be there!' and the ethereal staircase faded.

Tony became annoyed and almost lost his footing as the mysterious substance the staircase was made of became slightly warped. 'Don't say that, Brian! Just accept its there!'

'I'm not breaking my neck going up that, it's giving way,' Brian took a step backwards and he let go of Tony's hand and then his arms flailed about as he tried to keep his balance. 'We're walking on thin air!' Brian yelled.

The prisoners fell to the floor. Tony looked up and saw the staircase to freedom – wherever that freedom was – fade away into something that resembled cobwebs. Tony picked himself up off the floor and placed his foot on the gossamer step hanging in mid-air, but it was like stepping through smoke. He turned to curse Brian, but could hardly see him in the darkness now that the lighter had vanished along with the stairs.

'This is called dabbling with the Devil's work, this is!' said Brian, getting to his feet. 'God knows what would have happened to us if we had gone up that thing! I'm seeing the prison priest tomorrow, Tony, and I'm telling him about you.'

Tony suddenly threw his fist at his cellmate, but missed and hit the side of the bunk. He yelled in pain, then launched another blind jab, and he felt Brian's teeth graze his knuckle. Then came a muffled expulsion of air from Brian as he hit the wall, then slid down it to the floor.

'You bastard!' Brian groaned, 'I never thought you of all people would do that to me.'

Tony cried and struck Brian again, hitting him in the nose, and he almost knocked him out. Tony was now sobbing like a baby as he groped about for the lighter but he was unable to find it. His belief had gone with that lighter, evaporated into that mortal quagmire of self-doubt. No matter how hard Tony tried to recreate the staircase, it never materialised again after that night.

Can mere belief inside the human mind produce physical effects in the real world? If you really imagine a slice of freshly-cut lemon, and picture it being placed on your tongue, you will probably salivate, and that is just a tiny example of a suggestion from the mind causing a physical process in the real world. A blindfolded person who is told that he or she is about to have their face slit with an icy steel blade of a knife will feel momentary pain or feel the actual blade – even if the "knife" is just an ice-cube. In one of my stories somewhere I recall the true account of the callous medical men who killed a blindfolded condemned man by telling him they were about to siphon off his blood through a tube inserted into his back, and they merely switched on a tap and the victim died of shock, because he imagined the gush of water was his actual life-blood being drawn from a tube inserted into his back. That is the misuse of hypnosis to turn a thought into a physical action, but in recent years, physicists have started to formulate a very alarming theory about reality which will really make your head spin if you read on. In the world of computers, everything – every piece of data or simulation – can be reduced in its most simplest form to a binary digit – a zero (0) or a one (1), so no matter how realistic a computer generated effect might seem or even the most advanced computer game, if you reduce the program or the scenes and pictures in the program to the smallest unit, you will have a binary digit which can be either 0 or 1. Please remember that a 0 or a 1 are a 'bit' and a bit is the smallest unit of information in a computer. Now, in what we call reality, we can also reduce everything down to a smallest unit of information, and this basic unit is known as the qubit – short for quantum bit. The qubit is the smallest piece of information in quantum computing. Now, without boring you by going into the intricacies of Quantum Physics, let me explain my point this way. Let us say, for the sake of argument, that you are merely a character in some computer simulation – a game, like, say, *Grand Theft Auto*. Someone in the game tells you that you and they are merely living in a computer generated world, and this person proves it to you by fetching you a microscope. He tells you to look at your skin under the microscope and you discover that, instead of cells of tissue, you are made up of pixels. A pixel is, as you probably know, a tiny point of light in a digital image, and when you see a picture on your computer or mobile, its made up of these tiny picture elements. So, you discover you are not as real as you thought, but merely made up of tiny pin-points of light – pixel elements in *someone's computer*. Sounds like something out that film, *The Matrix* doesn't it? Well now for the eerie punchline. It turns out that what we call reality – the place where you and I and everyone and everything in the Universe exists – is also digital, but instead of pixels, we are made up of quibits – quantum bits. This discovery has led scientists to consider the intriguing possibility that we are all living in some computer simulation of life – in a holographic universe, and someone or something has programmed all of the constants and variables and equations into the simulation of life. This mysterious programmer has set the speed of light at a certain value, and has done the same with the gravitational constant and so on. So, in other words, you and I are not real in one sense – we are merely a computer simulation, and a simulation can only be run in a mind or a computer (and a vast, almost unimaginable computer). Some scientists who were previously atheists now think that the programmer of the universe simulation may be what we could call God. Two obvious questions are: where is the master programmer and where is his/her supercomputer? Now, if we accept that we are merely sophisticated programs running in this phenomenal computer, we may be able to affect 'reality' – perhaps through sheer will power, and it's a big "if" but if someone inside of a program can affect the 'quantum code' in some way, they'd be able to produce what would seem like 'real' physical – but apparently paranormal - effects – such as the bending of a spoon, or the creation of a staircase in a prison cell and so on. The Holographic Theory of the Universe is slowly gaining ground in the world of physics, and I recommend a book called *The Holographic Universe* by Michael Talbot, an American author who tragically died of leukaemia in 1992, aged just thirty-eight.

THE HAND

In the many years I have spent researching and collecting accounts about the supernatural, certain stories have come my way which I could not easily forget, either because they have dovetailed with similar tales, or simply because the story was very eerie; the following tale stands out in my memory because it's both eerie and fits together with other stories I have researched over the years. Can I explain it, though? No, I must admit defeat on this one, and I suppose that this inability to rationalise the story makes it even more uncanny. I have had to change the names of the people involved in this strange tale for legal reasons, but I have changed nothing else.

It all started – as far as I can tell – back in the autumn of 1966. Liverpool was being visited by one of those ghastly smogs which are thankfully absent nowadays because the smoking chimney is now a rarity. We'd had a sunny October day, and the autumn sun - which had raised a salty mist from Liverpool Bay – was now a dying blood-orange disc, slinking downwards behind the chimney stacks and silhouetted television aerials. Now we had to pay the grim price for that sunny day. The insidious fog rolled into the town from the Mersey like an invading army of seaborne ghosts. There was a strange chill in the air that late afternoon – the type of chill which feels as if it is invading your marrow and your very mind. The sun deserted the streets of Liverpool and left the world slate grey, and despite the lights of the lamp-posts and the car headlights and the little squares of light from the windows of the town, the chill and the fog and carboniferous chimney coal-smoke – together with the mournful echoes of the fog-horns on the river – conspired to dominate our mood. Through the sodden smoggy late afternoon, old Mrs Fisher pushed a pram across Waterloo's Victoria Park. The poor old soul was, as they said in those days, 'not right in the head' and she had been collecting litter and putting it in the pram to sort it all out later in her little ground floor flat at a terraced red-brick house on nearby Lawton Road, a road of about five hundred feet in length, where most people knew their neighbours, but not one of them wanted to know Mrs Fisher, the old lady who hoarded rubbish in her front parlour. She had even brought a dead starling home from the park the other day.

Well, upon this foggy afternoon around 5.45pm, Mrs Fisher was heading towards the gates of the park that lead onto Ferndale Road when two young men bolted past her, and one of the running youths threw something at the old lady which landed in her pram. Before she could see what the object was, three police constables came running through the gates of the park, and the fattest and oldest of the coppers slowed down and between pants and wheezes he asked Mrs Fisher if two 'deadbeats' had passed her, and the old woman got the feeling he was asking the question just for an excuse to stop running while he recovered his breath.

'Yes officer, they went that way, two big fellahs,' Mrs

Fisher pointed backwards with the thumb of her hand and then she tightened the knot of the dark blue polka-dotted headscarf under her chin. 'What have they done, officer?'

The corpulent constable leaned forward, hands on knees, and took a few quick breaths. 'Broke into a widow's house…Thorndale Road…robbed the gas meter and the woman's purse.'

'Give them the birch if you catch them, lad,' Mrs Fisher ground her gums in anger and made a fist with her gnarled arthritic fingers.

The policeman, still gazing down at the park path as he recovered his breath, nodded with his hands gripping his kneecaps, and then he straightened up and walked on into the darkness.

Once she had left the park, Mrs Fisher turned right at the first corner and walked down Lawton Road, absolutely aching to see what the house-robber had thrown into the pram, and as soon as she got into the hallway of her home, the elderly eccentric turned on the dim 40 watt bulb and pushed down the hood of the perambulator.

Amongst the empty crumpled cigarette packets, the screwed-up roses of newspaper pages, shrivelled leaves, discarded bus tickets, sweet wrappers and a withered condom – sat a doll. It was about fifteen inches tall, and had long straight black hair which was either dyed mohair – or real hair. It certainly felt real to Mrs Fisher. The pale moulded porcelain-like face had no colour to it – even the thin lips were white, but the eyes, they were something else; they looked like smoky grey glass marbles with a blob of black oil suspended in their centres, and the eyebrows were mere black arches — semicircles inscribed with not a trace of artistic flourish. The doll therefore looked as if she was eternally shocked at something with her wide-eyed raised-eyebrow expression. The clothes the doll wore were all black; the shawl, the long-sleeved blouse with black velvet-covered buttons, and the knee length skirt, which felt as if it was made of some cheap coarse material. The stockings were painted on the legs in glossy black paint, but the tiny black boots had miniature hooks around which the laces had been strung and tied.

Mrs Fisher lifted the skirt up and saw the doll was wearing a pair of white silky bloomers, and she chuckled at the sight of them. She sat the doll on an old scuffed armchair with its legs dangling over the edge of the greasy cushion and its back resting against a bundle of old newspapers. Mrs Fisher lit the gas fire set into her old fireplace and then she went into the kitchen as she lifted her skirt and scratched her bare backside. She opened a drawer and searched for a can opener so she could make two incisions in the tin of Carnation evaporated milk. Her fingers rummaged through old rusted nails, assorted brass and iron keys, washers and the skins shed by woodworm. She looked back at the doll on the armchair, visible through the kitchen doorway. She listened to the hiss of the gas fire's jets, and realised she now had some sort of company with that doll sitting there. Then she noticed that the doll's face was looking towards her, and yet Mrs Fisher distinctly recalled turning the head to face the fire.

'Your mammy's going to give you a saucer of milk soon,' she promised the doll, then went to the toilet.

When she returned, she saw that the doll was now looking towards a corner of the room. How odd. Mrs Fisher walked over the bare lime-green linoleum and stood with her back to the fire as she gazed down at the doll. 'What are we going to call you, eh?' she wondered out loud, and she rubbed her fingers over her forearm and the friction created little black rolls of grime and skin flakes which she flicked into the blue and white flames of the gas fire.

There was a rap at the bay window.

Mrs Fisher walked over to the mildewed net curtain and lifted it to see the face of 'the bummer' as she called him, a fifty-year-old man named Stan O'Hare who was always cadging money so he could bet on the horses. In return, he sometimes did little favours for Mrs Fisher, like going on errands for her, unblocking her sink, and sometimes even sleeping with her when she was feeling particularly lonely. Stan came in, made himself a cup of tea, then came back into the parlour. He picked the doll up off the armchair and threw her onto the lino, and Mrs Fisher swore at him as he sat on the edge of the armchair the doll had previously been placed upon.

'Sorry lover,' he told the pensioner, and grinned as Mrs Fisher picked up the doll and cradled it in her arms as if it was her baby.

'You will be sorry you stupid thing!' Mrs Fisher rocked the doll in her arms.

Stan nearly spat out the tea with laughter. 'I wish I had a camera now!' he cackled.

'Come on, get off that chair, its dolly's speck!' the old woman said with a stone face.

'What? Ah come on lover!' the gigolo replied, but

seeing how serious the old woman was he slowly got up.

Mrs Fisher sat on the edge of the cluttered armchair with the doll and she gazed up at Stan, and then she glared at him. She said: 'And by the way I haven't got two halfpennies to rub together so go and bum off someone else!'

'Not even half a crown?' Stan asked, horrified at what he perceived to be stinginess. 'Come on, lover, I'll do *anything* you want.'

'Leave us alone you cadging bastard!' Mrs Fisher screeched. 'Get a job you old layabout!'

Stan recoiled in shock and then a smile broke out on his face. 'What? Me? Old? Ha! You're that old you've got cobwebs in your crotch you dirty old slut!'

'Get out of here before I slit your gizzard!' Mrs Fisher tried to get up, but Stan hurled the tea into the flames of the gas fire, and then he grabbed the doll from the old woman's arms and threw it hard onto the floor.

As Mrs Fisher screamed, Stan laughed and ran for the door. The elderly lady was on her knees, picking up the doll and checking if she had been broken as Stan ran out into the street. He slipped down an alleyway and went straight to his dilapidated house on St John's Road, a few minutes' walk away from Mrs Fisher's flat. The old lady was in tears as she held the doll, but was relieved it had not sustained any damage after being thrown by Stan.

That night, just after 1 am, Claire and Billy, a couple of teenagers, were kissing in Victoria Park under the partial cover of the smog, when Claire happened to gaze over Billy's shoulder as he pressed her against a tree trunk. 'Who's that?' Claire asked.

'I don't care, face this way,' Billy replied, and tried to kiss her, but Claire turned away and said: 'Look, down there – who's that?'

Billy swore under his breath and turned to see what Claire was referring to. Through the park gates he could see the silhouette of a woman in the smog, and she was walking in funny, jerky movements, as if she was acting like a robot. Claire could see that the woman had long hair and was wearing a calf-length dress. She was becoming fainter and fainter as she walked further into the mists – towards St John's Road.

Around this time, Charlie Davies, an asthmatic coalman, left his bed and opened the window. 'Close that window, Chuck,' said Mrs Davies, lying in bed with curlers in her head. 'It's too cold.'

'I'm trying to get my breath,' her husband replied, 'get back to sleep.'

As his wife cocooned herself in the bedclothes and coats in a huff, Mr Davies saw the same peculiar figure – that of the shadowy woman who walked in a weird stiff manner – coming down the street. 'Hey love, is this Mr O'Hare's daughter?' Mr Davies addressed his wife, who was too comfortable and warm to come to the window.

'His daughter's moved to Australia,' Mrs Davies reminded him. 'Hilda O'Hare, I told you about it a fortnight ago.'

'Well has he got another daughter? He hasn't got a wife, has he? Didn't she die?' Mr Davies couldn't see the silhouetted woman now.

From the inner roll of blankets came the muffled

reply from his cosseted wife. 'His other daughter is married and she lives in Blackpool. His wife's alive but she left him ten years ago and went on the game. He won't ever have her back.'

'Well this one was wearing some funny clobber; old fashioned like,' Mr Davies said, and inhaled the cool smoggy air.

'Close that window before you catch pneumonia!' Mrs Davies said, and yawned.

'I will in a minute, love, just having a breather. Feel as if my lungs are closing up,' Mr Davies was saying, when he suddenly squinted into the murky night. The light came on in Stan O'Hare's bedroom – and the silhouette of a woman could be seen on the drawn curtains there. Then came a scream, and it was that loud, even Mrs Davies heard it and she wrestled out of the swathes of blankets and coats and went to the window, where she elbowed her husband Charlie out the way. 'Who was that?' she asked, scanning the rows of dark windows in the still terraced street.

'O'Hare! Over there love, look!' the coalman pointed to the bedroom window now dimmed somewhat by the fog. Mrs Davies saw movement of a figure there, and then she and her husband heard another scream.

'That's a man's scream, that,' Mr Davies said, and he went to put on his trousers and braces, and his wife also got dressed. They went to the house of Stan O'Hare and saw that someone had forced the front door. They went into the hallway and Charlie Davies shouted "Mr O'Hare! Are you alright?' In his hand, Mr Davies wielded a roofing hammer – just in case he encountered any burglars.

The couple went up the stairs and rapped on a

bedroom door. This proved to be Mr O'Hare's bedroom door, and when they opened that door and switched on the light, the couple saw Stan O'Hare lying on his back in his underpants, gazing at the ceiling with a face twisted by sheer terror. The eyes were bulging and the toothless mouth was wide open. At the side of the body a bedside lamp lay on its side with a broken bulb. Mrs Davies felt for a pulse – but there was none. 'He's dead,' she said in a trembling voice.

'You sure?' Mr Davies asked. He wanted to get out of that room as soon as possible.

'Yes, let's go and phone the police Chuck,' Mrs Davies said, and she grabbed her husband's hand and the couple hurried out the room, intending to go to the nearest public telephone box. Outside, on the bottom step, Mrs Davies noticed a strange thing. It was a little doll's hand with its fingers and thumb clenched – except for the index finger, and this tiny hand was resting on the step with its knuckles upwards. It was pointing at the door of Stan O'Hare, and Mr and Mrs Davies thought there was something eerie about the presence of the doll's hand.

Alerted by Mrs Davies, the police soon visited O'Hare's house and an ambulance turned up minutes later. There was no evidence of a break-in and the coroner opined heart failure as the cause of Stan O'Hare's death.

Days after the mysterious death of O'Hare, Mrs Fisher caused a scene on Lawton Road by running about in her dirty old nightdress one night, saying her doll had changed into a fully grown woman. Most laughed at the bizarre claims but one resident got in touch with the police because he had an early start in the morning and wanted this nutty behaviour nipped in the bud. Mrs Fisher told a grinning policeman and a bemused policewoman that her doll had changed into a tall woman before her eyes as it lay on the bed. It had left the house and gone in the direction of Victoria Park. The coppers reassured Mrs Fisher that they'd try and find the 'living doll' and bring her back home in the morning, and left after warning the old woman to stay indoors.

That morning around 2.20 am, the two robbers who had stolen the doll from the widow's house on Thorndale Road were sitting on a bench in Victoria Park smoking marijuana spliffs and sipping bottles of cider. They were contemplating another robbery in the area. The names of the burglars were Martin and Simon, and they were both aged eighteen. They heard dull, padding footsteps approaching, but when they looked towards the source of the sounds, it suddenly stopped.

'Is that somebody there?' Simon asked, and he pointed at a vague shape in the depths of the fog. 'Look, over there.'

'Nah, that's a tree,' Martin said, and grinned uneasily. His eyes were red and watery from the effects of the cold and the cannabis.

'It's a bleedin' movin' tree then,' Simon told his friend with a grave look.

Martin produced his flick knife and Simon nervously urged him to put the weapon away.

'No, I won't sky it,' Martin gritted his teeth stubbornly and rose from the bench. He knew it wasn't the outline of a copper; it looked more like a woman or one of those long-haired jessies copying the Beatles' hairdo.

The youths were suddenly startled to see the figure run towards them. It was a woman – or at least that is what they thought at first, but the way she moved was very odd indeed. She moved as if she was a robot with straight legs that could hardly bend at the knees. It was both funny and sinister somehow.

'What the bleedin' hell – ' Martin saw that the face of the woman looked like one of those wax dummies he'd seen at the waxwork shows up in Blackpool, and he thought it was someone messing about with a mask at first, but as the creepy figure got close, Martin and Simon could see it as something very unearthly-looking, and the two young men turned and ran off. The figure gave chase, and the lads ran over a hundred yards north and scaled the railings to get away from the weird thing pursuing them. They crossed Park View and ran along Cedar Grove – straight into the path of a well-known policeman on his beat – PC Eggar. He was one hard knock of a copper, the spitting image of Stratford Johns, the corpulent actor who played Chief Superintendent Barlow in *Z Cars*. He naturally challenged the two young crooks, and they told him that a weird-looking woman had just chased them from the park.

'Oh, is that so is it?' the PC Eggar replied sarcastically, but then he saw the pallid face of the woman concerned, peering over the railings of the park on the other side of the road. She was standing in the shadows of a clump of trees, and as the policeman looked on, the face withdrew into the darkness of the park.

'You – get home now!' the policeman indicated the direction of Martin's home – Winchester Avenue – with his thumb, and then he grabbed the forearm of Simon and told him: 'And you live up on er, Lyra Road, don't you?'

Simon nodded and watched his friend walk away down Cedar Grove. 'Yeah, constable, but I'm staying with my granny at the moment – ' the delinquent lied, but the streetwise copper wasn't buying it.

'And you're out at this friggin' hour?' PC Eggar said with a sneer. 'Get home to Lyra Road now or I'll take you in.' Eggar shoved the youth – in the direction of the park, for that was the direction he lived, but there was no way Simon was going through that park with that eldritch figure knocking about. He went the long way round, and got home at five minutes to three that morning. Simon told his mother what had happened that morning over breakfast and she said she had heard about the weird-looking woman prowling Victoria Park and the streets around it, and she asked her son to stop going out at night and to try and find a decent job. Later that day in the afternoon, around 2pm, Simon went to Winchester Avenue to see his mate – and got the shock of his life. There was no one at Martin's home, but still Simon ran-tanned on the door-knocker until a neighbour came out – an elderly woman named Jean who Simon vaguely knew by sight. Jean said Martin had been found dead in his bed. He had awakened half the street around four in the morning, screaming at the top of his voice, and the lad's parents had tried to wake him, but he died when they did. Jean said the poor lad's mother had told her he had been having some sort of nightmare, and the doctor said he'd died of "night terror" (a real medical condition). The parents were staying with relatives and the body was in the mortuary.

Simon mouthed the F word with nerves, and then apologised to Jean – and then he looked down – and there, just to the left of the front doorstep of his late friend's house, there lay a little doll's hand. Simon didn't really think it was odd at first, for he was so shocked and upset at the news of Martin's death, his thoughts were elsewhere – but later on, his mother mentioned the doll's hand that had been found outside of Mr O'Hare's home – pointing its tiny index finger to the dead man's door. Simon later went back to Martin's house to try and find the little hand on the floor, but it wasn't there.

It is said there were more and more strange deaths and sudden fatal heart attacks – all in the vicinity of old Mrs Fisher's house on Lawton Road, and on each occasion, a little doll's hand with closed fingers – except for the index one –would be found, always pointing to the door. I mentioned this strange case on the radio and was inundated with accounts from people across the north west who had either lived in Waterloo in the 1960s or had relatives who had been living near Lawton Road. I was told that a well-known priest in the area died from a brain haemorrhage after he attempted to destroy the doll belonging to old Mrs Fisher, and that on the morning of his funeral, when the mourners were going into the priest's house, one of them noticed the accursed omen of the little doll hand pointing at the door. Someone believed hoaxers had planted it there, but when the person who found the hand took it to the police station in her purse, she found that it had inexplicably vanished. This is a very bizarre case, because I myself was warned not to bring up the strange goings-on about the doll, because the entity – or whatever it was – would always become active again, allegedly stirred up by talk of its uncanny agenda. One lady named Penny, who lived near Lawton Road in the late 1960s, said her mother told her about the little doll's hand, and later on in the week, a doll's little hand was found outside Hulme Hall, Port Sunlight, close to the place where Penny's mother worked. Her mother died of a stroke that month, aged just 54. A milkman named Tony Mere also told me how, one March morning in 1967, he had found a doll's hand on the doorstep of a terraced house on Heald Street in Garston, and never really thought anything odd of it at first, although the hand – which measured about two-and-a-half inches in length – looked as if it had been carefully placed in the middle of the step. Tony later found out that a young man who lived at the house on Heald Street where the hand was found had died that morning in a car crash. The milkman also overheard a conversation between three drinkers in a pub about doll's hands being found on the doorsteps of people who had suffered bad – and fatal – luck, and all of these spooky incidents had occurred in the Garston area. As I stated at the beginning of this chapter, I cannot rationalise the doll's hand omen, but if it's true that even discussing it can evoke this sinister portent, there may be something outside *your* door right now…

LOVE AND TELEPORTATION

In the late 1990s my publisher held a booksigning event at the old branch of WH Smith which stood on Church Street, and amongst the many members of the public who attended the event, a couple in their sixties named Grace and Harry turned up – and they had an amazing story to recount. In 1959, Harry was 27-years-old, single, and living with his mother, father and grandfather on Lorenzo Drive, Norris Green. He had moved out the family home three years earlier to live with his friend Alan at their bachelor flat in Wavertree, but when Alan met a girl and started going steady with her, he kicked his old mate out. Harry's mother and father were forever telling their son to take a leaf out of Alan's book and settle down with a girl, but Harry thought wedlock would be a padlock and that a wife would "cramp his style". On this particular day – a Saturday – Harry's mother Eileen warned her son: 'A man without a wife is but half a man!'

'Advise none to marry or go to war,' said Eileen's old father, 'marry in haste and repent at leisure.' And Harry nodded in agreement and said, 'They are wise words they are, thanks granddad!'

Harry had his tea, and by 7pm he was in the bath, singing his head off, getting all keyed up for a night on the town. He couldn't find his shampoo so he used a bar of Lifebuoy soap to wash his hair, and then came the shave, and Harry whipped the brush on the soap stick into a lather and applied it to his face – and then everything went black.

'Mam!' he shouted, getting up out the bath, 'Have the lights gone?'

The lights came back on, but Harry found himself in a tiled shower cubicle. He swished the green plastic shower curtain aside – and saw a woman who looked as if she was in her mid twenties, looking in a bathroom mirror as she put lipstick on. This woman, who looked as if she was dressed up to go out with her long white fashionable gloves and an expensive-looking red evening dress, gazed at Harry's reflected image with a look of utter astonishment – and then she screamed and ran out the bathroom in her high heels. As a confused naked Harry covered himself with the shower curtains, the woman returned to the bathroom with an older lady, who glared at the audacious intruder. 'Come on Grace, this is a matter for the police!' the lady gasped, and she and Grace went to the telephone in the hall of their Heswall home. In a panic, Harry examined the tiles of the shower cubicle for a way back to his bathroom, as he was naturally perplexed by this surreal state of affairs. Finding no way back, he left the shower, wrapped a towel around his loins, and within minutes the bathroom door burst open and two policemen seized him. It looked as if they'd caught some sex pest, but Harry told them how he'd been in the bath at the house on Lorenzo Drive one moment, and then he'd found himself in the shower cubicle. Then the policemen and Grace, and the older lady (her mother), heard an unfamiliar voice coming from the shower: 'Harry! Where are you?' It was the voice of Harry's mum, Eileen. Grace convinced her mother not to press charges because something very strange – supernatural even - had obviously taken place. The voice in the shower faded, and the policemen seemed spooked by this. The police made a thorough search for Harry's clothes and shoes, but could find nothing, and when he gave his address as being ten miles away in Norris Green, the coppers knew this would be a hard case to present to their superiors. So, no charges were brought, and Harry later started to see Grace because of what seems to have been a teleportation – the mysterious transference of a physical object across space by paranormal means, usually in the proverbial twinkling of an eye. I have not only investigated many teleportation incidents over the years, I believe I was also teleported myself when I was in my teens. This occurred at the house of a friend as I was running towards a flight of stairs. One moment I was at the bottom of the stairs, and then a splt-second later I was at the top of the stairs. Because of the strange teleportation from Norris Green to Heswall, Harry and Grace dated and married a few years afterwards. The strange thing is that Grace had been due to go to a party at her friend's house that night when Harry appeared in her shower, and the girl's mother had made a comment which has an eerily familiar ring to it, for she told Grace: 'Never mind parties and drinking, you won't find a husband like that.' Grace's mother had been nagging her to find a suitor for the past month, and told her that she wasn't getting any younger. To this day Harry and Grace think some higher force literally brought them together. A few months after the 10-mile teleportation of Harry, towels and tubes of toothpaste would go missing from the bathroom on Lorenzo Drive, and these items would always end up at Grace's Heswall home.

SEFTON'S HAUNTED PUNCHBOWL HOTEL

People often ask me if there are any places they can visit that have ghosts, but most of the haunted locations I know of are on private property, with the exception of buildings open to the public at certain times, such as Croxteth Hall, Knowsley Hall and Speke Hall, but there are a few pubs in our vicinity that are allegedly haunted. I am told that the New Johnny Todd pub in Kirkby even has a ghost who is occasionally seen, and what's unusual about this ghost is that the entity has also been encountered in the Fantail (just up the road from the New Johnny Todd on Whitefield Drive). This ghost in question is that of a man in old-fashioned black clothes who fixes his gaze on the unfortunate drinker, and then looks him up and down before taking out a cloth tape measure to 'size him up' – recording his length from feet to head in a little notebook. The legend goes that the measured person dies not long afterwards, and is of course duly measured for a coffin prior to burial or cremation. The sinister man in black is thought to be the ghost of a local undertaker who died in the 1930s. I have a few very peculiar supernatural stories concerning the New Johnny Todd I'll regale you with in future editions of *Haunted Liverpool*.

If you want to go in search of spirits of the non-alcoholic kind whilst perhaps indulging in a cordial drink and a tasty bite to eat, then I heartily recommend a haunted inn which has a long history of ghostly goings-on, and this is the Punchbowl Hotel up in Sefton, situated next door to the ancient (and haunted) Sefton Church. I have been in this pub, which dates back to the 1850s – possibly even earlier – on many occasions for a drink and the odd Sunday roast, and the building definitely has an 'Olde World atmosphere' about it which harks back to Pickwickian times when travellers from far and wide arrived by coach and horses. In 1971, the barmaid and landlord's daughter of the Punchbowl saw the ghost of a man twice within the space of a fortnight, and on both occasions the pub was closed. The apparition was said to be a man in dark blue who had the air of a sailor about him, but there are other ghosts that haunt or call into the pub as well, and one of them is a cheerful Regency figure, resplendent in a top hat, monocle and walking cane, who struts with a purposeful stride, and many who have seen him say he looks just like the famous character found on the label of a Johnnie Walker Scotch whisky bottle, except that instead of the red hunting waistcoat Johnnie wears, our ghost wears a dark blue one, and his breeches are also of a bluish colour. For many years, people wondered who this ghost in blue was, and so I undertook research into the matter and found a very credible contender – Sir Nicholas Blundell. Back in the middle of the 17th century, Sir Nicholas Blundell, Lord of the Manor of Little Crosby, passed away at Ince Hall, and his dying words to his faithful steward were: "Let me be interred at Lydiate Abbey and not Sefton Church." The steward honoured his deceased master's last wish, even though the rest of the Blundell family arranged for Sir Nicholas to be buried in the graveyard of Sefton Church. The steward removed the corpse of Sir Nicholas from the coffin on the night before the funeral and propped him up in a closet, and then he fetched a hundred-weight of stones and put them in the coffin, which was then screwed shut. Then came an even more risky piece of business – the transportation of the dead body to Lydiate Abbey. For this, the servant hired an expert rider from Aintree named Jack Kildare who was bribed with money and ale to keep his mouth shut. The body of Sir Nicholas was dressed in a dark blue waistcoat and blue breeches and black boots, and a monocle was jammed into his eye and a hat shoved onto his head. The body was then strapped to the rider Kildare so it looked as if he had a man clinging to him on horseback, and that rider rode like the Devil himself through the night to Lydiate Abbey. He thundered past Sefton Church as the clock struck the hour of twelve, and suddenly, the luminous ghost of Sir Nicholas Blundell appeared in the road ahead of the rider and scared the horse as it stood there with a horrible angry expression on its face as it lifted its protesting arms into the air. The rider regained control of the horse, dug his spurs hard into the steed and rode around the terrifying ghost, reaching Lydiate Abbey in a dreadful state, for Kildare said the displeased ghost had followed him most of the way. The Catholic priest at the Abbey, who had been sworn to secrecy, carried out a brief Requiem and the body of Sir Nicholas Blundell was laid in the ground by three burly gravediggers. On the following day, the coffin of stones was solemnly laid in the graveyard of Sefton Church, where people wept, unaware of the grotesque charade which had taken place under their very noses. Not long afterwards, the ghost of Sir Nicholas was seen marching past the Punchbowl Inn, headed for Sefton Church, dressed in the blue attire he'd been clothed in after death, and some think that because Sir Nicholas changed his mind about his intended resting place, he now walks in a type of purgatory in a tormented state, forever back and forth between Sefton Church and the ruins of Lydiate Abbey (which belong, incidentally, along with the land it stands upon, to an unknown descendant of the Ireland family).

Surely then, it is Sir Nicholas Blundell who haunts the Punchbowl Hotel? Many years ago I talked to a gravedigger from Sefton Church who told me how, one late afternoon, while he was digging a grave, he found himself showered by something which giggled as it hurled the excavated soil and clay back at him. He ran into the Punchbowl, and the thing followed him in there and caused havoc in the bar by hurling chairs and stools about and smashing glasses. Perhaps this same malevolent force was at large in 1985 when a couple in their thirties from Huyton – named Barry Evanston and Ann Stanley – visited the pub one evening, and openly scoffed at the tales of a poltergeist that was currently doing the rounds in the area. The violent ghost had hammered on the sides of buses and cars in the neighbourhood, and had even thrown a man in Lunt Road off his bicycle, breaking his arm. Barry Evanston laid a bet that he'd give anyone present a hundred quid if they could prove such a ghost was real, and he shouted out: "If you can hear me, show yourself!" and he and his girlfriend Ann laughed when no response came. Then an old man came into the Punchbowl and asked: "Has anyone in here got a red Mini parked outside?"

Barry Evanston nodded to the oldster and nervously enquired: 'Why do you ask?'

The old man replied, "Something's tossing it about," and everyone in the pub went to the window – including Barry and Ann. All could see that the headlights of Barry's Mini were on, and the car was moving back and forth – even though a steering lock was fitted in the vehicle. It was as if an invisible giant was throwing the vehicle about as if it were a child's Dinky Car. As Barry and Ann went outside the pub to challenge the suspected jokers, the Mini stood on end with its headlights pointing skywards, and then it crashed to the ground, and something was heard to hammer upon it, leaving massive dents in the body work. The couple tried to take their car back to Huyton but the Mini kept veering off the road, as if the steering column had been damaged. In the end, Barry had to call out the AA to fix the Mini, and he and Ann never visited the Punchbowl again.

ANFIELD APPARITIONS

The origin of the place-name Anfield is lost in the mists of time. We know the area Anfield now covers was once called Hangfield – a sloping field upon which cattle grazed, but it's a documented historical fact that these pastures were known earlier in time as the Hanging Fields, perhaps because of some association with the lynchings that took place there when cattle thieves and other miscreants met rough justice at the end of a rope. The etymological origins of Anfield's ancient name remain a mystery, and on the subject of mystery, Anfield has been the backdrop to some strange conundrums over the years, and we need only think of the infamous Man from the Pru murder case in which Julia Wallace, the wife of an insurance man, was battered to death by a sinister killer who called himself "Qualtrough". Julia's husband was suspected of the murder, and arrested, tried and found guilty, but subsequently appealed and the Court of Appeal in London did an unprecedented thing – they freed

Wallace, a man who had been convicted to hang, simply because there were too many question marks hanging over the case, and it seemed as if Wallace could not have carried out the murder. The full story is in my book, *Murders of Merseyside*, and my solution to this world-famous whodunit caused a storm of controversy, but now has a surprising amount of growing followers.

Aside from inexplicable crimes, Anfield has been the scene of many peculiar mysteries of a paranormal nature. From the 1950s to the 1980s, strange gigantic footprints were reported on seven occasions in Stanley Park after a snowfall. In January 1951, a 40-year-old woman named Agnes Taverner went out one morning around 7.45 am to walk her dog before setting out for work, and she strolled into Stanley Park as she did most mornings to be greeted by the serene sight of a terrace covered in an ivory blanket of newly-fallen snow – but as Agnes and her dog set off into the middle of this 110-acre park, she noticed something very odd indeed – huge pointed shoeprints in the snow, some five feet in length, heading in a northern direction with gaps of about ten feet between each imprint. Agnes followed the gargantuan tracks – which ran parallel to a path - for about two hundred yards, but her dog, normally a very docile creature, began to act very strange and he made whimpering sounds and dug ihis claws into the snowy ground. Agnes halted, and thought she saw shadowy movements near the trees on the Priory Road side of the park, and was suddenly gripped by an inexplicable sensation of panic. She picked up the little dog, turned and went home, leaving the park in a dreadful state. She never told her husband what she had seen in the park because she thought he'd laugh, but later that day when she returned from work, her 13-year-old daughter Linda said she and her friends had seen the "giant's footprints" in Stanley Park, and many other people remarked on them, but most rationalised the huge prints - which had partially degraded because of a thaw – as a trick of the weather: mere patterns caused by uneven thawing of snow because of the wind, but Agnes thought otherwise; the massive footprints, she told me, looked as if they had been caused by a giant who had worn a pair of "winkies" (slang for pointed 'winkle-picker' shoes which were worn in the 1960s). The edges of the prints were too sharply defined to be natural, Agnes thought, and she believed that whatever had made them must have been colossal, and she'd had the feeling that this mysterious towering being had been hiding behind the trees that morning. I mentioned the Stanley Park tracks on the Billy Butler Show one afternoon in 2001 and the switchboard at the radio station went haywire as people from across the region telephoned to tell of their memories of tracks in the park over the years. One caller named Graham Taft told me how, in 1965, he had been a 13-year-old lad living near to Stanley Park, and in December of that year, he recalled a strange rumour that giant footprints had been found after a light snowfall by kids who had gone to play football in the park. Against his mother's wishes, Graham sneaked out of his house on Alroy Road and went in search of the giant footprints – and he was astounded to find five of the prints, with people milling around them in the moonlit park. Some thought the prints had been created by pranksters, but Graham thought they looked real, and like Agnes he saw how well-defined and even the impressions were. A few of the prints were still there on the following morning when Graham returned with his best mate, and he distinctly recalls an elderly man taking a photograph of the prints. I would dearly love to see any photographs of those mysterious shoeprints. One caller to the radio station told me that the giant prints were seen as late as January 1980, and that strange lights had been seen in Stanley Park the night before during a blizzard. Just what made these prints remains a mystery.

Let us now cross priory Road from Stanley Park to that vast kite-shaped 57-hectare necropolis known as Anfield Cemetery – the scene of many supernatural mysteries. The cemetery was designed by the same person who designed Stanley Park – Edward Kemp, a landscape architect and writer who also designed Flaybrick Cemetery (where Kemp was later buried in 1891). The first internment at Anfield Cemetery was on 5 May 1863, and since then, thousands of people from near and far have been interred or cremated within Liverpool's answer to Père Lachaise. As a rule, most cemeteries – contrary to the popular imagination – do not have many ghosts, as the latter tend to haunt the places they frequented in life – but Anfield Cemetery has quite a few paranormal entities. One gloriously sunny day in the summer of 2006, Lyn Staunton, the first woman to become chairman of the Variety Club in the North West, was paying a visit to the grave of her father in Anfield Cemetery with her mum Georgina when Lyn saw something very unusual. She was driving through the cemetery at the time, near to the crematorium, when she noticed a soldier standing there on the pathway ahead, almost directly in the path of the vehicle. Lyn pointed the soldier out to her mother, but Georgina could see nothing, and then Lyn realised he had inexplicably vanished. The soldier had made eye contact with Lyn and she was certain he had deliberately attracted her attention for a while before he vanished. Close to the spot where this ghostly soldier is regularly seen there are a group of soldiers' graves, and figures in both Army and naval uniform have been seen in the vicinity of these graves, close to the crematorium.

In August 2010, two women in their sixties from West Derby named Barbara and Angela went to visit the graves of relatives at Anfield Cemetery. Angela had brought flowers to put on the grave of her aunt in the southern part of the cemetery, and Barbara had brought a bouquet of roses to place on the resting place of her grandmother who was interred in the northern end of the cemetery. The graves were therefore some fifteen hundred yards apart, quite a stroll on a hot sunny afternoon. The two ladies visited the grave of Angela's aunt first, and lingered there for about ten minutes, and once the flowers had been placed before the white marble headstone, Angela kissed her fingers then touched the gravestone with those fingers as she said, 'Bye auntie,' and then the two women walked northward, bound for the grave of Barbara's Gran. About 300 yards up the path, the women heard a soft padding of feet behind them, and both turned to see a woman of about fifty years of age in a knee-length black and red floral dress hurrying towards them. 'Excuse me,' the lady said, with a self-conscious smile on her face, 'but could you tell me where the lodge is?'

Barbara didn't understand what the lady was referring to at first, but then she thought she meant the lodge of the cemetery on Walton Lane, but before she could respond, Angela was already pointing that lodge out. Angela then said, 'But there's another lodge to the south, you know? Which one do you want?'

'Er, it's not the one on Walton Lane, I think it's the one that's er, is that south, you say?' the lady said, and seemed all flustered. 'They've made a terrible mistake you see,' she stammered, then walked away saying: 'Aw, I'm so grateful love, sorry to have bothered you.'

'No, you haven't bothered us,' Angela said with a smile, and she and Barbara walked on in the blistering heat as they saw the woman in the floral dress trot away among the rows of gravestones, heading south – the very opposite direction Barbara and Angela were headed for.

'She seemed all "airyated" didn't she?' Barbara remarked.

'Yeah, I thought that,' Angela replied, and she stopped to look back, and she could see the woman in question as a speck in the distance. 'Wonder what she meant about a terrible mistake?'

'I should have brought me sunglasses today,' Barbara squinted at the merciless sun. 'I'll have a migraine tonight.'

The two women walked on, and Angela took a bottle of Evian mineral water out of her handbag and offered Barbara a swig – when a familiar voice came from their left. It was that woman in the floral dress again. She had her hand to her grinning mouth, and she said, 'I'm sorry to bother you, but er – oh! Haven't I just asked you two where the lodge is?'

Although the temperatures were in the seventies, Barbara and Angela went cold, for they knew there was no way that woman could be in front of them. They had seen her about 200 yards away seconds ago to the south of them – so how could she now be in front of them – unless she was some identical twin dressed in the same red and black floral dress – but the woman herself had just admitted to speaking to them before.

'Yes, you did,' a stunned Barbara replied to the woman's question.

'Only they made a mistake you see,' she explained – again.

Angela was lost for words, and she stood close to her friend, feeling very uneasy.

'I'm sorry to bother you, bye bye,' the woman said, and again she walked south down the path. Barbara and Angela walked as fast as they could in the other direction, and when they finally reached the grave of Barbara's grandmother, the women were astonished to see that same woman in the floral dress standing near to a headstone just thirty feet away. This time the woman said nothing, and Barbara literally dropped the roses onto her Gran's grave before she and Barbara left in a hurry. They were too scared to look back, but they heard the woman shout: 'Bye bye!'

When the woman related this story to me, they were flabbergasted when I showed them a sketch of the ubiquitous lady. That sketch had been made by an art student who had seen the same lady back in the late 1980s when the student had been making sketches of

Anfield Cemetery for an art project. The woman is of course, an earthbound ghost, and she has been seen by many visitors to Anfield Cemetery over the years, and some reports I have recorded date back to the late 1960s. She says the same phrases to those who she meets – the question about the location of the lodge and the "terrible mistake" that has been made, but no one knows just what this terrible mistake is. If you should happen to bump into the lady in the red and back floral dress, try and put your fear aside, and ask her what the terrible mistake is, because I think once she tells someone what it is, she may be able to rest.

In Anfield Cemetery there stands a fairly tall arch-shaped headstone, dating back to the 1870s, and it is black with the soot and air pollution of almost a century and a half. This gravestone has been reported to me on several occasions because it is said to be haunted by a very sinister ghost. The first case in my files regarding this headstone concerns a man named Jim Gallagher, who paid a visit to his uncle at the cemetery one sweltering day in July 1976 – the year of the infamous drought. It was around 4pm when Jim entered the cemetery on his way home from work. The cemetery was almost devoid of any other living soul except two elderly men who were talking near to the entrance gate. As Jim walked along to the grave, where his favourite uncle had been laid to rest seven years before, he thought he heard a voice calling his name – not Jim – but James. Jim stopped and looked around, and all he could see were the two old men in the distance. They definitely weren't calling him, for they were too far away and looked as if they were chatting to one another – so *who* had called him?

Jim walked on, but once again he heard someone with a rather deep voice shout: 'James...James.' Jim tried to rationalise the voice. Perhaps, he reasoned, it was merely the sound of the rush-hour traffic in the distance coupled with the acoustics of the cemetery. He walked on and stood at his uncle's grave for a few minutes, and heard nothing but the odd drone of a passing bumble bee or the occasional car horn in the misty shimmering distance. Jim then walked back the way he had come, and once again he heard someone – definitely a male voice, calling his name. Given that the unseen caller was in a cemetery, most people would have made a speedy exit from the place, but it was a bright sunny summer afternoon, and the two old men in the distance made Jim feel fairly safe from any vague thoughts of the supernatural. And so he stopped and listened carefully. The voice was coming from a western direction. Jim walked in that direction, and slowly, the voice became louder and clearer, but still he could see no one about. After about five minutes Jim reached a spot in the cemetery where the voice sounded very close indeed, and this time the caller shouted: 'Oh James..'

Then Jim saw where the voice was coming from, and his stomach turned over at the surreal sight. Upon the tall black arched headstone, among the jumble of blackened and chipped sandstone, Jim Gallagher saw a mouth – opening and closing as it called his name. 'Oh James, your time has come...' the voice from the headstone announced in a rich deep voice.

Jim Gallagher turned and bolted as fast as his legs could carry him. He flew past the two startled old men in their cloth caps at the entrance to the cemetery, and he kept running until he was about half a mile from the cemetery. When his wife came home around tea time she found Jim sitting with the TV and radio on for company with a glass of whiskey in his hand. He told her about the speaking headstone and his wife believed him, for she knew when he was telling the truth. Jim never talked about anything remotely supernatural and yet his missus could see the goosebumps on his arms as he told her about the terrifying warning from the grave. It might have been a black coincidence, but a week later, in the middle of the hottest spell the British Isles has ever experienced, Jim Gallagher somehow contracted pneumonia and died, but was successfully resuscitated. To this day, Jim believed that "talking headstone" had somehow warned him about the impending health scare. What Jim didn't know was that the headstone he had seen the mouth on has quite a reputation for producing weird sounds and others have heard their name being called in that part of the cemetery. A woman in her seventies named Phyllis once told me how, one wintry morning in February 1977, she had visited the grave of her brother in Anfield cemetery with her niece, and they had both heard someone crying nearby, even though no one else was around at the time. Phyllis and her niece Donna went in search of the mysterious crier and were shocked and scared when they realised that the sobbing noise was coming from the tall black arched headstone – the very same one Jim Gallagher had seen the mouth upon the year before. Aunt and niece soon left the cemetery! At the time of writing I am investigating this headstone. The names upon it are faded but I have managed to extract a few names and dates which I will research to see if they will throw any light on the eerie phenomenon associated with the headstone.

Wenlock Road in Anfield spans Pinehurst Road and Priory Road, (some 650 yards east of Liverpool Football Club's ground) 800 feet of terraced houses; typical of most streets in Liverpool in its layout. From the early 1950s to the late 1970s this street was the backdrop to an eerie supernatural mystery - the strange case of the Beckoning Girl. It all started one sunny Sunday afternoon in June 1960, when a ten-year-old boy named Ollie from Anfield's Hornsey Road went to call on his friend Ian who lived on Wenlock Road. He held an old "casey" football in his hands and was looking forward to a game of footy with his friend. As Ollie was passing an entry on Wenlock Road, he noticed a girl's head pop round the corner of the alleyway. She had huge baby blue eyes, a very pale face and a mop of curly "Shirley Temple" type of hair, and she looked about a year or so younger than Ollie, who stopped and said: 'Who are you looking at?'

The girl beckoned Ollie to come to her with her little hand without saying a word, and Ollie said: 'No – you come here.'

The girl continued to beckon the lad, and curiosity got the better of him, but as he approached the entry, the girl retreated and ran silently down the 'jigger'. She wore a pretty pale blue dress. Ollie threw the ball at the girl's back but she turned a corner just in time. Ollie turned that corner, and what he saw in the entry scared him so much, he ran off, leaving his beloved football behind.

On the floor of the entry was the mutilated body of

the girl, and at first, Ollie only knew it was the girl because the disfigured and dismembered thing on the floor wore the same pale blue dress as the girl who had beckoned him. Her face had been smashed inwards by something – or someone – and one of her eyes was missing from its socket. The temple of the forehead had caved in and the brains were visible. The upper arms had deep scarlet slashes as if the child had been struck with a meat cleaver, and part of the girl's right kneecap had been sheared off – presumably by the same instrument that had inflicted the deep grooves in the arms. A mass of bluebottles and flies were swarming and buzzing over the corpse, and Ollie was struck mute by the horrific sight. That girl had only just turned the corner into this alleyway, so who could have killed her that fast? Ollie wondered as he felt nauseous and panic-stricken, and then he naturally reasoned that the killer must be close by to have struck so fast. Ollie tried to cry out for help as he turned and ran round the corner, but he was so deeply in shock he couldn't force a single sound out of his throat. He staggered into Wenlock Road and raised his arms to a passing woman, gesturing for help, and the passer-by could plainly see that the lad was distressed. She asked him what the matter was as she crouched to look at him, and Ollie burst into tears and gave a garbled account of the girl's body down the entry. A man in his fifties passed by at this point and the woman told him what Ollie had just said, and so the man went down the alleyway and turned the corner. He returned seconds later shaking his head and shrugging. 'No one there,' he said to the lady.

Ollie ran home to Hornsey Road and told his

mother what he had seen and she and her three older daughters went to the entry behind Wenlock Road and saw nothing except Ollie's football. Ollie's mother later heard a strange thing at the local laundrette. She mentioned Ollie's strange story and an old woman said that she had seen 'that girl' many times over the years in that entry on Wenlock Road, and so had many others. She always beckoned people into that entry, and some had seen her corpse, whilst others in that street had reported a terrible stench in the alleyway that could never be traced. Some believe the "Beckoning Girl" is the ghost of some murder victim of long ago, but no one seemed to know of such a murder. I have researched murders in that area and cannot find one that took place in Wenlock Road. Perhaps the girl was murdered in that alleyway a long time ago and her body might have been efficiently disposed of by the killer. When I mentioned this weird case on the radio, many older people rang the station to say that they had either seen the ghostly girl in the blue dress or had heard about her. Perhaps some researcher will uncover some piece of evidence in the archives one day which will throw some light on the strange case of the Beckoning Girl.

To the north west of Wenlock Road, on the other side of Anfield Cemetery, you will find Bardsay Road, just a stone's throw from Goodison Park, and here a rather bizarre but terrifying number of incidents took place over a 3-year span in the 1980s. It all started one October night in 1982 when a 14-year-old girl named Justine was stripping the wallpaper of her bedroom with her best friend Carmel when the girls uncovered a drawing of what looked like a teddy bear with a pair of walrus-like tusks. Both girls thought the drawing was creepy and Carmel tried to scrape the image off the plaster wall with a butter knife but when the girls came back upstairs after having a short break, they saw that the tusked teddy bear's image had somehow returned. Justine painted over the drawing with greyish white primer, and Carmel went home, but around 3am, Justine woke up from a graphic gory nightmare about the sinister teddy in which he was giving her clear orders (in an accent-less deep voice) to send chain letters to people telling them that they'd die in their sleep unless they in turn wrote three chain letters of their own and posted them to people who would then generate even more menacing letters.

Justine woke in a sweat from the nightmare and switched on her bedside lamp, and immediately she saw that the drawing of the tusked bear had somehow come through the coat of primer on the wall facing, and what's more, the drawing seemed to have changed, for now the face on the creepy teddy was grinning. Justine got out of bed, turned on the main light in her room and then she covered the spooky wall sketch with a pop poster which featured The Jam. She then went back to bed, but at ten-past four that morning she woke again from the same horrible nightmare featuring the tusked teddy bear entity. It had been leaning over her in bed, playfully biting her hand with its tusks. The thing told the girl it could easily kill her and that she'd never wake up and she'd be his forever.

Justine went downstairs and slept on the sofa and later told her mother over breakfast about the weird drawing she and Carmel had found under her wallpaper and of the associated lucid nightmares, but the girl's mum said she'd just had a nightmare and told her – and her friend Carmel – to get a move on painting the bedroom. A strange thing happened a few nights later. Justine's younger brother Billy, who was just aged 7, woke the whole house up one morning at two o'clock with his screams. Carmel was staying over at the time and she heard Billy's shrieks first, as she was passing his bedroom door to go to the toilet. Carmel swore she saw something dark flit from the boy's room and breeze past her on the landing. It looked tall – about six feet in height – and was rather stout. Carmel thought there was some brown to the thing, but wasn't certain because it moved that fast. It seemed to vanish into the wall at the end of the landing. Billy's parents barged into his room, followed by Justine and Carmel, and the little boy was in a hysterical state as he cried his eyes out. When Billy managed to tell his mother what had scared him, Justine went cold.

'A big teddy bear with horrible teeth,' Billy gasped to get his breath, for all of the crying had taken the wind out of him. 'It tried to pull me out the bed!'

Carmel turned and looked at Justine, and immediately thought of the grotesque and menacing tusked teddy bear that had been haunting Justine's dreams.

Justine's mother turned to her daughter and asked: 'What have you been bleedin' filling his head with hey? You soft cow!'

'Mum, I haven't said a word to Billy about anything,' Justine protested, and she asked her friend to back her up: 'Have I Carmel?'

'No, she hasn't honest,' Carmel told the girl's

mother.

'Well someone has,' Justine's Mum said, and she cradled Billy in her arms and stroked his head. 'Look at the state of him!'

That morning, Justine's dreams were infiltrated by the ghastly tusked entity again, and this time, Justine asked the thing who it was. She seemed to be in some old-fashioned classroom in this dream.

'My name is Looey,' the demonic being told Justine, and wrote its name on a blackboard with a piece of chalk. 'I collect people like you once they die,' he said, and Justine saw his fearsome-looking mouth, with the huge tusks on each side, turn up into a grin. The eyes of the entity were just black, almost triangular-shaped sockets. A few days after this nightmare, Debbie, Justine's older sister paid a visit to her former home on Bardsay Road with her husband Eddie. Debbie was heavily pregnant and she let Justine put her hand on her bump to feel the baby kicking. In those days, establishing the sex of the unborn was virtually unheard of, and Debbie said if it was a boy they were calling him Daniel and if it was a girl her name would be Danielle – as Debbie liked those names (and Eddie never had a say in the matter).

That night, "Looey" appeared in Justine's dream once again, and this time he said: 'You didn't write the letters [referring to the chain letters], so this is what you get.'

And he produced something that looked like a limp doll at first and he lifted it high with his clawed paw.

It was a baby – a male baby – and it looked inert as the bear-like creature shook it as it dangled there. The mouth of the entity broke into a grin and Justine could see the red fleshy gum at the top of the great tusks, and she drew back, for she somehow knew that the dead baby was Debbie's, and she started to cry. She woke up in a terrible state and found her mother and father leaning over her with very concerned faces. 'Justine! Are you okay?' the girl's father said, and he seemed near to tears. Justine had never seen this side of her father; he was usually a man who showed no emotion whatsoever.

Justine recalled the inert baby and said to her mother, 'Mum! Is Debbie okay?'

'What are you talking about?' Justine's mother asked, baffled.

'I dreamt she lost her baby, and it was a boy! It was horrible!' the girl told her and began to cry so hard she almost threw up.

'I'm sending you to a psychiatrist if you don't stop this!' Justine's father told her. 'Acting the goat! Is this all attention seeking is it? Eh?'

'Oh shut up,' Justine's mother told her husband, and she stroked Justine's back. 'She's had a nightmare, that's all,' she said, and then her daughter embraced her.

On the following morning, the sad news reached the family in Bardsay Road: Debbie had miscarried, and a week after that Debbie revealed how the baby had been a boy.

Justine began to make secret trips to a church where she begged a priest to bless her, and this he did. She told him about the terrifying bear with the tusks in her dream and thought he'd laugh, but he said a curious thing in reply. The priest asked, 'Is this thing like a teddy bear?'

'Yeah!' Justine replied excitedly, and the priest did not explain how he knew this, but Justine had the impression that the same thing had been reported to the priest by another parishioner – but of course, what people tell a priest in confidence remains off the record, so Justine never found out if others had been plagued by the terrifying being which had haunted her dreams. Thankfully the nightmares of Looey ended after the blessing, but then it was Carmel's turn. One night she had an absolutely horrific nightmare of a man, curled up in a foetal position while a huge mob of people stabbed him and kicked him, and cut off his fingers as he screamed. As this went on, Carmel could see the vague outline of Looey standing there in the distance, watching the gory goings-on. Then the scene would change, and Carmel would find herself unable to move in her bed, yet she knew she was awake – and she knew he was in the room. Then she would hear the distinctive low accent-less voice telling her to send chain letters to people she knew, otherwise he'd kill her in her sleep and she'd be in his dark world forever. Justine took Carmel to the priest and had her blessed, and the priest also visited the families of the girls and told them he believed the thing with tusks was some sort of demon. Around this time, the priest heard about the sickening and brutal murder of one PC Keith Blakelock down in Tottenham on the Broadwater Farm housing estate. The policeman had been surrounded by a mob in a riot and had ended up stabbed fifty-odd times. He was found with the six-inch-blade of a knife rammed into his neck up to the hilt, and had lost several fingers trying to ward off knife attacks. Blakelock was found in a curled-up foetal position and had screamed - in vain - for help before he was cruelly murdered. The circumstances of the policeman's death matched the details of Carmel's gruesome nightmare of the man receiving multiple stab-wounds by the frenzied people - who ended up cutting his fingers off.

Justine's family ended up moving – just in case the thing ever returned to haunt their dreams, while Carmel's family stayed put, but thankfully, they had no further nocturnal visits from the bizarre and evil creature. Years afterwards, I heard of a girl down in Devon who had died in her sleep after she had told her sisters that a weird, creepy-looking teddy bear had started haunting her dreams. She never mentioned the tusks but I feel there is some connection with the dream figure and the malevolent Looey.

A CULT OF BLOOD LUST?

Every single day we hear of some horrible incidents in the world, via the newspapers, the internet and the TV, but there are good people out there too, though they don't get much publicity, because bad news travels quicker than good news and sells more newspapers too. Many of us started out as budding helpers when we were kids (I know I did) but the world often eventually knocks any good intentions out of us, and its true what they say, the kindest hearts are the first to be wounded. Now and then, however, a Samaritan or a do-gooder will cross our path to help us regain our faith in human nature. In the sultry August of 1967, a 22-year-old woman named Dee Fearon was driving her car down Lodge Lane, bound for her home off West Derby Road, when the vehicle began to act strange. The car – a pale green 4-door 1962 Morris Minor – had been left to Dee by her late uncle in his will, and it had never given her trouble in the two-and-a-half years she'd owned it, but now it was shuddering and increasingly difficult to steer, and inconsiderate motorists behind her were beeping their horns, and the disharmonious cacophony made the girl panic. She managed to steer the troubled car down a side street (this would be Beaumont Street) and put the handbrake on. Dee got out of the vehicle and looked at the rear left wheel. It had lost its hubcap and the wheel was at a strange angle. At this moment a tall thin man of about 35 years of age came around the corner. He was carrying a square black case – similar to an attaché case but a bit thicker. 'Having car trouble?' he asked, and he did not have a Liverpool accent, but it was hard to say what part of the country he was from. His eyes looked red and sorrowful, as if he had been crying, Dee thought, but there was a kindness in those eyes which really put her at ease.

'I think the wheel's coming off,' Dee told him, crouching in her floral slack dress.

'Yes, it is,' the stranger replied and stooped down alongside Dee.

'I have a spare wheel in the boot – ' Dee was saying when the stranger shook his head and told her: 'No, this wheel's okay – just needs fixing on again.' He rested his case on the pavement, undid the catches and opened it. He rooted about in a green canvas bag and Dee heard a lot of metallic clanking in the bag before the man produced the strangest-looking car jack she'd ever seen. It was black, shiny and looked like a bedside lamp minus its shade. The man put the top of this thing under the car, located the jacking point, then began to turn a small lever on the device.

'I've got a more modern one if you want to use it?' Dee suggested, and grinned at the size of the jack, but the man muttered something unintelligible and shook his head – and the jack worked, because the car lifted a few inches. He tightened the loose wheel nuts with impressive speed and then lowered the car.

'Thankyou so much,' Dee nodded and smiled to the man as he packed the miniature jack back into his case, and the stranger smiled briefly and said, 'The least I could do.'

Dee walked around the car and waited until a van passed before she got into her car. She saw the face of the stranger peering in at her through the front passenger window, so she leaned over and wound the window down to see what he wanted.

He asked: 'Do you know what number bus I should take to Clubmoor? I'm not familiar with this area.'

'Where about in Clubmoor are you going?' Dee asked. 'I'm going to West Derby Road so I can give you a lift that far if you like?'

'No, I don't want to impose, I'll get the bus,' the man insisted, but Dee wouldn't have it and she opened the passenger door and beckoned the man in.

'Come on, where about in Clubmoor?' she asked, and started the car.

'Elquin Crescent,' the stranger told her.

'Well you'll have to give directions, I've never heard of that place,' Dee said, checking her mirrors.

Dee was driving along about a minute later when the stranger said 'My name's Dean, by the way.'

'Mine's Dee,' Dee gave a little giggle. 'We sound like a stage act – Dean and Dee,' she said, giving her passenger a sidelong glance.

'You're really good at the backstroke," Dean told her. There was a pause. Dee realised the man had been in the baths earlier, watching her swim and this really freaked her out. She began to panic now. The sordid truth of the situation slowly dawned on her: this man had obviously pretended to be a Samaritan just to inveigle her. She should have been suspicious of the fact that he just happened to have a car jack in a case after she'd pulled over with the wobbly wheel. She was too scared to even turn to face him. 'You realised you were on and you suddenly left,' the stranger remarked in a slow, deep measured voice which made her flesh creep. The car halted at the lights at the junction of Tunnel Road and Wavertree Road, and in the right lane alongside Dee's vehicle, a police car cruised to a halt. Dee looked right at the driver of the car; he was staring straight ahead, beyond the junction, towards Durning Road. She had to grab the policeman's attention so she bleeped the car horn, startling her weird passenger. The policeman turned left reflexively and as the creepy passenger realised what she had done, he reached into the right inside pocket of his jacket and produced something that glinted. Dee mouthed the words 'help me' to the driver of the police car, and his curiosity was immediately aroused. He got out of the vehicle and the lights changed.

'Go! Go on! Go! Step on it!' Yelled the stalker. Dee had not secured her seat belt, and took a chance; she left the car and hurled herself at the policeman. She fell against his chest and looked up at his face.

'What's wrong miss?' the policeman asked, and Dean – or whatever his real name – bolted from the other side of Dee's Morris Minor and ran towards Harbord Street. 'I think he was trying to kidnap me!' Dee yelled and turned to point at the wiry figure sprinting off with his case.

'And I think he's got a knife!' she added as the policeman gave chase.

Dee watched the figures run into the distance

towards Edge Hill, and just when the policeman was closing in on Dean, he threw the case squarely at him with such force, it opened on impact, knocking the policeman to the ground as its contents spilled all over the roadway. The car jack, screwdrivers, hammers – all sorts of tools hit passing vehicles as the stunned copper sunk to his knees. Dean ran on, laughing, and managed to escape.

Dee made a statement at Derby Road police station in which she mentioned the destination given by Dean as Elquin Crescent in Clubmoor – but it turned out that no such a place existed. There was no Elquin Crescent or Street or Road of that name in Clubmoor or anywhere else in Liverpool for that matter – nor was there any place-name that sounded remotely like Elquin in any of the street directories. Dee drove homeward in a terrible state of nerves. Every time she set eyes on a thin tall man she imagined it was Dean, and when she reached home, she told her mother and father what had happened and they assured her the bogus Samaritan would not come after her after having such a hairy encounter with the police. That evening, Dee grimaced as she recalled what he had said about her "being on" in the baths. How had he known that?

Just under a month later, Dee was asked to mind her cousin Rose's house on Kingsway in Huyton for a few weeks until Rose came back from a holiday in France. Dee would visit the house when she came home from work (a factory in Speke) and spend half an hour there before she went home. She also made occasional visits of a night and stayed over for an hour on Saturday and Sunday afternoons. It was on the second Sunday afternoon at the house when the phone rang. Dee assumed it was Rose, telling her she'd be coming home soon, but instead a chillingly distinctive voice spoke to her. It was *his* voice – Dean – there was no mistaking it, even over the phone. He said, 'Hello Dee, I see you're on again.'

Then he hung up.

Dee called the police and told them what had happened and at first they suggested it might have been a prank caller who had merely telephoned a random number, but Dee insisted it was the sinister Dean. She drove home soon afterwards and told her parents what had happened. They tried to reassure Dee that the obviously unbalanced caller was not going to try and attack her in her own home, but Dee would jump every time someone called at the house. A whole year passed, and Dee thought – or hoped – she had seen the last of the demented Dean. She got a new job as a secretary for a law firm in the city centre and became good friends with another secretary at her place of work named Helen. The two girls would often go for a drink after work and chat about all kinds, and one day, Helen said she had met 'a lovely girl' named Mona who was very shy, but very intelligent, for she could speak German, French, Italian and Swedish – and she was good at shorthand. Helen said she'd met Mona in a pub called the Lisbon when she had gone for a drink with her boyfriend Gordon. 'There's a position for a shorthand typist which has just come up, and I think Mona could fill the vacancy easily,' Helen said.

'She sounds like a decent girl,' Dee remarked, and said she'd like to meet her one evening.

Helen said she'd arranged a meet-up at the Rigby's

public house on Dale Street in a few nights' time.

When the meet-up occurred, Dee saw that Mona was very tall and rather awkward in her movements – the exact antithesis of Helen, who was graceful as a swan.

And then Dee's blood ran cold. When she went to shake hands with Mona, she could see, without a shadow of a doubt, that it was Dean. He was wearing a wig and was in full make-up. As Dee backed away in shock, he didn't seem to be surprised, and grinned, and Helen grabbed Dee's arm and said, 'What's the matter Dee? What's wrong?'

'It's him! That's not a woman, it's a man!' she jerked backwards and almost knocked a man's pint out of his hand.

'Hey, watch it will you?' the drinker said.

'Well, I've never been called that before!' Dean said in a very feminine voice, and he shot a puzzled look at Helen, who was both puzzled and annoyed at Dee's behaviour.

'Get away from me! You freak!' Dee screeched, and she ran out of Rigby's and kept looking back. She went into Cheapside police bridewell and told a bemused officer about the transvestite stalker but he merely advised Dee not to drink with such people. Dee left the bridewell and got a bus home. She could not believe the audacity of this weirdo. Surely Helen had plainly seen Mona was a man? Apparently not, Dee discovered on the following morning at work, but Helen did tell her something very strange about Mona that made Dee's stomach turn over. Mona had seemed fixated with menstruation and had asked Helen three times if she had heavy periods. Then Mona had gone to powder her nose – and that was the last Helen had seen of her.

'She *is* rather strange, Dee,' Helen reflected over her coffee break.

'She's not a "she" at all – she's a *he* - why can't you see that?' said Dee.

'I admit she doesn't have much going in the looks department – ' Helen admitted.

'Because she's a bloody man!' Dee interposed, 'Do you even know where this Mona lives?'

'Yes, she told me, er, Elquin Crescent, up in er – '

'Clubmoor?' Dee cut in.

'How did you know that?' Helen wanted to know.

Dee told her about the ersatz Samaritan a year ago who had given that destination. Helen was dumbfounded.

'Why in heaven is he so fixated with periods?' Dee wondered out loud.

The telephone rang on her desk, and Dee put on her professional posh voice and answered. It was him again. But before Dee could gesture for Helen to listen in, Dean said: 'I'm not alone. We target you by your blood cycle.' And then he hung up.

Both women lived in mortal fear of bumping into Dean in the guise of either sex, but thankfully there were no further encounters with him. However, Dee's younger sister Patricia, said she had met a 'funny' man at the Grafton club who had seemed okay at first, and had bought her drinks. But when he left the Grafton with her and a friend named Mo, the man – who gave his name as Keith – started going on about women's periods and how some women were evil the way they went looking for men in clubs. He talked of the first woman of the Bible – Eve – and how she had started to menstruate as punishment when she was thrown out of the Garden of Eden. Patricia told Keith to beat it, but he followed her along West Derby Road and started quoting the Bible. Patricia and her friend ended up taking off their heels and running along West Derby Road to get away from the Bible-thumper. Dee asked her 18-year-old sister to describe Keith, and she said he was tall and thin and pasty-faced.

And then, in 1969 Dee happened to read in the newspapers about a series of very odd murders up in Scotland, committed by an unknown serial killer nicknamed Bible John. Her heart skipped a beat when she took in the weird details of the unsolved murder case. On Sunday, 23 February 1968, the naked body of a 25-year-old nurse named Patricia Docker had been found in a secluded lane near Carmichael Place in Glasgow. Patricia had been raped and strangled (with her own pantyhose), and police soon pieced together the murdered young lady's movements prior to her murder. Patricia had gone out to an over-25s night at the Barrowland Ballroom – where she had apparently met her killer, and he had left the venue with her under the pretence of wanting to escort her home. The murder victim's clothes and handbag were missing, and they were never found despite an intensive police search. Then, in the middle of August 1969, 32-year-old mother-of-three Jemima MacDonald also went out for a night at the Barrowland Ballroom, and on the following Monday, Jemima's body was found in an old derelict building. She had been raped and strangled – with her own nylon tights - but unlike the previous victim, Jemima's body was still clothed when it was found. People at the ballroom recalled that Jemima had danced with a tall fair-haired man in a blue suit most of the night. He looked as if he was in his 20s – possible early 30s – and he had a short back and sides haircut. Detectives who realised the same killer had raped and strangled the two women noted that both victims were menstruating at the time of their deaths. The police quizzed everyone at the dance ballrooms as well as family members, neighbours and workmates of the women, but could not find a lead and could not trace the man in the blue suit who had been seen dancing with Jemima MacDonald on the night she was raped and murdered. On Devil's Night (October 30) of that year, the night before Halloween, 29-year-old Helen Puttock went out for a night at the Barrowland Ballroom while her husband stayed at home to mind their two young boys, but being mindful of the two previous murders associated with the ballroom, he told Helen to be careful who she danced with. Helen said she'd be okay because she wasn't going alone to the Barrowland Ballroom – she was going with her sister Jean, and she'd make sure she was always surrounded by people. Not long after the sisters arrived at the ballroom, Helen Puttock met a tall man with fairish, possibly reddish, hair, and grey-blue eyes, and she partnered with him for most of the night thereafter, while Jean, who danced with a few men, looked on. Sometime around midnight, the sisters decided to go home, and Helen's new 'friend' the dancing partner she'd been with all night, said he'd see the girls home in a taxi. He gave his name as 'John'. Throughout the taxi journey, John seemed to resent Jean being there, as if he wanted Helen all to himself, and Jean, being curious to know a little about the man who had taken a shine to her sister, asked him a little about himself. In a well-spoken voice, John gave a potted history of his life. He came from a strict religious family, and this was borne out by the way he seemed to be able to recite passages from the Bible from memory. On a lighter note, John also happened to mention that he was lousy at golf but had a cousin who was something of an expert player who had recently hit a hole-in-one. The cab came to Jean's house in the Knightswood area, and that was the last time she would see her sister alive. On the following morning, Helen Puttock's body was found, fully clothed, but she had been raped and strangled with her pantyhose. Her handbag was never found, but the contents of the bag were scattered nearby. Once again, it was discovered that the murder victim had been on her period during her death, and there was a curious clue to the killer's mindset on this occasion, because when Helen's body was examined, her sanitary towel had been removed from her underwear and tucked into her armpit. The killer had also left a bite mark on Helen's leg and a semen stain was also detected on her clothing. Police embarked on one of the biggest investigations the city of Glasgow had ever seen and the husband of third murder victim – Helen Puttock –used most of his life savings to put up a £100 reward to anyone who could supply information to catch the killer the Press had now dubbed "Bible John" – because of his citing of scripture. The police received around four thousand tip-offs from members of the public who thought they knew Bible John from an artist's impression that had been circulated in newspapers and on TV, but none of the leads were productive. The BBC even staged an early type of "Crimewatch" reconstruction with a policewoman dressed in the same clothes as Helen Puttock, but again, that provoked no worthwhile information from the people of Glasgow. Scores of young police officers went undercover and frequented the dance ballrooms of the city in the hope of collaring Bible John in his hunting grounds, but the sinister religious maniac was nowhere to be seen. The bite mark left by the killer on Helen Puttock's leg was analysed and a dentist noted that one of Bible John's upper teeth overlapped another tooth, so dental records were also searched – but to no avail. Detectives contacted golf clubs throughout Scotland to see if any members had recently bragged about a hole in one - in order to see if there was any truth in Bible John's hole in one story regarding his cousin. No club members could remember any such recent occurrences. The police were back to square one. Bible John was never found and no one is sure to this day if the rumours of the investigating officers knowing more about the case than they divulged are true, but there were whispers that the killer targeted women who were menstruating – but to my knowledge, not one investigator of this strange case, nor any report on the three murders has ever explained how Bible John knew his victims were on their periods. Is it possible that someone working in a pharmacy might have known each woman was menstruating because the woman in question may have purchased sanitary towels at the chemist? If that was the case, then surely Helen Puttock would have told her sister in the taxi that she had seen John before in a certain pharmacy –

unless, of course, John was just an assistant in the chemist's shop who had seen the woman receive the towels. As far as I know, no such checks were made on staff working in pharmacies.

Anyway, when Dee learned of the eerie Bible John murders, and when she read about the three menstruating victims, she immediately thought of the weird stalker who had somehow known she was on her period when he watched her in Lodge Lane baths, and she thought of his unnerving message over the telephone at her workplace when he had told her: 'I'm not alone. We target you by your blood cycle.' If that crackpot's statement had some truth in it, did it mean there was some cult of blood lust targeting menstruating females? And if so, how would these blood-obsessed fetishists know when their prey was having her period? The idea frightened Dee.

It's possible of course, that all of this is down to synchronicity – that the joker in pack of life's playing cards – coincidence – is to blame for all of these strange references to menace and menstruation – but I'm not so sure, because I recall a woman I interviewed many years ago named Karen. She told me how, in the summer of 1965, she went to visit the Liverpool Show at Wavertree Playground with her best friend Elsie. Both girls had just turned eighteen at the time. Karen soon realised she was being followed all over Wavertree Playground by a tall brown-haired man in a dark blue suit who looked as if he was in his early thirties. Wherever Karen and Elsie went, this man would be watching Karen, and at first Elsie seemed to think he was just some older admirer and she waved at him and giggled when she got on the fairground rides at the Show, but Karen thought there was something very creepy about the way the man stared at her. The Liverpool Show was a three-day event, and on the second day, Karen turned up again with Elsie, and the park was crowded with a record attendance for the event – later calculated to have been in the region of almost 130,000. Karen bought some candy floss as Elsie had a go at shooting an air rifle at a target, and the same weird stalker turned up, and this time he walked directly towards Karen, who felt so afraid, she felt her legs go numb. The man halted about four feet away from the teenager and in a low voice which seemed monotone and devoid of accent, he said: 'You're on, aren't you?' and he smiled.

Karen could not understand how the man knew she was on at the time, and the comment appalled her. She swore at the stranger and suddenly spotted a policeman in the distance next to a fortune-teller's caravan. She ran to the policeman but the stranger sneaked away into the milling crowds. Karen went home to her house near Old Swan, and told her mother and grandmother about the 'headcase' and his vulgar question. Karen didn't want her father to know because she knew she'd be embarrassed talking about periods to him.

Karen's mother Pat said something which frightened her. Pat said that five years back, in July 1960, she and her neighbour's daughter Lindsay, who was then nineteen, had gone to the Liverpool Show for the day, and a man who matched the description given by Karen had followed them all over the park. When Lindsay went to the toilet in the park, the man had approached her and said something about her being on her period, and Lindsay hadn't understood what he was talking about. The man then said something disgusting about Lindsay's sanitation towel, and when Karen asked her mother exactly what he had said, Pat said she'd never repeat the man's words because they were so disgusting, but the top and bottom of it was that he somehow knew Lindsay was on her period. Lindsay was so creeped out by this man, who continued to follow her (and Pat) around the park, the girl decided to go home. That evening around half-past ten, there was single loud knock at the door of her house off St Oswald's Street, and when Lindsay opened the front door, there was a packet of sanitation towels on the doorstep, but not a sign of the person who had placed them there, and this naturally scared the teenager. She never saw the man who had shadowed her all over the park, but for weeks she had the unsettling feeling he was watching her.

When Karen heard this, her stomach turned and when darkness fell, she was too scared to even look out of her window in case the nutcase was out there. A few days later around half-past nine there was a heavy knocking at the front door of Karen's house, and Karen's grandmother answered the door to find Elsie, Karen's best friend, trembling on the doorstep. The girl was usually very courteous and would wait until she was invited into the house, but on this occasion she flew past Karen's grandmother, and bolted down the hall into the back kitchen, where Karen was watching the TV with her father. Her mother had gone to bed because she had a bad summer cold.

'Karen!' a wide-eyed Elsie yelped as she burst into the kitchen, 'That man was looking through my window!'

'What man?' Karen asked, and then she suddenly realised just who Elsie was referring to.

'What?' Karen's father asked.

'Some man who was following us round the park at the Liverpool Show, Dad,' Karen explained. 'Another admirer, eh?' Karen's father said, gazing back at the television screen, not realising the gravity of the situation. He imagined the girls were talking about some harmless soppy lad with a crush.

Karen left the kitchen and took Elsie into the parlour where she and her grandmother asked the girl what had happened. Elsie said she had been on the toilet in her yard (for outdoor toilets were very common in 1965) when she had seen an eye looking at her through a hole in the old wooden door. She had screamed before pulling her knickers up and making herself decent before dashing from the toilet in the backyard to her kitchen doorway. The girl was at home on her own at the time, which was about 9.10pm. Elsie then saw the unmistakable face of the man who had stalked her and Karen at the Liverpool Show, gazing through the kitchen window at her.

As Karen and her grandmother listened to Elsie's story there was a loud ran-tan on the front door, and everyone jumped at the hammering knock. It was Elsie's mother and younger brother, Peter. They had come home from a visit to relatives and found the house empty. Karen and her grandmother backed up Elsie's story about the man spying on her in the toilet, but the girl was told to come home immediately, so she accompanied her mother and brother and went back to the house, and on the doorstep, they saw that someone had left a packet of sanitation towels there. This was an odd thing to find, but Elsie was on her period at the time and believed the man who had stalked her friend in Wavertree Playground had left the packet there.

Karen and Elsie never set eyes on the unbalanced stranger again, but neither of them could ever bring themselves to attend any of the Liverpool Shows after those uncanny encounters with a man who seemed obsessed with the girl's menstruation. How he knew they were on their periods is as mysterious as Bible John's knowledge about the periods of his victims.

PARADISE FOUND

I seriously believe some misguided genius is dabbling with weather control technology. We used to have fairly regular weather patterns; sunny summers and snowy winters, but now even the top meteorologists are admitting that 'something strange' is happening to our climate, and it may not be down to a change in the direction of the Gulf Stream or Global Warming. Believe it or not, the first serious proposal for weather control was put forward by Liverpool University physicist Sir Oliver Lodge in January 1914. Pre-Marconi radio pioneer Lodge suggested flying kites wired to electrodes into clouds to electrically stimulate the upper atmosphere to manually start or stop rainfall. The idea was hooted at in the Kelvin Lecture, but Lodge's ideas were later taken up by American scientists and by March 1951 a top secret machine was produced, partly funded by the US military, to 'drastically modify weather patterns'. The Senate considered a Weather Control Act, but never passed it, citing the dangers of weather control as a weapon – but research has continued since then, of course. Now, in 2007 I met a man in his nineties we shall call Vince (not his real name) at a booksigning in the city centre.

'Tell Tom your story before you snuff it, Dad,' his son insensitively told him, and Vince told me how, in

March 1958, he had been allowed out of prison on compassionate grounds to attend his mother's funeral in Cheshire. Vince was a small-time criminal at this time, serving five years for aggravated burglary. After the funeral he went into a pub toilet, but climbed through a tiny window and managed to escape and make his way back to Liverpool, where he tried to find a safe house. 'Still in my funeral clobber,' Vince told me, 'I went to a mate's flat in the Bull Ring but he wouldn't let me in.'

Vince went downtown and visited the shop of a relative on Hanover Street but the person wasn't in, so in panic he went down School Lane in a downpour, wondering if she should give himself up. He passed the Bluecoat Chambers, and was hit by a heat wave. Now the skies were clear blue. It was so hot, Vince could hardly breathe, and he walked up an alley to be greeted by a very strange site: a Church Street of white-painted buildings lined with towering palm trees. The people passing by were all wearing white clothing like the citizens of Mexico or Spain, and there was now no road running through Church Street; it was pedestrianised, as it is today, only instead of grey paving flags, most of the ground was taken up by well-kept diamond-shaped lawns . Vince wandered through this surreal paradise and saw massive unfamiliar buildings in the distance, and he halted at a huge fountain at the bottom of Bold Street next to a whitewashed Lyceum. He cupped the cool waters there, bathed his face, and asked passers-by: "When did they do all this?' – thinking the Council were responsible for the transformed city centre, but when the people talked back, Vince could hardly understand them – for they sounded as if they were Russian or Polish speaking in broken English. All of the familiar shops Vince had known on Bold Street were gone, and in their place he noticed there were continental style bars and café's with people sitting outside in deckchairs of some sort as they sipped oddly-coloured drinks and coffee.

One elderly man – in a white trilby and matching smart white suit, "dressed like the man from Delmonte", Vince recalled, kept a close watch on him, and Vince told him he was confused. 'I've been away for a while, and this all looks foreign to me,' he told the old man. The man, and several other passers by, looked at Vince's black suit. He obviously stood out starkly in this white-suited society. The old man, who later identified himself as Val, spoke good English, but there was a slight foreign accent to his voice, and he cryptically said to Vince: 'I know where you've come from, but you must abide by the rules here or you'll go back.'

Vince thought the old man knew he'd escaped from prison, and he said, 'I'm an innocent man, I was framed, so I had to get out.'

'Look, sonny, just don't upset the boat,' the oldster advised with a grave look, 'because those in power will have you sent back pronto.'

Vince could not make sense of this remark and asked why it was so hot, and after a long pause, the man looked skyward, squinted and replied: 'They knocked the earth off its axis – fifty years ago.' He never explained who these people were who had carried out this act of planetary vandalism, but he did explain because the world had been tipped over, the

North Pole was near the East Indies and Europe was now on the Equator. The South Pole was now Sumatra, and whole cities had become encased by the new polar icecap there. Vince was not a man who thought on a global scale, and so he couldn't really take any of this in. His everyday concerns about carrying out petty crimes and evading the police kept him in a little parochial world bounded by Blackpool to the north, Manchester to the east, Runcorn to the south, and Birkenhead to the west. Anything outside of that world of small-time crime, horseracing, drinking, smoking, clothes and women was terra incognita.

Still, Vince remained paranoid, and expected the police to turn up any moment and nab him. If this had happened to you or I, we'd suspect we had somehow entered a timeslip, but in 1958, the year Vince hailed from, such concepts were only known to people who read science fiction books and pulp magazines. Vince discovered that there was no money in this communistic society, and that if you wanted food, drink, shelter or clothing, you merely asked for it, and it was given to you. He accompanied Val into a bar with strange glyphs written over the entrance, and he and the old man were served blue liquid in large bulbous glasses. Vince had no money on his person because he'd only been allowed out the prison for the funeral before he absconded of course, but he saw that no money changed hands between Val and the barman. The music playing in the bar sounded like some sort of mandolin with an odd beat to it, and was reminiscent of Russian folk music Vince had seen on TV and in films. The drink had a strange effect on

Vince, and in hindsight he thought it must have been some hallucinogenic. He saw tiny sparkling stars everywhere he looked after taking just a few sips, and a strange peaceful feeling came over him. He felt friendly all of a sudden, and as he drank more of the blue beverage he was almost moved to tears by the intense bliss, so Val prevented him drinking any more and took him out into the harsh sunlight. The rest of Vince's stay – which seemed to last about a week - was almost one blur to him after that. He vaguely recalled drinking at other bars in what seemed to be the Hanover Street area, and he also had recollections of a visit to some amazing crystal temple with psychedelic patterns in its stained-glass window and jewel-encrusted walls. The drinks he and hundreds of other people had who attended the temple made them actually *feel* the strange music that was played on some organ there, and it was a type of religious experience. Vince also had fragmented memories of having sex with people at the temple, but it was dreamlike and he was obviously under the influence of the mind-bending drinks.

Vince did remember becoming quite ill, and he was taken to what seemed to be a circular room in a hospital with intense white light shining down on him. Next thing he knew, he was shivering in a dingy hospital ward, surrounded by two doctors, male nurses and several policemen. He knew he was back in the cold dreary grey world he had temporarily escaped from. He found himself in custody in 1958, and the detectives wanted to know where he had been for a week. Vince told them everything he could recall, about the world knocked off its axis, a tropical city centre, and of the shops where no one used money, but the detectives thought he was 'taking the piss' (as they put it), and they interrogated him over and over until Vince collapsed. It was later discovered that he had somehow contracted malaria – an infective disease normally found in a much hotter climate than wintry Britain. Still, no one believed his seemingly far-fetched story; the detectives noted his tan and believed he had somehow gone on the run abroad, but Vince angrily refuted this and said: 'Do you think I'd be stupid enough to come back to all this shite if I'd been abroad?'

Vince was treated for his malaria for a few years, because it was evidently a very hardy strain. Only decades later did he happen to read about the many timeslips people had encountered in the Bold Street area in my books, and he realised he had probably visited some future state of Britain. I tried to make arrangements to have Vince hypnotically regressed, but his son contacted me a week after the interview to say that his father had sadly died in his sleep. When I briefly mentioned this strange case on the Billy Butler Show on BBC Radio Merseyside, I was contacted by one of the detectives who had quizzed Vince about his week-long absence, and he told me that Vince was thick as two short planks and could not have dreamt up a story like that, and he did find it hard to believe that Vince would have come back from some sunny place abroad when the police of three counties were on the lookout for him. So what are we to make of Vince's story? If we accept it, will this world of ours be knocked off its axis by some meddling scientists? I can't think of many things that could tilt this planet of ours at such an angle so Europe would be placed on a new equator; a thermonuclear explosion perhaps? Or perhaps the world could be flipped over if some huge wandering planet passed by the earth at close enough proximity – it's probably useless to speculate. The British Isles were certainly tropical in the Carboniferous era of around 340 million years ago and their exotic fern forests eventually became the fossilised coal we once mined, and India and parts of Australia were once covered with ice, so we know that the climate of our world has undergone drastic changes in the past. What seems just as curious to me regarding Vince's account is the description of the people in future Liverpool speaking in what seemed to him to be English and a mixture of a language that was either Polish or Russian. Polish is now England's second most-spoken language, and the third most popular language in Wales. This fact was gleaned from the data gathered in the 2011 census; that of the 56.1 million inhabitants of England and Wales, 546,000 speak Polish. Just a few thousand more people speak Welsh (562,000) in comparison. There were 32,000 Russians living in the UK in 2009, and there are about 300,000 people of Russian descent living in Britain (2014 figures). The Baltic states joined the EU in 2004, and although Vladimir Putin, the president of Russia, has stated that it would not be in the interests of Russia to join the European Union, this could easily change if Putin retires, dies, is deposed or assassinated in the future, and if a reformed and democratic Russia accepts the EU's invitation to join its growing club, Russian citizens would be perfectly entitled to come to the UK to live and work in their millions. In the light of these facts and possibilities, the story of Vince and his possible inadvertent trip into the future seems entirely plausible.

A CRISIS APPARITION

In February 1979, a 45-year-old Woolton man named Gene said goodbye to his wife Susan and their two daughters, Tammy, aged 5, and Laura, aged 10. In some detail he had told his wife he had to attend a crucial evening business seminar in Crosby, and that meant staying overnight at a friend's house, but he was in fact, going to spend the night with a 22-year-old work colleague named Erika at her flat in Prenton, over in Wirral. Affairs are a fact of life, and people have them for various reasons; sometimes people perceive their relationship as being a little stale and boring, and some embark on a liaison out of a longing to recapture some lost youthful part of their lives, whilst some people in relationships happen to meet someone else and – often against their will and better judgement - fall hopelessly in love with them. In Gene's case, he was having an affair out of lust – but the shapely Erika believed his spiel about love at first sight. So in a way, there were two victims in this affair, Gene's wife Susan - and Erika, who really believed Gene would marry her in the near future and start a family. Upon this wintry February night, Gene went to have a bath, and he read the A to Z street atlas he'd brought with him to research his lies. He wasn't too au fait with the local geography of Crosby – the place where he was supposed to be having the long business seminar with his bosses – and so he did a modicum of swatting as he lay soaking in the bath, and he grinned as he scanned the maps of the roads of Crosby and Brighton le Sands – when suddenly, he thought he heard a girl sobbing somewhere.

'Erika? You alright, love?' he shouted, but he could hear Erika in the kitchen, singing, as well as the sounds of pots clanking on the cooker. Then he heard the crying sounds again, and all of a sudden, what looked like a fuzzy oval-shaped hole opened in the air in front of him, about two feet above the bath, and within this hole, Gene clearly saw Jo, the 15-year-old daughter of his friend Barry. She had her face in her hand as she sobbed. 'Dad, please come back...' the girl cried – and then Gene noticed she was holding a bottle of pills. The disturbing vision then vanished. Gene instantly recalled that his friend Barry had left his wife and daughter recently. He jumped out the bath, quickly dried and dressed himself, and told a perplexed Erika he had to go and save his friend's daughter from a suicide attempt.

'What do you mean?' Erika had laid the table and was about to serve the dinner she'd been preparing for hours.

'You'd never believe me,' Gene said, and seemed very confused to the 22-year-old. He drove back to Liverpool as fast as the law would allow him and reached Barry's house in Mossley Hill. He hammered on the door and Barry's wife, Rose, answered. Gene pushed past her and bounded up the stairs two at a time to search each room. He found Jo lying on her bed with a half-empty bottle of sleeping tablets in her left hand. Her face was slicked with tears.

'What the hell are you playing at?' Rose yelled at Gene, but then she saw the ghastly scene; Jo was lying face down on the bed and Rose recognised her bottle of sleeping tablets in her inert daughter's hand. Within seconds the woman's trembling finger was dialling the telephone for an ambulance.

Jo was pumped at the hospital and eventually recovered, and Barry and Rose were astounded at Gene's story about the 'crisis vision'. Gene then realised how much his own wife and daughters loved him, and he ended the affair with Erika immediately. Gene had never had a psychic experience before that night, and he hasn't had one since, but he believes something supernatural took place that wintry night which saved a teenaged girl's life and also saved Gene's marriage.

WHISPERING JACK

Quite a few years back I was testing a man named Stephen who claimed to have psychic powers, and many of the tests I subjected him to indicated that he did indeed have mediumistic abilities. The tests involved such things as reading Zener cards from another room, dice forecasts, the reading of an object's history while it was concealed in a box (psychometry) and so on, but the most intriguing test took place outdoors. I took Stephen to Howard Drive in Grassendale and we walked the length of this street, which is about 125 metres, when he suddenly halted in front of one particular house. The three-storey dwelling Stephen gazed at in dread is typical of most of the houses on this street – yellow brick with a pointed, Gothic-looking gable. Stephen said we were being watched by a being that was "ancient, odd and very sinister." I tried to press Stephen for more information as his eyes - which were full of fear - scanned the upper windows of the house in question, but he hurried away from the street. The house he had homed in on has a spinechilling history. In the 1970s, an 11-year-old girl named Natalie used to stay over at the house at least once a month at the invitation of her Aunt Celia and Uncle Jim. Then, one night in March 1977, Natalie went to bed in the spare room at the Howard Drive house. The time was around half-past twelve and the girl was feeling rather sleepy. Aunt and Uncle said goodnight from the landing outside the door of the room Natalie was staying in, and then they retired for the night, but around 2am, something woke Natalie up. It was a male voice whispering her name outside her door. It was not her uncle's voice, and this realisation scared her. The door handle squeaked as it turned, and Natalie hid under the bed in terror. She saw a pair of weird, pointy-toed jet-black shoes walk past the bed in the moonlight. The girl then ran from under the bed and straight to her Aunt and Uncle's room. They said she'd been dreaming. Each time Natalie stayed over, the whispering entity would visit her, and one morning around three, the girl awoke to find an unearthly silhouetted figure sitting in an old high-backed chair in the bedroom. There was a full moon shining into the bedroom and Natalie could see the shadowy entity was impossibly thin, and resembled an artist's mannequin model – as if it was jointed like a doll.

'Hello Natalie,' the eerie figure whispered, 'my name is Jack.'

'Leave me alone,' Natalie sobbed as she hid her head under the covers, but the creepy entity said: 'Don't be scared, I've come to tell you some stories.' And Natalie felt paralysed all of a sudden. The weird visitor then narrated a terrifying story about children trapped in a cupboard while their house was on fire, and suddenly the walls of the bedroom lit up with orange flickering light – as if illuminated by flames. Natalie tried to scream, but was unable to. The sinister storyteller ended his narrative with: 'And the children died, but they can do all sorts of wonderful things now. Would *you* like to die, Natalie? It doesn't hurt.'

The girl suddenly managed to let out a scream and ran out the room in hysterics, and never stayed at the house on Howard Drive again. I've discovered that "Whispering Jack" was seen at the house as recently as 2009, but just what he is remains a mystery.

THE SHIEL ROAD GHOST

Time and time again I hear about certain apparitions from members of the reading public, and what follows is just one of these oft-reported ghosts. I'll start at the beginning. One grey March morning in 1977 at around 7am, a 27-year-old woman named Frances and her 5-year-old daughter Patsy were standing at the bus stop at the Rocky Lane end of Kensington's Sheil Road. Mother and daughter were from nearby Sunlight Street, and were waiting for the bus to take them to the house of a relative in Toxteth who was getting married at Brougham Terrace later that day. At this time in the morning the rush-hour hadn't really started yet, and Frances stamped her feet with the cold as she looked northwards – towards her right, for the Number 26 bus. Patsy, meanwhile was gazing in the exact opposite direction – southwards down Sheil Road, when she noticed something which struck her as odd. The distant figure of a man was walking, and Patsy watched him for some time, but he didn't seem to be getting nearer. She told her mum about this peculiarity, and Frances squinted into the wind and asked, 'What fellah?'

'There,' Patsy pointed at the speck in the distance,

and then she added, 'three lamp posts down. See him?'

'Oh yeah,' Frances said, then looked north again, hoping to see the green bus.

'He's walking and he's been walking for ages but he's still there,' Patsy told her mother, and became annoyed at no response. 'Mam!'

'Yeah, I saw him!' Frances replied, irritated by the sharp wind on her stockinged legs. 'God, where's this bleedin' bus gone?'

Ten minutes passed and Patsy was still looking at the pedestrian in the distance, and, as the girl had observed, he had not moved further away or advanced towards her and her mum. 'Mam, this is quite strange – he's still there.'

Frances sighed and turned to look down Sheil Road, and she saw the man, who was about 300 yards away – was in the same spot she'd seen him in ten minutes ago, and yet she could see his legs were moving, and unless he was walking on the spot, he was somehow remaining stationary as he walked – an impossibility of course. She took a tissue from her handbag and dabbed her eye, and looked again. 'He's walking away from us,' she said.

'No, he's not, he's walking towards us – I can see his face, Mam,' said Patsy, leaning forward with her hand over her eyes like a ship's lookout.

'I used to have eyesight like you, love,' Frances said with a smirk. 'Oh, Patsy! Here's the bus love, come on, come here!'

The bus slowed and Frances held her daughter's hand as she got her purse ready to pay the fare. Patsy leaned southwards, pulling her mother's arm as she continued to gaze at the paradoxical walker in the distance.

Patsy ran to a vacant seat and pressed her face to the window as her mother paid the fare, and then Frances staggered towards her child as the bus jarred and began to move off from the stop. Frances wanted to see the walker pass by and she looked out the windows on the left side of the bus. Patsy and Frances could see the figure getting nearer, and then, when the bus was about fifty yards away, the walker vanished, and Frances couldn't take in the eerie disappearance at first, but Patsy turned her little cup face to her mother and exclaimed: 'Mam! He disappeared!'

Frances was speechless.

Suddenly, a black woman in her sixties who was seated in front of the mother and daughter turned, and she smiled at Patsy, then turned further around and said to Frances: 'I've seen him a few times,' and then, mindful of the child's presence, the lady mouthed the words: 'He's a ghost' to Frances, then turned away.

Frances was naturally intrigued, and she leaned forward and said, 'Excuse me,' to the black lady. 'Is he really a ghost?'

The lady nodded and said, 'I've seen him a few times. He has a cap on but you never get to see his face became he vanishes as the bus gets close.'

'Wonder who he is?' Frances asked, and the woman merely shrugged in reply.

When I mentioned this story on the radio some years ago, I received many letters and emails from listeners – some of them bus drivers, and some of them passengers who had travelled on that bus route. I received one letter from a man who worked for a well-known car sales business, and he told me how, in the

1990s, he had seen that ghostly figure many times on Sheil Road, apparently walking in the same spot. I got a lot of correspondence from people who had waited at the bus stop Patsy and Frances had been waiting at when they saw the ghost, and all of the stories I was told said that the ghost had been seen, and no one could make out if the man in the distance was approaching them or walking away – he merely seemed to be going through the motions of walking and yet he never moved, which is quite strange. A local of Sheil Road named Phil told me how, in the late 1980s, he had waited at the bus stop for a few days, hoping to catch a sight of the ghost, when he appeared one afternoon around three. Phil had a pair of 25x50 bird-watching binoculars on him, and he eagerly had a look at the apparition through them. What he saw was surreal. The man seemed to be walking away and yet his face was visible – he was facing Phil and yet walking backwards with a strange gait, but not physically moving from his observer or towards him, and then, after about twenty seconds the ghost vanished. Phil said he had on a brownish tweed cap and a dark grey raincoat. The face of the ghost was deathly pale. The entity used to be reported to me quite regularly, although I haven't had any reports of this Sheil Road ghost for a while now, so maybe it has stopped walking, but if you're ever passing along that part of town, keep a look out for the apparition.

ONE LUCKY CHILD

Some of the greatest dramas are not to be found on film or the stage, but within the theatre of everyday life, especially in the kaleidoscopic brouhaha of Liverpool street life. Budding authors, script-writers and playwrights in search of a muse, get out of your stuffy studies and take yourself off to the city centre of Liverpool, for every citizen you meet is a walking book of short stories – and some are absolute novels. One such font of stories was a man nicknamed "Mac", a cabby who has long left this arena of existence, and the following story is just one of many his son related to me, which I have researched and vindicated.

It was a hot and sunny April afternoon in 1957 when Mac's ancient rust bucket of a taxi pulled up at the grass-green wooden hut known as Mrs Farrimond's Café in the middle of Williamson Square. This café was exclusive to taxi drivers, and 58-year-old Mac took his afternoon coffee break here, where he and the other cabbies would always end up in heated arguments about sport, politics and metaphysics (which usually concerned the whys and wherefores of human existence), and on this day the drivers were talking about premonitions. One of the lads had talked of a vivid dream he'd had on the previous night in which Mac had either knocked someone down or caused their death through dangerous driving and was jailed for manslaughter as a result. Mac said he didn't even believe in the weather forecast, never mind "airy-fairy dreams". The cabby who had had prophetic dreams come true before warned Mac to have his eyes checked, as he felt as if his colleague's poor vision had something to do with the crime he'd dreamt of. Mac wore thick pebble-lensed glasses and thought the whole premonition thing was all some late April Fool wind-up and so he left the café in a huff.

Later that day, Mac dropped off a woman and her two young children on Church Street, and as the lady paid the cabby her 3-year-old daughter Daisy spotted a butterfly and followed it. The colourful butterfly landed on the bonnet of the cab. The child giggled and climbed onto the front of the taxi, then knelt on the fender, and tried to grab the butterfly – when Mac drove off, unaware that a child was clinging on for dear life to the radiator grille! The mother went into shock when she saw Daisy had seemingly vanished into thin air.

Mac drove on, meanwhile, oblivious to the terrifying situation, and wondered why some people were waving and shouting at him as he went by. He wondered if his exhaust was spewing out black smoke again, and checked his mirrors. No, the exhaust was fine. He went down Victoria Street, where a policeman had just arrested a 17-year-old Teddy Boy named Jimmy for throwing an egg at him as part of a dare, and as Mac cruised past, the delinquent spotted poor Daisy and told the stout constable: 'Hey, there's a little kid hangin' on the front of that taxi!'

'Button it, Billy's Weekly Liar!' the copper replied, his fist securely gripping Jimmy's shirt collar, but then he saw a well-to-do woman shriek and point at Mac's cab as it approached traffic lights.

'I'm not kiddin' mate!' Jimmy said. 'I swear to God there's a kid clingin' onto that cab!'

'Well go and stop him then! Go on!' the policeman released the ted, and Jimmy hared it to the taxi, the tails of his midnight blue jacket flying up as he went, but the lights changed and the vehicle moved off. Jimmy's suede crepe-soled shoes pounded the tar macadam and he caught up with Mac's noisy vehicle, and the lad somehow jumped onto the back of the ancient cab. Jimmy climbed onto the roof as the policeman's whistle pierced the air. The constable was overweight, and could only chase the taxi as far as North John Street where a sharp stitch in his side brought him to a halt, and he removed his egg-splattered helmet and wiped his brow, gasping for air. Jimmy, meanwhile, was lying flat on the roof of the taxi, telling the crying Daisy to hang on as he pounded on the windscreen. Mac tried to slow down – but to his utter horror he discovered that the brakes had gone. He had a flashback to Mrs Farrimond's Café and to the premonition his colleague had had about him getting nicked for manslaughter.

'Oh Jesus,' he mumbled, and felt beads of sweat form under his cap on his bald head.

Pedestrians fled out of the way as the cab hurtled down Lord Street. Jimmy bravely climbed into the cab through the wound-down front passenger window and yelled, 'There's a bleedin' kid hangin' on the bonnet you stupid old get!'

'What?' Mac asked, and felt his legs going numb with shock. 'The brakes have gone! I can't friggin' stop!'

'Let's try this!' Jimmy reached for the handbrake.

Mac swore hard at him at the top of his voice. 'The car'll flip over you stupid bastard!'

'There's a kid gonna die here!' Jimmy yelled back and his hand seized the handbrake, pressed the little button on it and operated it in one swift moment.

The car shook as if it had hit a wall and Jimmy felt his teeth clatter as his jaw vibrated. The cab shook violently, spun around twice and screeched to a halt in a cloud of dust and black smoke from the tyre friction.

'That kid'll be dead you soft 'arl get!' Jimmy cried, and opened the door as Mac sat there, stunned. His glasses had been thrown onto the fascia from the inertia of the highly dangerous handbrake manoeuvre.

A crowd encircled the car and Jimmy walked through the smoke and dreaded what he'd see.

Daisy calmly hopped off the fender with a smile on her face.

'You're – you're alright!' Jimmy gasped in amazement before a row of silent observers wondering what was happening.

Daisy was later reunited with her mother, and she told her something quite odd. The little girl said 'some woman in blue' had held her that day as she clung to the car. At first she could only feel her hands around her waist, but then she saw her, and she had 'such a kind face,' Daisy recalled, and then the little lucky girl added: 'but then she said she was going back to Heaven and she went up.'

That lady in blue could possibly be the same 'angel' or spiritual helper who has been reported to me quite a lot over the years. I have written about her somewhere in my books, and I must publish more reports of this sort, for I have a feeling they may be all describing the same entity, but who or what she is I do not know.

A WOOLTON SUCCUBUS

Let me take you back to simpler, yet admittedly politically incorrect times – a certain well-known pub in the Woolton area, in the blistering hot summer of 1976. The backdrop to this true story was atypical of the era: clinking pints of Greenall Whitley beer, lazy dart games, drowsing domino players and a couple of young virginal lads ogling the barmaid and giggling as they repeatedly made strategic purchases of bags of Big D roasted peanuts from the card featuring a topless model hanging next to the till. A little rotund plasterer named Roy stood at the bar in this unprecedented summer heat, alternating glances between *Crossroads* on the pub telly, Alison the barmaid, and his swanky digital watch. It was nearly 5.45pm and there was no sign of Roy's mate Tony. They always met in this pub after work. Then the door opened and in came Tony, a dead ringer for the Carry On actor Jack Douglas with his John Lennon specs and flat tweed cap. He looked very pale, and Roy produced a pound note and slid it across the counter to Alison, saying: 'Two pints of bitter and get one yourself love.'

'Sorry I'm late, Roy,' Tony said, gazing down at the bar counter, 'but erm, well – Roy - you know if you went a bit top twenty, would you know you'd gone nuts or wouldn't you know at all?'

'Come again?' Roy said and smiled at Alison, who was eavesdropping as she lined up the glasses.

'Do people who go mad know they've lost their marbles?' Tony queried with great concern on his face.

Roy squeezed his eyebrows together, puzzled, then shrugged. 'Dunno. I'm not Bamber Gascoyne, Tone, but I should imagine people who go tappy don't realise they've gone nuts – why?'

'Come over here,' Tony indicated with a turn of his head that he wanted his friend to come and sit in the corner with him, and Roy sighed and followed. The two men sat, and Tony took a deep breath, and then he came out with it. 'I got home around half-four and no one was in. I went up to get a shower – '

Roy tutted. 'Tony –'

Tony waved his hand dismissively at Roy's preachy attitude. 'Yeah, I know, because of the water ban and the drought and all that, we're not supposed to shower a few times a week –'

'Every single day mate,' Roy told him with a smirk. 'Every bleedin' day you've had a shower. Me and the missus bathe together, and I know I'm a big fellah but you've seen how big Marie's ars –'

'Here's our pints,' Tony interrupted his friend's aesthetic description of his other half.

Alison plonked the pints of bitter on the little oaken table, smiled and put the four pence change in Roy's clammy hand.

'Thanks sweetheart,' Roy said, detecting the barmaid's beautiful scent.

The two men were parched, and lifted the pints to

their lips simultaneously, and then Tony explained his odd questions about the nature of insanity.

'As I was saying, I came home, at half-four, no one was in, so I went up to the bathroom, had a shower, and something happened, and you're not going to believe this Roy, but I stood there in the shower, and the water was ice cold and it was lovely and that – then all of a sudden, everything went bright, as if the roof had come off the house and the sun was shining in. I opened my eyes and saw light – like sunlight – coming out the shower head. It was like thousands of little beams coming out instead of water, and then I felt a naked woman – a young naked woman put her arms around me.'

Roy's eyes darted left and right to see if any of the drinkers had heard this last sentence of Tony's, then the plump plasterer said in a low voice: 'You what?'

Tony continued: 'A nude woman, and I'd say she was about twenty, maybe twenty-two – and – '

'And what?' Roy lifted his pint, unaware that the beermat was stuck to the bottom of the glass.

Tony whispered: 'I had it off with her.'

'You what?' The beermat fell off the end of Roy's glass onto the carpeted floor.

Tony was deadly serious, and Roy didn't know the turmoil of guilt his friend was going through. Tony felt as if he had betrayed his wife Joan, even though the woman he'd had sex with had subsequently vanished. 'Am I going mad, Roy?' Tony asked, and seemed ready to burst into tears. Roy had never seen this side of his old friend before.

'Look, Tone, just calm down a sec, and let's go through this one bit at a time because what you're saying doesn't make sense. Now, your eldest, Michelle is back with that fellah – the student – '

'Ambrose?' Tony asked, puzzled. 'Michelle's left home now and she doesn't come near - '

'Yeah, Ambrose – now, didn't you say he was into LSD?'

Tony closed his eyes and shook his head. 'Roy, I have *not* taken any drugs. This was not an 'illusionation or whatever you call it – this really happened and I can't explain it.'

'So what you're saying then is that you goosed a ghost?' Roy put him on the spot and gulped down his bitter. He was now so concerned about Tony's mental wellbeing.

'No, not a ghost, but – but – I can't explain it, Roy' Tony struggled to put into words just what had taken place in the shower. 'Roy, you know me more than anyone, and you know I have never even told a white lie to you, agreed?'

'Yeah, but – '

'No, hang on, Roy, listen to common sense mate. What would I get out of making up a story like this? I would swear on a stack of Bibles – '

Roy took out a new box of twenty Woodbines, took the cellophane wrapper of it, and offered one of the filterless fags to his friend, but Tony shook his head and ranted on about how honest he was. Roy uncapped his lighter, lit up and then accidentally blew smoke in Tony's face. 'Tony, hang on a minute. Look, what did she look like? This young woman in the shower?'

'You'll laugh – ' Tony said, with that wallowing-in-self-pity look Roy had seen so many times before in their long friendship over the years.

'I won't, go on,' Roy assured him. He really needed this cigarette for once.

'Okay, here goes. She had a fantastic figure, and her bristols were pretty big, and her face was lovely, but this is the part you won't believe and I wouldn't blame you: she had like purplish hair in a sort of bob – '

'Purple hair?' Roy replied, and Tony caught him grinning behind his hand as he held the ciggie to his mouth.

'You said you wouldn't laugh. Forget it, Roy.'

'I didn't bleedin' laugh, go on.'

'Nah, it's alright. Thought you'd be the one person I *could* talk to,' Tony sulked, eyes glistening.

Roy eventually convinced his friend the grin had been more borne out of nerves than the description of the 'ghostly' girl's unusual hair colour, and Tony told him the rest.

'I don't even know why I did it with her, it was like I was in a trance, and that light coming down on me made me feel dizzy. I really got stuck into her – and that has never happened before – even with Joan. It was lovely, but it was wrong, Roy – I'm married. I feel terrible now, guilt-ridden.'

Roy saw a tear in his friend's eye. 'Calm down, Tony,' the plasterer patted him on the shoulder. 'Cor, I wouldn't mind having a shower in yours sometime, ha!'

'That's not funny, Roy,' Tony gritted his teeth, took off his spectacles and wiped a tear away with the back of his finger. 'What the hell is going on?'

'There are more things in Heaven and earth – ' Roy began the famous Shakespearian quote, but couldn't recall how the rest of it went, and so he turned to face Alison and then he gestured for two shorts by gripping an imaginary little glass in front of his face between thumb and two fingers and rapidly turning his wrist twice. 'Two large whiskeys, love – and one for yourself.'

'I might go and see me doctor,' Tony mused, putting his specs back on.

'And say what?' Roy asked all matter-of-fact about the half-hearted suggestion, 'That you made love to a woman who wasn't there?'

'You're really not helping, Roy – '

'Has anyone ever seen anything strange in your house over the years?' Roy pondered and dragged on the Woodbine.

'How do you mean, strange?'

'Ghosts. Cold spots, footsteps when there's no one there, and that,' Roy thinned his eyes and gazed up into the billowing exhaled smoke, meditatively.

'That house isn't haunted,' Tony told him, 'its got a nice welcoming atmosphere. And the fellah who lived there before us is still alive and well.'

'Yeah but what about the people who lived there before him?' said Roy, and he seemed to be taking on the air of some professional psychical investigator.

'Ghosts put the willies up us, not the other way around,' quipped Tony, with a very shameful expression. 'Oh, that was a horrible thing to say, I didn't mean it.'

'Drink this, mate, you'll feel better,' Roy passed a double whiskey towards his perplexed friend.

'Hey, it was my turn to get the round in – ' Tony objected.

'You can - in a minute, drink up,' Roy placed the glass in Tony's hand. 'It might get our cogs going and we can fathom this thing out.'

Tony and Roy were sipping the scotch when the door of the pub burst open and in came Tony's wife, Joan and 15-year-old daughter Nicola.

'What are you doing here?' a startled Tony asked his wife.

'I want to see you about something, come on – ' she beckoned him with a sidelong tilt of her head as she walked out of the pub. Tony got up and went to see what the matter was, and outside in the harsh evening sunshine, a worried-looking Joan said: 'Tony, did you know we've got a ghost in our house!'

'A what?' Tony replied, feeling ever so relieved. He gazed at his daughter and she nodded and added: 'We both saw it, Dad, a girl at the top of the stairs - dead clear.'

'Come inside and tell me,' Tony said with a half-smile on his smug face, 'I want Roy to hear this.'

'Piss off!' Joan dismissed the suggestion. 'I'm not talking in pubs about this!'

'Calm down Joan, I saw her myself – ' Tony told her, and blushed, but it wasn't noticeable because he was so tanned in this heatwave.

Joan's mouth went o-shaped and she looked at her daughter Nicola, who returned the same look of astonishment like a mirror, then they simultaneously asked Tony: 'Did you?'

'Yeah, she had purple hair – ' Tony began to reply but they both butted in.

'Oh my God!' Joan said and clamped her hand on her own mouth.

'Ah! Yeah! That's her!' Nicola said, and gave a succession of nervous blinks.

'She appeared in the shower, on Nicola's life, Joan,' Tony told his wife, 'I thought I was going mad. I told Roy and I think he thought I was making it up.'

Roy appeared in the pub doorway at this point and said, 'What's up, Joan?'

'Tony was just telling me that he'd told you all about the - ' And Joan mouthed the word "ghost". 'Isn't it weird?' Joan said to Roy. 'I'm getting a priest in – '

'I was just telling Joan what I told you, Roy, about the girl with purple hair in the shower.'

'Yeah, Tony was in the shower with her, yeah, and she was trying it on with him,' Roy told mother and daughter, assuming, from what he had heard, that Tony had come clean about the incident.

'What?' Joan recoiled with a look of disgust mingled with disbelief, and she turned to face a speechless Tony. 'You were in the shower with her and she what?'

'No, Roy's got it wrong, *I* was in the shower but *she* was in the doorway of the bathroom,' Tony lied, then as an afterthought he said: 'Fully clothed, she was.'

'Ooh, I've just gone all cold,' Joan shuddered, and her hands gripped Nicola's hands.

Roy tried to reassure Joan and her daughter. 'The thing with ghosts is that they appear and then usually you never hear from them again, Joan, honest. Don't you and the girl start worrying. My Nan used to say: "Ghosts can't harm you, it's the living you have to worry about." '

Tony was glaring at Roy over his wife's shoulder for nearly dropping him in it.

'Hey Roy, I don't suppose you want to come back with us?' Joan asked, 'We'd feel safer with you there as well.'

'Yeah, come on, I'll sort this ghost out,' Roy laughed, and walked with the family to their semi-detached home off Woolton Road.

Roy stayed at the house till 10.45pm , regaling Joan and Nicola with every hackneyed story about his adventures in the plastering trade until Joan became so bored, she actually dozed off in the middle of a long-winded yarn Roy was telling.

'Mam!' Nicola giggled and tapped her mothers arm and Joan let out a yelp and said, 'Oh my God, I dreamt that ghost got hold of me.'

'I'll have another coffee and then I'll have to love you and leave you,' said Roy, leaning back in the armchair.

'We're out of coffee, mate,' Tony fibbed.

'Ha! You said Coffee Mate Dad,' Nicola joked, 'Uncle Roy wants coffee, not Coffee Mate.'

'Tea then, I don't mind,' Roy said with a shrug.

'It's nearly eleven,' Tony informed his talkative friend. 'I'm knackered and Joan can't keep her eyes open.'

'Your funny, Roy,' Nicola told her 'uncle' and gave a toothy grin. 'Did anything funny ever happen to you when you plastered your own house?'

'Oh yeah – ' Roy was about to tell another story but Tony intervened.

'Nicola, it's time you went to bed, girl,' her father told her sternly, 'or you'll have big bags under your eyes the way you're going on.'

Joan and Tony finally saw Roy off and then they

wearily climbed the stairs and as they brushed their teeth they both couldn't stop laughing at the way Roy had dominated the evening. Tony knew Nicola was a bag of nerves over the ghost, and so he let her stay downstairs with the television on till "Closedown" around one o'clock and then she'd be allowed to take the radio up to her bedroom.

The couple slept soundly that night, and nothing remotely supernatural took place – until a fortnight later. The heatwave was still going on, Britain was now facing very serious drought conditions, and most people could hardly get a wink of sleep because of the smothering heat. Opening the bedroom windows at night seemed to make people even more hot and bothered, and holy men of all denominations began to actually pray for rain.

It was a Tuesday afternoon one boiling cauldron of a day when Tony got home earlier than usual from his job. The time was ten minutes to four, and despite the Government restrictions about using water, Tony decided to get a shower. He took off his sweat-soaked clothes and rubbed a brand new bar of soap over his body and felt the icy water run down his face and chest and limbs in rivulets, and he started to feel so fresh. He aimed to shower for just three minutes, and it felt so wrong - but so luxurious.

Then the very same thing occurred which had happened two weeks back. A bright solar light – as if a noonday sun was shining down through a hole in the ceiling – fell down on the crown of Tony's hair. He felt his heart palpitate as he realised what was taking place. The light was warm, and it rapidly filled the shower cubicle and became so intense he squinted. He was just about to get out of that cubicle when he felt the soft hairless arms of a female embrace him. Cool breasts cushioned against his dripping chest, and he felt full lips upon his. He opened his eyes and the light was still bright but not as intense as before, and he saw green eyes looking into his. It was her again. He tried to push her away, but it was impossible, and Tony found himself going into a trance-like state in which he became very aroused – even though he was afraid. This time though, he heard a voice shouting – echoing in the distance. It was Joan calling his name, and suddenly the frosted transparent cubicle door of the shower opened and the light faded – and the girl vanished in an instant.

Joan stood there in shock, gazing at her drenched husband with his hair hanging down and stuck against his face.

'Did you see her?' Tony managed to say, for he had felt paralysed from head to toe for a moment.

'Yes,' Joan said, and she grabbed Tony by his forearm and guided him out the shower cubicle and into the bedroom.

'Did you see her clearly, love?' Tony asked, sitting naked on the bed. He was shivering, despite the infernal heat of day.

'Yes, it was horrible,' Joan replied, and she told him that she only saw a distorted image of the ghost because she had glimpsed it through the frosted panes of the cubicle, but it had been the ghastly greyish colour she had noticed, and the white hair.

Tony was puzzled at this description, and still seemed to be in a daze. 'No, she was beautiful, love, with purple hair.'

'Not this time, Tony,' his wife told him, 'she looked horrible. Oh God, we are going to have to get out of this house. I asked a priest to bless it and he said they don't do that nowadays.'

Tony was adamant that the ghostly seducer had been a beautiful young woman, but he had heart-stopping nightmares almost every night after the incident in which a grotesque, heavily wrinkled grey-skinned hag with one tooth was performing all types of perverted acts upon him. Her skin felt leathery and she seemed reptilian. Roy asked a cousin who was into the occult to look into the matter and he refused, but this relative got in touch with an amateur investigator who turned up at the house in Woolton and carried out all sorts of tests with self-made electronic gadgets. The researcher seemed a very level-headed man, and he gravely warned Tony that the entity which had seduced him twice in the shower was some sort of demonic creature that had been recorded since ancient times. One of the names given to this paranormal persecutor was a "succubus" – a demon which targets and seduces certain males – and occasionally females too – in an attempt to draw off the very essence of their souls. These 'succubi' (a plural term for such demons) often appear beautiful at first, but it's just an illusion to hide their true ugly forms and facilitate seduction. They are also said to sit on the chests of sleeping men to cause paralysis, loss of breath, graphic nightmares and intense anxiety attacks in their victims.

'How do we get rid of her?' Joan wanted to know. Her sister had irresponsibly given her valium that had been prescribed for herself, but Joan was close to taking the pills as she had hardly slept because Tony screamed and thrashed about in his sleep almost every night.

The investigator was at the end of his tether, and just before he left the house, he stood in the hallway and bluntly told them: 'You could try your best to convince someone from the Roman Catholic Church to perform an exorcism in this house, but don't hold your breath, because the modern priest thinks this type of thing is all nonsense.'

'So what do we do then?' Tony asked, holding his wife's hand tightly as they stood there, feeling so lost.

'This is probably impractical, Tony, but if I was you, I'd leave,' the investigator told them. 'Are you owners or renters?'

'Owners,' Joan said, sombrely.

And so Tony and his family made plans to sell the house in Woolton. They also made plans to stay at the house of Tony's older brother in Whiston, but before then, something extraordinary happened one night as Tony came into the bedroom. He saw Joan lying in the bed asleep, and the time was about 2am, perhaps a little later. Tony had finished packing most of their stuff away into tea chests and suitcases, and as he got into bed, he felt so sorry for his wife, lying there. She had put up with all this and remained by his side throughout.

She opened her eyes – and immediately Tony saw that they were green.

Joan had blue eyes, and even by the light of the bedside lamp Tony could plainly see that these eyes were green – that same shade of green as the eyes of that evil entity in the shower.

In an instant the woman in the bed changed into that

young woman again, but this time Tony ran out of the room, and straight into Nicola's room, where Joan was sitting on the bed as she talked to their daughter. Tony didn't want to upset his daughter so he waited until his wife said goodnight to Nicola, then told her what he had seen in the bedroom: the thing, and how it had taken on her form. Joan trembled when Tony told her this. Joan slept with her daughter and Tony slept on the sofa downstairs with Rosary beads and a Bible in his hands. Five prospective couples called to view the house over weeks that seemed to last for an eternity, and then a Swedish couple decided to buy the house, and Tony and Joyce and Nicola bought a house in Ormskirk, and although Tony suffered all sorts of nightmares about the succubus (if that indeed is what this things was), he was never stalked by it again.

THE DEVIL'S TIP

The following is a true story which happened many years ago, and it was related to me by the son of the man at the centre of this tale – Arthur, a very down-to-earth individual who did not believe in ghosts nor hold any interest in the supernatural.

One foggy March afternoon in 1947, a 60-year-old man named Arthur rode a tram from his home to an allotment in Wavertree. Being such a cold and fogbound day, there were just two other people on the allotment and they were all getting ready to go home. But Arthur had a terrible home life, and this was down to the continual squabbles he had with his wife Lizzie over her two brothers, who were always coming round to cadge money and food. The hut on Arthur's allotment was like his second home, with a padded, patched-up leather armchair and a radio he'd hooked up to an old accumulator battery. Rationing was still in progress, but Arthur had brought along a bottle of milk, a few eggs, a couple of ounces of butter, a few spoonfuls of tea, three rounds of his sister Dot's home-made bread and a jar of her lovely marmalade. And there was the copy of the *Liverpool Echo* to provide him with a leisurely read and a packet of Churchman's cigarettes obtained from the black market via "Edgy" the local spiv. The old metal drum with holes knocked in it was packed with stick-wood Arthur had collected from the bombsites, and now all he needed was paper – and he'd clean forgotten to bring the bundle of old newspaper to his plot. He had no intentions of burning his new unread Echo, so he looked around his hut for any paper. There was none. There were cherished volumes of *Greene's Gardening Encyclopaedia*, given to him by his late father, sitting on a shelf, but they certainly weren't for burning. How about that old Bible Lizzie had left? She'd read that book throughout the war and had left it up here in the hut last summer. Arthur associated the Holy Book with his hypocritical wife, who had been forever going on about the value of honesty while she was secretly giving her sponging brothers Arthur's old boxing magazines and items of prized food like powdered egg and rounds of bacon. He had lost count of the times when Lizzie had blamed the cat for eating Arthur's tiny cuts of brisket and minute portions of corned beef. It was just a book, Arthur reasoned, feeling the March chill on his chest. He knew the message of the Church by heart at sixty, so why freeze and go without tea and toast and a boiled egg because of that old dog-eared book?

'It'll have to go,' Arthur decided, 'I want me scran and my cup of hot char.'

He found himself feeding the fire in the drum with pages of Genesis, Deuteronomy, Matthew, Luke, Revelation… and all the time he wore a faint smile, thinking how his wife would react if she knew he was burning her family Bible. 'Silly old cow,' he muttered, watching the pages blacken and shrivel and send sparks up through the limbo of fog. 'Wants to bleedin'' practice what she preaches, sour-faced bat.'

And a priest caught him red-handed; at least he thought it was a priest, for a stranger, all in black with a sort of short black cape and a cassock, coughed behind him and in a well-to-do accent he asked: 'Is Mr O'Gaucho about?' Arthur had never heard of anyone of that name on the allotment and shook his head. The tall stranger spelt the surname out, but then he saw the pages being fed into the drum, and there followed a sharp intake of breath, and a crooked smile. 'Burning the Holy Book eh?' he asked, then tutted and shook his head of glossy, well-oiled black hair.

Blushing with guilt and firebug fever, Arthur said: 'Sorry Father, I'm cold and hungry, and well, I – I don't really know what to say. It's not like me to do this, but well – '

The man laughed and said he *was* a father, but not a priest, and he said, 'Ah, you don't need to explain to me, that book is just a bloody historical novel. Starts with that stupid far-fetched story about a couple in the Garden of Eden, and the big fellah tells them they can have anything in paradise except the Tree of Forbidden knowledge!'

'Yes, it is a bit far-fetched,' Arthur chuckled.

'And you know what women are like,' the visitor said with an infectious grin, 'they can't help themselves where secrets are concerned. And the big fellah tells a woman of all things not to have anything to do with the Tree of Forbidden Knowledge – and he bloody points it out and says "That's the tree! Don't eat the fruit of it!" Now, she's naturally going to want to know why, isn't she?'

'She certainly is,' Arthur pulled out a whole chapter

of the Bible and fed the hungry flames. 'Anyone would I suppose, if you told them not to do a certain thing without explaining why.'

'Precisely! And she goes and has a look at the Tree and a serpent – a *talking* serpent – comes down the branches and tells her to try the apples!'

'That would be scary, a talking snake,' Arthur imagined the slithery creature.

'Women are terrified of spiders and mice, never mind big bastard talking snakes! And yet this woman doesn't flinch, because she's such a nosy bitch, she *has* to know what will happen if she eats the apple, but she isn't stupid enough to try it herself – she talks her dumb fellah into biting the apple – and he does!'

'Yeah,' Arthur grinned and wiped a tear from his smoked left eye. He didn't feel at all bad about incinerating this blasted book now.

'And they ask you to swear on this bloody book in a court of law!' the stranger's voice went up an octave. 'You swear to tell the truth, the whole truth and nothing but the truth!'

'Ha! I never thought of that,' Arthur mused upon the visitor's deep comments and fed the leather cover into the flames.

He nodded and continued. 'No one does! It's all baloney! If we are all descended from Adam and Eve, isn't that incest? We are all related according to that book!'

'Well, I tell you what mate, you've really cheered me up on this foggy day. You're welcome to have a cup of tea with me and some toast – just a round is all I can spare though.'

'Is that salmon there, eh?' the entertaining man

pointed at the table in the hut. Arthur was amazed to see a huge red can of salmon there. Arthur had only tasted snoek fish for the past seven years, and he was absolutely dumbfounded by the appearance of the tinned salmon. This incident made Arthur very suspicious. Here he was burning a Bible and this man in black had appeared. There was a pause, and time seemed to stand still. The stranger who'd come out the fog, suddenly said. 'Yes, it's *me*. ' And he shrugged, and his eyes seemed as dead as the eyes of a doll.

'What do you mean?' Arthur stepped back. 'Who are you?'

The sinister man looked at the burning Bible in the drum, then turned to face Arthur. 'You're a betting man, aren't you? The Grand National's soon, too.'

Arthur hoped the visitor was merely a nutter who'd planted the salmon in the hut. He ignored the man for a while, but glanced at the pair of shears hanging up in the hut. If this fellah tried to attack him he'd stab him, and it'd be self-defence. The man became silent and his pale face became expressionless as he lingered in the doorway of the hut for a while. This behaviour really unnerved Arthur, who decided that this visitor really was the Devil. No wonder he had mocked the story of Adam and Eve! And yes – it all came back to Arthur now from his schooldays. He had read in the Bible that the Devil was known as the Father of all lies, and this abomination *had* admitted to being a father, but not a priest.

'Would you like me to tell you the name of that winning horse, Arthur?' the Devil asked, and leaned against the doorframe.

Arthur began to doubt his intuition again – began to

pooh pooh the warnings from his unconscious mind, but asked the question that was on his mind anyway. 'You're not the Devil are you?'

'You could have unlimited wealth – and power over people! Beautiful women will fall at your feet!' was the reply – but no answer to Arthur's question.

Arthur put his suspicion to the test. 'God bless you,' he said to the creepy man in black, just to see how he'd react to the mention of God in the half-hearted blessing, and immediately the man turned in the doorway and fled into the fog. Arthur rushed to the doorway to see where the uncanny figure was going, but already there was no sign of him, but whether he had vanished into thin air or had simply become obscured by the fog was unknown, and Arthur never discovered where the visitor had gone, and thankfully he never saw him again. That tin of salmon could not be found either once the unearthly caller departed.

Arthur believed the man had been the Devil in earthly form, and naturally regretted burning his wife's Bible, merely out of spite. He told a priest what had happened and the clergyman said it was possible that it could have been Satan or one of his cohorts, and Arthur asked to be blessed. The priest complied.

Arthur loved crosswords and anagrams and wondered what the significance of the surname "O'Gaucho" was – the person the visitor had been supposedly searching for. Well, Arthur discovered that O'Gaucho was an anagram of "Caughoo" – which happened to be the name of an 8-year-old horse running in the Grand National at 100/1 odds, so Arthur backed this outsider, and a strange thing happened. A thick fog descended on Aintree racing course, that day – Saturday 29 March, 1947 – as the world's most famous steeplechase got underway. The fifty-seven horses running in the National vanished into the swirling mists, causing havoc for the announcers and the man attempting to do the commentary in the radio broadcast. Caughoo finished first, but some doubted this, as the horse had only cost £50 to buy, and had been regarded as something of a joke. People claimed that Caughoo had only completed one lap of the course, but somehow, expert photographers managed to take snaps of the horse which proved that it had indeed run the course and won fair and square. Arthur won £51 that day on Caughoo, and felt a bit uncomfortable, because he wondered if the Devil had given him a tip in a devious roundabout way. Arthur decided to give £25 of his winnings to a charity for blind children, and he never betted on the horses or gambled in any form again.

THE NECROMANCERS

I recall the first incident in this chapter being reported in the newspapers many years ago, and when I first went on local radio to talk about the supernatural, I appealed for the couple in the newspaper story - who had seen something very strange in a cemetery - to get in touch. The couple did, and provided me with all of the details of a very scary encounter with occultists.

In the late 1970s at a certain cemetery on the outskirts of Liverpool, a couple, both aged fifteen, were kissing and petting under the shadows of a large Yew tree when something terrifying took place. The time was 1.10 am, and the teenagers, Marc and Gail, should have long been in their respective homes. Gail's mother and older sisters were out looking for her, and Marc's parents were about to call the police, because it was not like their son to stay out so late. Marc, however, had been persecuting Gail to have sex with him for weeks, and upon this warm August night it was beginning to look as if he'd finally have his carnal desires fulfilled – but then there came sounds somewhere in the distance near the cemetery. The soft thuds of what sounded like car doors being shut. Gail's wide eyes looked towards the gates of the cemetery, which were always open – and she saw movement there in the dull orange illumination from a solitary sodium street lamp filtering through the trees. Police, Marc automatically assumed, perhaps coming to investigate some report by an old biddy that had seen him and Gail loitering in the cemetery.

Silhouetted figures – first three, then a fourth, and then two more, came into the place of the dead and the steamy couple cooled somewhat as they became nervous because the strangers were headed towards them. The six shadows – three male and one female from their outlines – were filing down the path when the full moon appeared through a gap in the clouds, and by its dead light the couple saw that two of the figures were carrying what looked like spades. As the night visitors came down the pale path in the moonlight, Gail zipped up Marc a little too quickly and he squealed.

'Ah, You idiot!' he freed himself from the zipper and turned to see what was going on.

The six shadows were getting nearer and nearer, and the only way the couple could get away from this suspicious-looking gang was by climbing the six-foot railings, and Gail was a lousy climber – and when she had last asked Marc to give her a boost over the railings (a week ago), he had pushed her clean over them. She had landed on her elbows and her chin had smacked her forearm so she bit her tongue.

'What the hell are they doing?' Marc stepped back behind the tree and squinted at the approaching people.

'Ssshh!' Gail got behind him and now she could see their pallid faces and triangular black eye sockets. Not one of the group looked remotely trendy. In this era of long hair for men and women, the girl among the group of men had a big helmet of blonde puffed up-hair – like some 1960s bouffant – and the short-haired men were all in black suits with "shit-stopper" straight trousers – not a flare to be seen on any of them – and these guys had on white shirts and narrow black ties. Gail reckoned all six of them were in their early to mid-twenties.

They were still advancing.

'Marc, give me a bunk over the railings, I think we should go now,' Gail whispered with some urgency.

'Are they gonna dig someone up?' Marc muttered, oblivious to his scared girlfriend's request.

'Marc, I said can you give me – '

'Shut up a sec, they're stopping,' Marc crouched and peeped over the top of a barberry bush.

The sinister six halted and the woman among them with the Dusty Springfield hairdo crouched and seemed to read the moonlit inscription on a white gravestone. This woman wore a pale – possibly pale blue – jacket, and a whitish mini skirt. Her legs were bare, and she wore white flat strappy shoes. She got up slowly from her crouching position and turned to the two men with the spades. The teenagers could hear the woman's faint words on the warm breeze.

The men with the spades began to dig.

Gail swore under her breath, and turned to look at the railing. 'Come on Marc, let's get out of here.'

'What the hell are they doing?' Marc's curiosity was getting the better of him.

Gail gently grabbed Marc by the tails of his tee shirt and tugged. 'Marc, I said let's go.'

'We will soon, let's just see – ' he replied without even looking at her.

The men were digging in a very energetic fashion, and from the looks of it, they had done this before. It was a warm night and yet neither of the excavators even loosened his tie or removed a jacket. The moon went behind a cloud for seconds, but then emerged into a vast dark gap in the sky, and now the couple could see the perfect rectangular outline created by the spades. There had been no grass growing on the grave so perhaps the person they were digging up had not been buried for long, Marc reasoned.

'Oh!' yelled Gail and grabbed Marc's arm with both hands. He turned in a flash, startled, and saw just what had given Gail such a start: a vagrant known as Dirty Johnny was walking slowly past the black railings of the cemetery with his eyes fixed on Gail. He wore a bushy grey beard and a head of curly white hair. He had on trousers tied with a length of clothes line for a belt and he was scratching his hairy chest through his string vest as he drifted past.

'Beat it, you stupid old foggy,' Marc whispered as he made a v-sign to the tramp.

Dirty Johnny spat out a disgusting pale-green blob of phlegm onto the pavement and walked on, swearing under his breath.

'Did they hear me?' Gail wondered, and looked anxiously back towards the possible grave robbers. They seemed too engrossed in their morbid work to have noticed Gail's yelp. 'Let's get the friggin' hell out of here, Marc,' Gail said, and she placed her little foot in a white Dunlop tennis shoe on the ledge of the railings' base, ready to attempt a climb, but Marc crouched behind the bush again and continued his edgy surveillance, even though Gail slapped the back of his head and made subdued guttural sounds to incite him to leave.

The men were pulling the coffin up now with either some sort of ropes or straps that had presumably been looped under the coffin or tied to its brass handles. It was such an eerie unnatural sight, seeing these shadowy figures resurrecting a dead person by the light of the moon. Usually there was a constant faint white-noise din from the distant traffic, but tonight a hard silence was hanging in the air. The silhouettes gathered around the coffin, and some of the desecrators must have been unscrewing the lid, because when two of them moved away, Gail and Marc gasped together in horror as they saw something white now showing in that coffin: the body in its shroud. The coffin lid was placed on the pile of excavated soil and clay, and the blonde knelt at the side of the open coffin and put her hand on the face of the corpse, which seemed to be wearing a type of white balaclava. Marc had the better eyesight of the two teens and claimed the exhumed body was that of a woman. He could see the face – the only bit of flesh visible amongst the ivory shroud.

'Oh my God,' Gail unconsciously dug her nails into Marc's forearm. 'What *is* she doing?'

Marc screwed his eyes up. 'She's giving her something from a bottle – with a spoon.'

'Let's go Marc, I'm scared,' Gail was near to tears now.

The blonde put the bottle down and seemed to open the mouth of the dead woman. The horrified teenagers could see the dark spot in the pale face where the mouth had opened. The spoonful of God knows what went into that mouth.

Then the men in the black suits started to chant something. Neither Marc nor Gail could understand the words being intoned.

The corpse began to move.

Gail came close to wetting herself at the sight of the corpse convulsing.

Enough was enough, and Marc got up from the cover of the barberry bush, turned, and hurried just a few feet to the railings with Gail clawing at his back. He joined his hands together with interlocking fingers and formed a step, and Gail's right tennis shoe was lifted and placed on his joined hands. He did what he had done last time – he over-boosted her and pushed poor Gail clean over the railings, only this time she managed to land on her feet, but she felt a little winded upon impact with the pavement. Then Marc quickly climbed over the railings and landed quietly in the silent lane. The couple ran across this lane and slowed for a moment in the shadows of the sycamores hanging over a wall. They both looked back to the cemetery, in case any of the weird people were following, and then they bolted off into the night, but they hadn't covered much ground when they heard the noise of an accelerating car engine. They turned and saw a white car tearing down the road. Marc was into cars at the time and was well-acquainted with all of the various models and makes of vehicles from Abarth to Zaporozhets, and he knew without a doubt that the white car - which mounted the pavement and overshot him and Gail as it almost knocked them down – was a four-door Vauxhall Victor saloon. Gail screamed and froze in terror as the car reversed and came zooming towards her and Marc, but just when the trunk of the vehicle was about ten feet away from impact, Marc pushed Gail down an entry and dived with her. The teens then got to their feet and ran to Gail's home via a labyrinth of alleyways. Gail was in a terrible state when she and Marc reached her backyard. The girl sobbed hysterically and told Marc to bolt the back door because she believed the people who had defiled that woman's resting place were about to appear. When the girl's parents admitted her and Marc into the house via the kitchen door, they could not get a coherent word of sense from Gail, and when Marc told the adults what had happened, they seemed to think he was exaggerating.

'Well. That's what you get for staying out so late,' Gail's father said condescendingly, 'especially in a graveyard for Christ's sake.' And then he turned to Marc and chided him. 'What the hell did you take Gail into a cemetery for anyway? You nut!'

Gail suddenly broke out of her unintelligible sobbing voice and shouted: 'Leave him alone, Dad, we weren't doing anything!'

'From now on, you get in at ten o'clock!' Gail's mother bawled, 'Or you're grounded, and I'll have words with *his* mother and father!'

Marc was terrified going home that night, even though he only lived about four hundred yards from Gail's house. Every time he heard a car he thought it was the white Vauxhall Victor closing in on him. Both teens had nightmares when they finally managed to get some sleep that night, and the next day, when the desecration incident was reported in the newspapers and on the radio and TV news bulletins, the parents of Gail and Marc finally realised that something ghastly *had* taken place and the young couple had not been lying. Marc and Gail were forbidden to go anywhere near the cemetery in question – not that they intended to do their courting there after the weird exhumation they had seen, followed by what seems to have been a concerted effort by the desecrators to bump off the teenaged witnesses.

About a week after the desecration, Gail was sitting in bed around 11.40pm at night, reading a magazine about pop stars, when she began to feel drowsy. She turned off the light and went to the window to open the curtains a little to allow some light from the streetlamp into her room, for she had become too scared to sleep in total blackness with the curtains drawn.

As Gail glanced out the window, she saw the solid black silhouettes of two tall men standing just outside her front gate. Behind them a car was parked – a white car, just like the one that had tried to run Gail and Marc down a week back. Gail backed away from her window and went into the room of her parents. She woke them up and told them about the men downstairs and the white car, and the girl's father went to the bedroom window to see that the men were not there now, but he could see a light-coloured car moving off, and it had no lights on. On the following morning around 6.30am, Gail's father was leaving for work (he was a postman) and he noticed something on the front door: the symbol of an upside-down cross carved into the wood. Throughout that week, the telephone would ring in Gail's home and whenever the call was answered, the person at the other end would say nothing, but their breathing was barely audible.

After about a minute or so the mystery caller would hang up. An inverted cross was then discovered on the front door of Marc's home one evening as his father returned from the pub. A few days after this, the vagrant known as Dirty Johnny was found dead in the lane outside the cemetery with a look of absolute horror upon his face. His eyes were bulging in terror and his mouth was wide open. Cause of death could not be ascertained and the authorities said he had died from natural causes, but Gail and Marc thought otherwise.

When I mentioned this case on the radio I received a flurry of telephone calls and letters and emails from people who had witnessed some strange goings-on in the cemetery where the desecration took place. One woman named Maud had not seen any of the graveyard ghouls at work but her father, who worked as a night watch man, had seen the umbrageous figures flitting about in the cemetery near his place of work on many nights in the spring of 1977. He reported the matter to the police but nothing was done. One person – a young man named Shaun, who was 16 at the time of the incidents, actually witnessed a desecration and something very sinister after running into the cemetery at three o'clock one morning in April 1977 as he fled from the police. Shaun had been on the run since 2.40pm that day when a policeman arrested him for shoplifting in Liverpool City Centre. Shaun somehow wriggled out of his jacket as the policeman seized him by the collar, and the light-fingered teenager hid in Central Station. He had a small amount of change in his trouser pocket and with this he managed to pay for a ticket to take him to Aigburth. From there, the feisty felon embarked on a long roundabout journey to the house of a cousin on the outskirts of the city, but upon reaching his cousin's house, Shaun discovered that his relation had moved house just a week before. By now it was dark and Shaun was hungry. He ordered a curried meal at a chippy and told a trusting young girl behind the counter he would go and get change from a shop across the road. Shaun entered the chippy minutes later and saw his parcel waiting for him on the counter. He offered the docile girl a folded piece of paper he'd found on the street and then grabbed his curried chicken and rice and ran off. As the night wore on, Shaun realised he'd need somewhere to sleep, and thought the local cemetery would be a wise choice. He prowled the back gardens of several houses in the area and found some sheets and items of clothing that had been left out on washing lines. Some of these items were crawling with earwigs because it was such a warm but muggy and damp night. Just after Shaun had gathered his ad hoc blankets and pillow, he saw a police car crawling slowly down the road, and he ran off. The car roared after him but the sprightly teenager jumped clean over a garden fence and hid in a back garden until he thought the police had given up the search. He then made his way to the cemetery. The time was around three in the morning when Shaun finally chose a place to rest in the centre of the cemetery. A blanket was folded up around a pair of jeans to serve as a pillow, and someone's tablecloth served as a light blanket. The 16-year-old lay on the thick grass of a grave as he looked up at the stars wheeling ever so slowly across the sky. He thought of his loving mother and father and his little sister (who would be so upset when she heard about her brother going on the run). Shaun dozed off, exhausted, and because of the unusual surroundings, he woke up a few times and when he did he would see how the patterns of stars had moved a little across the black canopy of the sky. It must have been around 4am when a noise awakened Shaun from his alfresco slumbers. He thought it was the police moving in on him at first but soon realised the noise that had awakened him was voices – and a strange rhythmic sound. This noise sounded like a spade striking gritty or gravely soil.

Shaun slowly sat up (and felt a sharp pain in his neck because of the way he'd been sleeping with his head on the hard makeshift pillow) and he peeped around the gravestone. He saw a group of five men standing around a grave about 200 yards away. Two of the men were digging furiously into the surface of the grave, which, as in the previous account of the exhumation, was devoid of any grass because it was a fairly 'fresh' grave. There was some type of electric lantern on the floor with a red light, and this might have been the tail light from a bicycle. Shaun could see the men by the red illumination of this light source. There was no moon out on this night and the only faint light filtering into the graveyard was from streetlamps about three hundred yards away. Shaun obviously knew the men were up to no good and his immediate instinct told him to get the hell out of there but he thought he'd be seen - and heard - if he tried to run off. He therefore stayed put, and watched the sinister proceedings. Several times one of the strangers turned and looked around the cemetery, and at one point this man presented his pale face towards Shaun for some time, and the juvenile crook thought he had been seen for a while, but the man never came over to him.

It's hard for Shaun to calculate just how much time elapsed before the men dug up the coffin; it could have been fifteen minutes, perhaps a little longer. Shaun peeped from behind the gravestone just in time to see four of the men leaning over the coffin. They removed the lid and carefully took out the corpse. The same ritual which Gail and Marc had observed then took place. One of the grave desecrators seemed to put a bottle to the mouth of the female corpse, but whether this had a reanimating effect is not know, because Shaun freaked out when he saw the dead body being given something to drink. The lad left his crude pillow and improvised duvet and ran as fast as his legs could carry him out of that cemetery. As he ran, he definitely heard voices cry out, but what they were shouting is unknown. Shaun vaulted clean over the railings and landed in the lane, and from there he ran pell-mell towards the nearest main road – and when he spotted a police car crawling along, he actually ran over to it. The policemen in the car were told about the "oddballs" who had exhumed a corpse in the nearby cemetery, and they asked Shaun what he was doing out at such an unearthly hour.

'Never mind that!' Shaun replied, audaciously, 'Some fellahs have dug up a body in that cemetery!'

'Get home now!' the driver of the patrol car yelled at the teenager, then drove off at some speed towards the cemetery. Shaun then hid in a nearby front garden, where he crouched behind a hedge and looked in the direction of the cemetery. About three minutes later he saw flashes of blue light from the police car, and then there came the sounds of screeching tyres. A white car came down the road, followed by the police vehicle, and Shaun watched as the two cars hurtled past and roared on into the night. He held out till nearly 3pm on the following day, when, deprived of sleep and thoroughly starved, Shaun gave himself up at a police station. He asked if the police had 'nicked the graverobbers' but the desk officer at the station just returned a puzzled, condescending stare. According to reports in the local newspapers, the mysterious men who had exhumed a woman (who had been buried for just two days) from her grave had managed to give police the slip.

Many years ago I received an anonymous telephone call from a listener to my slot on BBC Radio Merseyside as I was still at the studios, minutes after making a broadcast in which I mentioned occultists disturbing graves. The man, who said his name was Anthony, supplied me with details which I had only heard from the many witnesses regarding the exhumations of the two women at the cemetery mentioned in this chapter. Anthony said many of the occultists were from people in very high positions in society, and they had stooped to their morbid pastime mostly out of boredom. The leader of the resurrectionists had been a weird man in his fifties who had genuine psychic powers. This man was an expert in chemistry and had made a medicine which could sometimes resuscitate a dead person for a minute or so, and this concoction was to be used to interrogate the dead about their experiences after death, and to obtain sacred information from them.

According to Anthony, most of those who were revived temporarily became hysterical when they realised they had died, and would ask for loved ones. Anthony asserted that one woman who was brought back to life for a few minutes bit clean through his finger and almost severed it, then bit into her own tongue as she convulsed. The poor woman's eyes bulged and then rolled back into her head and she vomited over her shroud before she became limp and lifeless again. Sometimes, Anthony informed me, the exhumed body was that of someone who had allegedly led a bad life, and their eyes would seem to glow and they'd come out with a string of disgusting language in a deep chilling voice – as if something evil – perhaps demonic – was speaking through them.

Anthony was cut off in the middle of further conversation, and the line went dead, but whether this was because of some telephonic fault – or because he was possibly silenced by some higher power – I cannot say.

Many occultists are fairly stable people who study a subject that is stigmatized by various religious groups, but there are a few students of the occult who go off the rails, and these are the ones who resort to necromancy – the ancient art (mentioned in the Bible) of raising the dead and controlling spirits to obtain secret information. I am told by reliable sources that the necromancers are just as active as ever – especially in this neck of the woods. If you are ever passing a cemetery in the dead of night, and should you see a group of these people at work, get as far away from them as you can. I believe many unsolved cases of people who have inexplicably disappeared are simply cases of people who have seen something they shouldn't have seen…

BACK TO THE EIGHTIES

Many of us have the occasional recurring dream – a dream in which specific events happen again and again. Such repeating dreams may be enjoyable or unpleasant, and they are difficult to explain. Common recurring dreams involve the dreamer being naked in a public place, losing control of a vehicle (often travelling backwards in a car or bus at high speed), or being able to fly, and psychologists have tried for decades to interpret these reoccurring dreams, and while some of them seem to be caused by stress, others are much harder to explain. The following recurring dream hints at some faculty of the human mind which allows human consciousness to travel back into the past – a type of involuntary mental time travel.

One evening in 2010, a 50-year-old Formby woman named Melanie went to bed, and as her husband David went immediately to sleep, she sat reading her Kindle. Around 2am, Melanie began to feel drowsy and she switched off her bedside lamp and rested her head on the pillow. She turned on her right side, and started to doze off. Her mind ventured into that twilit region between waking and sleeping, and strange surreal images appeared before her. Then came that odd process which psychologists find very hard to explain: the beginning of a dream. It's strange how most people wake up and recall how their dream ended, but no one seems to know exactly when a dream begins.

The dream Melanie had on this occasion was very realistic indeed – too real to be a dream in her opinion. She found herself back in her old house in West Derby, in her older brother Mike's bedroom, and there was her husband David – with hair! He was seated at Mike's Amstrad computer, and he looked about 25 – the age he started seeing her. Melanie laughed at his mullet hair-do because in 2010 David was completely bald. Then Melanie looked in a full length wardrobe mirror – and saw that she not only looked about 23 or 24 – she was dressed as she had been circa 1984 – all big hair, with fluorescent pink earrings, a lemon-yellow jacket with enormous shoulder pads and typical kitschy Eighties make-up. Pop-singer Nena's *99 Red Balloons* was coming from the laughably large and chunky ghetto-blaster radio/cassette, and David was waiting for a computer game cassette to load into the computer as he read a football magazine called *Shoot*. Melanie's mother came into the room whistling the theme to her favourite TV show – *Fresh Fields* which, Melanie recalled, had starred Julia Mckenzie and Anton Rodgers. Melanie's mother looked in her mid-forties. Sadly, in real life, her mum had long died from cancer. Melanie began to realise now, that this was so; that her beloved mum had died, so this had to be some dream, and yet she loved seeing her 'Mam' - as she had called her - again.

'That soft fellah Marty called for you before,' she told her daughter, and David looked up from his magazine and asked, 'Marty? Why is he calling for Mel?'

Marty was a melodramatic admirer of Melanie who had challenged David to a duel weeks back.

'Left this for you,' Melanie's mother handed her girl a pink envelope.

'Oh aye, what's all his?' David eyed the envelope, consumed with pure hot-blooded jealousy.

Melanie opened it under David's furious gaze.

'A birthday card,' Melanie said with a smile.

'Yeah, you're twenty-four tomorrow aren't you?' Her mum said, 'Hasn't that gone over, eh? Better get a move on and get married and have those babies.'

'Twenty-four tomorrow?' Melanie whispered, which meant it was 1 May 1984 tomorrow. Then she woke up from the lucid dream. She felt like crying, and in the silent darkness of her bedroom, she felt a warm tear escape from the tail of her right eye and bleed onto the pillowcase. 'Oh mum,' Melanie whispered, all choked up. She was so upset by the realistic dream of her mother, she reached out and hugged David, who was lying fast asleep beside her. Melanie thought about the dream, and her audio memory – her mind's ear – replayed that cherished voice of her mother until she dozed off again.

Melanie awoke around 10am to the morning light of midsummer shining into her room. David was not besides her. He was downstairs making himself some breakfast, ready to take the dog out. Melanie wanted to shout down to him and tell him of the strange lucid dream, but the mood of that nostalgic dream had lifted now and Melanie thought she'd be silly even talking about it.

On the following night, Melanie once again read a book on her Kindle as she lay in bed, and David was snoring lightly. Melanie did not even give the previous night's dream a thought as she started to doze off. Her last thoughts were a mental note to seek a certain recipe for a birthday cake she planned to make for a friend.

She had another dream which did not feel like a dream at all, and again, the setting was May, 1984. *The A Team* were on the big cathode ray tube television, and Melanie was sitting at a table as her mother cooked the tea. Melanie suddenly noticed her grandfather, Jack, sitting in the place he always sat in those days, the armchair in front of the telly. He was reading the *Echo* with his late wife's horn-rimmed glasses on as he tutted.

'That AIDS things getting worse,' Jack said without lifting his eyes from the page. 'There's going to be over a million deaths from it by the end of the century. Bloody nancy boys caused all this.'

'Gay people didn't start AIDS, granddad,' Melanie found herself saying. 'It's a virus that's been found in blood samples going back to the 1950s. Its – '

'Rubbish, the queers started all this – ' Jack butted in, his eyes glaring at Melanie through the lenses of the Dame Edna spectacles.

'Grandad! That's a horrible word!' Melanie gasped, but then recalled it *was* 1984, and not everyone was as educated and politically correct as they would be in the future. Then another realisation struck Melanie: the next door neighbour Adam, the 45-year-old bachelor her grandfather was forever praising because of his gardening know-how, had not yet come out. On a few occasions Melanie's mother had even suggested that Adam would make some lucky girl (meaning Mel) a great husband – despite the little age difference.

And – talk of the Devil – someone rapped on the living room window which looked onto the back garden. It was Adam. He'd stepped over the little fence dividing his back garden from Melanie's, and here he was smiling at the time-slipped girl with a thumb up gesture for some reason.

'If they found out you were one of *them* in the army you got a good hiding – ' Jack was continuing his homophobic rant.

Melanie went to the kitchen and opened the back-garden door, still feeling a little confused as she tried to adjust to this change in the era. Adam came in and said: 'Cor, Mel, you look lovelier every time I see you.'

'Oh, ta,' Melanie replied, and she followed him into the living room, where he grandfather said: 'Alright, lad, was it any good?'

'It was fab, Jack, Adam said, sitting at the dining table. It's true what they say on the telly, it really *is* less bovver than a hover!'

'Best thing I ever got that mower, the erm Concorde,' Jack struggled to recall its name.

'Qualcast Concorde,' Adam reminded him. 'Thanks for letting me have a borrow of it.'

'Put the kettle on Melanie, make Adam and me a cuppa,' Jack told Melanie, who was annoyed at his dictatorial streak – a trait she'd long forgotten about over the long years.

'No, I'll do it, Jack – ' Adam rose from the chair.

'Nah,' Jack protested, 'sit down Adam; can't have fellah's making tea. You're not a jessy are you?' The old man laughed.

Melanie froze and saw Adam's face pale at the

suggestion.

'Ha!' was all he could say to Jack as he pretended to watch the *A Team*. 'All these automatic weapons getting fired and no one gets a bloody scratch on them!' Adam remarked in a gruff macho voice.

Melanie went to make the tea and her mother said she'd do it, then whispered to Melanie: 'He really likes you, Adam. You can tell when someone has a crush, they go all funny in their company.'

'Nah, I don't think I'm his type, mum,' Melanie stifled a grin, and then looked out the window at the old forsythia bush that had been there since she was a child. All of a sudden she realised with crystal clarity that this was one of those lucid dreams again, and she was filled with utmost sorrow – so much so, she felt choked and it was hard to speak. The family cat Whisky was sprawled out on the roof of the garden shed, lazily watching sparrows fluttering about in the old apple tree. Whisky had died a long time ago. Melanie had let him out one night and the cat had stopped as he reached the gateway of the garden and looked back at her. She recalled that moment clearly – the last time she would ever see her beloved cat alive. They found his body at the side of a road three days later.

'Oh, mum!' Melanie turned and hurried to her startled mother with outstretched arms.

'Ah, what's wrong with you, eh, sulks?' her mum embraced her and that indefinable aroma of Melanie's mother was evident again. It seemed to be a scent of some sort – probably discontinued by the 21st century. Melanie had always felt so safe when she smelt it. She recalled how stable and lovely the world had been when she was a child with her mum. Sometimes she'd sit Melanie on the sofa and put *Bill and Ben* on the TV, or maybe *Play School* and Melanie would drift off, often dozing to the sound of the washing machine. All of these memories surrounded her as the girl's face was pressed against her mother's neck.

'I loved you mum! I thought you'd always be around!' Melanie could barely get the words out of her choked-up throat, and suddenly she realised she was hugging a snoring David back in 2010. The bedroom was still in darkness, and when Melanie checked the clock, she was baffled to see that she had only been asleep for a few minutes. She clung on to David, and wiped her tears away with her fingers. She began to wonder why she was having these cruel dreams of lost loves.

Every single night after that, Melanie returned to the 1980s in her dreams, and Marty – that long-time admirer of Melanie – began to feature in the dreams with increasing regularity, and whenever he appeared in the bizarre time-locked dreams he would fight David for her. After a fortnight of these distinctive – and exhausting - dreams, Melanie went to her doctor, and he said she was merely stressed, but still the dreams continued, night after night. Melanie was always in her twenties and the dreams were full of Rubik's cubes, Cannon and Ball, *Spitting Image*, Safe Sex TV ads, Roland Rat, Toyah, *Hi-De-Hi*, Boy George, Live Aid, Derek Hatton, and Wham. Melanie would wake up physically and emotionally drained from these gruelling dreams, and she'd be so relieved to see the 21st century, but she also feared she was going mad.

She visited her doctor again and told him about the

way she kept dreaming she was back in the 1980s, and the GP said that perhaps she should see a psychiatrist after all. This naturally worried Melanie, and for the first time in her life she hit the bottle. She thought that if she could drink enough vodka before bedtime, she wouldn't have those period dreams, but they still continued, and David started to notice his wife having sly drinks as bedtime loomed.

Then something quite strange happened. News reached Melanie that Marty, David's rival from long ago, had passed away after a long illness down in Brighton. A close friend of the ill man said that, as he lay dying, Marty kept rambling on about Melanie and how he would win her heart one day. This made Melanie wonder if Marty had somehow projected himself into her dreams as he lay reminiscing on his sickbed on all of those lonely nights. After Marty's death, the dreams of the Eighties ended.

GARSTON GHOSTS

Let us turn our attention now to a few inexplicable incidents in the haunted history of Garston, a place that dates back to the year 1235 at least, and whose name is derived from "Gaerstun" – Old English for "grazing settlement". Monks of the Benedictine Order established a settlement at Garston in the 13th century, but long before that, it's highly possible that there was a Viking influence at work, for the history of our region before the 10th century is rather murky to say the least. An old seaman named Ralph who operated a dredger on the banks of Garston in the 1950s told me of a very intriguing artefact that was brought up by the dredger's scoop around 1951. It was a barnacle-encrusted stone cross encircled by a ring, similar to a Celtic cross in appearance, but marked with Runic inscriptions. When Ralph's senior on the dredger saw this cross he went pale, and ordered young Ralph to dump it back into the Mersey. When Ralph asked why, his superior said that the thing was one of three ancient crosses that lay off the coast of Garston as a homage to some ancient Scandinavian God – and to disturb the crosses was sure to result in death and tragedy. The last time one of these crosses had been found was in January 1948, and the day after the cross was dropped back into the River by the superstitious operator of the dredging machine, a tugboat named

"Toxteth" – owned by R. R. Portus and Sons of Garston – was struck by the Norwegian steamer the *Basis*, a vessel of 2,444 tons. A strange gale had visited the Mersey the moment the ancient Scandinavian symbol was brought up, and the winds were of such ferocity, every vessel upon the river was perilously thrown about, and the barges in that part of the Mersey were driven to seek shelter against the walls of Garston docks. Four men of the "Toxteth" were drowned in this strange tragedy. Just after Ralph had heard this weird tale, a storm hit the river. The "Viking Cross" was quickly ditched into the heaving waters, and soon afterwards the storm suddenly abated, and sunlight broke through the clouds. Ralph boasted of his photographic memory, and so I asked him to draw the symbols he had seen upon that wheel of stone, and from what he could recall, I would say the wheel was some representation of the Eye of Odin, an ancient potent symbol which is almost identical to the Celtic Cross, only the arms radiating from the circle are of equal length, unlike the bottom arm of the Celtic Cross, which is elongated and reaches down to a base. The Eye of Odin looks more like a gun-sight with its encircled cross, and it is said that the Scandinavian warriors often had this symbol tattooed upon their bodies as a form of occult protection. Those of you who know their Norse mythology will know that Odin, the "Allfather" of all of the Gods, had a thirst for wisdom that was so powerful, he eagerly gave one of his eyes to the keeper of a Mimir's Well so he could drink from the waters of the well and gain incredible wisdom as a result. As far as I can tell, the three ancient crosses of Odin lay still amongst the silt near

Garston Rocks.

The shore of Garston has many more mysteries too, and what follows is just one of them. In the late January of 1951, a well-to-do Aigburth schoolboy of thirteen named John Hughes, was playing truant one afternoon, and wandered down to Garston shore. The worst fog of the winter had descended on Lancashire and it had brought traffic to a standstill. Visibility was nil, and bus services were suspended across the region. Police made the unusual decision to issue bulletins on radio and TV to advise commuters to take the train home, for the Met Office had predicted that the fog was about to become worse and was already spreading to neighbouring counties. Commuters who ended up stranded by the unusually thick fog ended up besieging police stations across Lancashire for advice. This all took place on Monday, 29 January, 1951. The schoolboy John Hughes could not have picked a worse day to "sag-off" school, and as he walked along the bleak icy shore of Garston, he saw a faint silhouette of a boat of about fifty feet, leaning at an angle of about 20 degrees. He had heard there were wrecks on this shore, and curiosity got the better of him, and the boy strolled through the fog, coughing and spluttering as the carboniferous vapours got on his chest. A square of light suddenly appeared in the shadowy beached vessel, and John realised it was a hatchway from which a lamp was shining. The rays from the lamp traced a vertical triangle in the mist, and the silhouette of a man's head and shoulders appeared in the hatchway. 'Who's that coughing?' said an old-sounding voice.

John halted and saw the dark figure of a hunched man climb out the hatchway and come to the rail of the boat.

'What are you doing down here?' the elderly stranger asked, and at that moment a loud foghorn from the upper reaches of the Mersey punctuated his question with an unearthly echo.

'I er-I'm lost,' John claimed, and remained rooted to the spot. Something told him not to go further.

'Well come up here and I'll give you some soup, come on!' the old man replied, and went back to the hatchway. He hesitated and turned back and said, 'Come on, laddy!' And he beckoned John with his waving arm, then went below deck.

John stayed put and looked back the way he had come. He thought he could hear the tide coming in with a faint rushing sound, and panicked.

The old man's head peeped out the hatchway. 'Are you coming or not?'

John Hughes hurried away from the approaching unseen waters and found a narrow steep ladder which he climbed, and its rungs were ice cold. He ducked under the rail of the boat and gingerly made his way to the hatchway, and already he could smell something tasty – but salty. John looked down into the interior of the vessel and saw it was lit by a fairly bright old-fashioned-looking oil lamp. A man with thin white hair combed over a shining bald head looked up, and his face was creased with wrinkles. His eyebrows were like thin pinches of white cotton wool glued over his eyes, and his curved Roman nose was pockmarked with dirty pores. The oldster's face had a yellowish weathered look to it, but is eyes were dark brown, penetrating and lively. 'Come on, come aboard,' he said, and he did not speak in a Liverpudlian accent, but

John was unable to say just what accent this was.

The schoolboy climbed down a short ladder and entered a cabin with the old man, and there was a table. On this table there was nothing but an old coiled tartan scarf and an unlit pipe. The aroma hanging in the air reminded John of the scouse stew his grandmother made, only with that odd salty scent to it. The man went through a doorway into a galley of some sort, where there was a hob or some sort of ancient iron cooker, and a blackened pot was brought from this cooker and plonked down on the table. The man carried the black pot with a towel around it because it had no handle. He went to fetch two bowls and spoons. 'Sit yourself down, and tell me your name,' the old man said, and he began to tilt the pot and pour out the stew of carrots and some meat – possibly mutton – into the bowl allotted to John.

A seated John gave the old man his full name, and then, for some reason, he felt he shouldn't have the broth, because he suspected it was poisoned. It was probably a silly idea, John thought, but he decided to wait for the man to sit at the table and have his soup first. The old man sat down and said, 'Well, my name's John too, so that's a good start isn't it?' And he grinned, showing a black square gap where his front teeth had been. 'Drink up, will you sonny?' he said, and looked at the bowl in front of John.

John just sat there, with the spoon poised over the steam of the soup, and suddenly, he decided he should leave. 'What's wrong?' the old man said, and became really annoyed. 'I was good enough to share this soup with you, and you won't even taste it!'

John got up and ran to the ladder, and began to

climb up it, but the old man was surprisingly sprightly for his age and he screamed with laughter and bolted after the schoolboy and seized his left shoe.

John screamed "Help!" and shrieked and kicked his other foot and booted the old man in the face. He kicked again and again and felt the heel of his shoe dig into the man's forehead, and he heard old John cry out and swear.

'Little ungrateful bastard! Come here!' the old man growled and pulled the boy's left shoe clean off. John climbed onto the deck and heard the old man coming up after him. He ducked under the rail of the boat and then decided to jump onto the shore rather than try and descend the ladder and end up captured. The lad's feet struck the stony shore and the impact was that hard, John Hughes thought the top of his legs had ripped upwards into his guts. He fell and landed on his hands, and could not breathe because the landing from such a great height – about 9 or 10 feet – had winded him. The boy couldn't even cry, and it seemed as if his lungs had burst upon hitting the floor with such a force. But he ran, and felt he wouldn't be able to run far without any intake of breath. He thought of his mother and father and grandparents and wished he was home.

'Little bastard! Come here!' shrieked the old man in a hysterical voice.

John Hughes realised he was running through ankle-deep water now, and believed he would drown. He somehow regained his breath and looked back to see nothing but a limbo of grey and a faint veil of paler fog swirling about. The horns of the river traffic were booming, and John kept running up the incline until he reached a roadway, and he started to cry. He eventually bumped into a man and told him what had happened and the man took the boy home and his wife sat the sobbing John Hughes down and gave him cocoa and some sandwich cake. When she heard his strange story the woman went out and telephoned the police. John Hughes was taken home by the couple and the police searched Garston shore for the old man and his boat, and found only an old wreck of a boat that had been left there years ago. They virtually accused John Hughes of making up the story, but the parents of the boy believed something had taken place, and John's father, George Hughes, drove down to Garston a few days later with his brother, and they found the same old wreck of the boat that the police had come across, but George and his brother had a better look at the boat because the fog had now virtually cleared. The timbers of the vessel were fungus-ridden and crumbled to the touch, and through a gaping hole in the wreck, the brothers saw a table standing on three legs. One of the men touched this table and it collapsed, and huge sewer rats scurried from under it and ran out of the wreck. A thick dusty web was strung across the hatchway set in the deck above, and a huge grey spider rested there. George and his brother could see the rusted hulk of some stove through a doorway on the right, which was blocked with fallen planks and rubble, but what was this in a corner of the cabin? George bent down and saw that it was unmistakably the brown shoe of his son, and it was pinned to a solitary wooden plank with a long rusted knife with a peculiar pale handle. It took some effort from George to remove the knife from the shoe, and he went home and showed it to his wife and son, and they shuddered when they heard how it had been fixed to the floor with an old-fashioned knife with a whalebone handle.

John Hughes rarely played truant after that incident, and never again ventured down to the Garston shore, even during the hours of daylight.

When a grown-up John Hughes was my guest on the radio, relating this story, many people telephoned the radio station and reported various strange encounters on Garston's shore. A few recalled the old wreck of the boat, and how they often saw a light burning in it on some nights. A few locals reported seeing the old man going in and out of that boat, all hours of the morning and night, even though that abandoned wreck had been there since around the 1930s. The boat was finally smashed up and removed, and the little wood that was left was put on a bonfire by the local children one Guy Fawkes Night in the 1960s. Just what the sinister motive of the ghost was in offering John some soup is hard to fathom, and will never be known now. Nor will we ever know just whose ghost it was that managed to pull off the shoe of John Hughes as it tried to drag him back to God knows what.

We move inland now to look at some more strange tales of Garston, and they don't get more stranger than the tale of "Brendan".

Being Liverpool born and bred I am probably biased but I think there is a superior zoological separation between Liverpudlians and the rest of the human race, whether it's in the sphere of sport or popular music, comedy, or art – and its definitely the case regarding the supernatural. Nothing fazes us, not even the paranormal sometimes. A few years ago a certain well-known solicitor in Liverpool told me that he had been visited by a bouncer who wanted to sue his employer because he had been attacked at work by a poltergeist. The bouncer had been in an office in a nightclub not far from the Cavern one morning around 3.10am when he was struck by a cashbox, then a typewriter and a huge framed picture that came flying off the wall. Then invisible hands began to throttle the bouncer and an ice cold "thing" that could not be seen, pinned him to a desk and started to punch his back. The bouncer fought back and even head-butted whatever it was which had attacked him, and the poltergeist activity soon calmed down. Anyone else would have quit their job or at least asked to be transferred to some other post in the firm, but the bouncer wanted compensation from his employer and when his boss said he was not insured for ghostly attacks, the bouncer attempted – unsuccessfully – to sue him. Such is the mettle of some Scousers. And here is another example that springs to mind of a Liverpudlian bravely facing the unknown. Many years ago, just after the Second World War, a world-wise West Derby sailor in his forties named Danny was dancing with an incredibly beautiful brunette in the Grafton. She was the daintiest thing Danny had ever set eyes on, and seemed to almost float as she danced. She had stunning green sparkly eyes and the face of a doll, and Danny felt unusually ecstatic – high as a kite in fact – as he danced with this sexy siren. Her name was Ciara. Around midnight in the middle of a dance, Danny happened to gaze down, and he noticed a green tail dangling down from under her skirt. This tail was writhing about the way a cat's does when it's annoyed.

'I think your garter's come lose, girl,' Danny said close to Ciara's ear, and he was quite unfazed. Many of the others dancing on the floor that night saw this strange spectacle and it would duly enter into the pantheon of Liverpool folklore. The girl stopped dancing, glanced down, cried out some unintelligible word, then vanished in an instant and people gasped, naturally thinking the young lady had been a ghost, but, the sailor matter-of-factly explained what his grandmother had told him: that the girl merely belonged to the "Fay" – a fairy race, and that she and her kin had a liking for Celts, especially of the Liverpool kind. She'd been sussed when her tail had fallen down from her knickers.

This brings us onto our next Garston tale. At the time of writing, Ellen Jones is in her forties, but when she was aged ten, she tells me she was – like many other children - in tune with the hidden world of fairies, ghosts, leprechauns, and angels. Ellen's Grandma claimed the unusual electric-blue eyes of the red-headed freckle-faced girl would allow her to see supernatural things, and this was so; even as a baby in her cot she would look past the shoulder of her mother at something no one could see, and she would laugh and seem transfixed by whatever it was. In May 1981, Ellen and her family moved into an old Grade II listed 4-bedroomed Victorian house on Garston's leafy North Road. On the third night at her new home, a very strange-looking man about 6 feet in height with enormous pointed ears and dressed in medieval-looking green clothes appeared in the corner of Ellen's bedroom. He peeped at her from behind her wardrobe, presenting half of his rounded face. His eyes seemed of a light green colour, and he had prominent rosy plump cheeks. He came out of hiding and Ellen could see that the only hair on the stranger's head were two small white tufts above each eye. The child gasped, blinked and her mouth formed a little "o" of surprise. 'Who the heck are you?' she asked.

Upon realising that Ellen could see him, and in a rich low voice with an Irish lilt to it, the odd-looking intruder said he was "a type of leprechaun" named Brendan who wanted to marry a human girl, and, furthermore, he had one in mind – Ellen's mother Rose. He excitedly asked Ellen to arrange a date with Rose for him and the girl said her mother was already married – to her dad – and she had no intention of breaking them up.

'I have no one you see,' Brendan sat on the end of the bed and looked towards the window, presenting a profile of his face. Ellen could see his double chin, aquiline nose and pot belly as he sat there. Most children would have run screaming from the room at the sight of this bogey man, but Ellen was made of sterner stuff and was more intrigued than scared. Children notice everything, and she took in all the details from the coarse weave of his green clothes to the grey hairs protruding from his nose.

'I thought leprechauns were supposed to be little,' the girl wondered out loud.

'Says who?' Brendan turned to face her. 'What do your lot know?'

The child thought there was something very sinister in the entity's eyes, perhaps evil or maybe just quite mischievous, but all of a sudden, Ellen felt a bit afraid.

'Anyway, you can't have my mum, now go away or I'll shout my dad,' Ellen told the weird being sternly.

'That's nice, isn't it?' Brendan said, getting up from the bed. It was strange seeing someone as tall as him in the bedroom; Ellen's father was only about five-foot-five. 'I shall "go away" then,' the unearthly apparition said in a sulky way, and his voice went up in pitch as he said the words 'go away'.

Ellen drew her legs up as she sat up in the bed and watched "Brendan" walk into the corner to the side of the wardrobe. She saw his big pointed dark-green shoes pad along until he vanished – but she somehow knew he hadn't gone, even though it was quiet enough to hear the ticking of her Mickey Mouse clock.

She was ready to run from the bed when Brendan's voice startled her. It came from the side of the wardrobe. 'Don't worry, I'm going now,' he said, out of sight. 'Just have to do this,' Ellen thought he muttered. Then a hard silence fell on the bedroom, and Ellen Jones got out of her bed and ran out the room. She went downstairs and informed her parents of the tall green visitor.

Rose Jones seemed alarmed and turned to her husband, who had been enjoying a TV show, and he rolled his eyes, then said: 'Oh come on, Ellen, a big tall leprechaun?'

'Maybe some maniac has got into her room somehow,' Rose told her husband with a shocked face.

Mr Jones hauled himself out of his armchair. 'I'll go and check,' he said, but his wife called him back and said she'd go with him, and she picked up an empty wine bottle from the table and went with him as he smirked.

The couple found no one – human prowler or any leprechaun – upstairs in Ellen's bedroom. They checked the other rooms and Mr Jones even checked the attic, but the dust and cobwebs there were undisturbed.

'I wasn't seeing things,' Ellen told her mum and dad, 'and I wasn't dreaming either.'

'Look, leave the nightlight on,' the girl's father advised, 'and if you hear or see anything unusual – and if it's not your imagination – shout me and your mum. Okay?'

Ellen nodded, and her father patted her head and her mother hugged and kissed her as she lay in her bed with the duvet covering her as far as her button nose. As soon as her mum and dad descended the stairs outside, Ellen looked over at the dark corner next to the wardrobe. Something moved over there, giving the girl a start, but it soon became apparent that the movement was the result of nothing more sinister than a little fluttering moth.

Ellen stared at that corner for a while, continually expecting and imagining the tall green stranger stepping out from behind the wardrobe. She turned on her side in the bed and looked at the nightlight. It was glimmering because there was a film of sleepy grit forming in the girl's tired eyes.

Something bulbous and dark came up from the floor at the side of the bed. It was the top of Brendan's bald head, and as he got up slowly the following words came from his silhouetted head: 'I'm sorry to bother you again – '

Ellen shrieked. 'Go away!' she screamed in the highest pitch she had ever attained.

Brendan's head dropped down, out of sight, and then came the sound of two pairs of feet bounding up the stairs. She heard her father tripping over the top step and heard him swear out loud. Then the door burst open and the main light in the room came on.

'He was here!' Ellen peered over the side of her bed, expecting the peculiar pest to be lying there on the floor, but he was nowhere to be seen.

'Ellen! You either nodded off and dreamt it, or you're seeing things!' her father told her, and he even knelt and looked under the bed.

'You've had a bad dream. Love,' Mrs Jones reassured her daughter, who was now looking under the bed - just in case her dad hadn't seen Brendan.

Thankfully, for the girl and the strained nerves of her parents, the leprechaun was not seen again that night, but on the following day, Mr Jones was in the back garden, snipping a hedge with a pair of shears when the old neighbour next door – a man named Graham, suddenly said: 'The lot who lived in your place were very rowdy.'

'Oh really?' Mr Jones replied out of politeness, but he wasn't really that interested in who had once lived in the house that he was now renting.

'Yes, they were Irish,' old Graham said, his eyes looking up at the blue sky as he thought back. 'One of them played the bodhrán at all hours of the night.'

'Irish, eh?' Mr Jones thought back to his daughter's account of "Brendan". He told his wife about this coincidental item of information later that day. She thought the whole idea of an overgrown leprechaun wanting her hand in marriage was quite creepy and something Ellen could not have dreamt up.

Just under a week later, Ellen came into her parents' bedroom at around 2am – and on this occasion she did not seem scared at all, but annoyed, and when Rose awoke to the sensation of her daughter tapping her shoulder, she was told: 'He's been again.'

Rose was afraid to wake her husband, but he opened his eyes when he heard his wife and daughter whispering, and asked what was going on.

Ellen told him. 'He's been pestering me again, Dad. Said he wants to marry mum again.'

'Ellen, this Brendan is just a figment of your imagination, love,' Mrs Jones told her daughter, but it was plain to see she didn't even believe her own words now.

'Go back to bed, Ellen,' Mr Jones said, squeezing his eyes shut and turning away from his wife with his left hand under his pillow. 'We'll talk about it later.' He mumbled, and was soon snoring.

'Go and get some sleep, love,' Rose Jones said, and she yawned too.

Ellen turned and left the bedroom in a right sulk and slammed the door behind her.

Later that morning, around four o'clock, Ellen felt the end of her bed go down as if someone had sat on it, and she opened her eyes. There, clearly visible in the moonlight, was the uncanny Brendan. 'Well, what did she say? Did you tell her about my proposal of marriage?'

Ellen was annoyed at being awakened by the persistent paranormal persecutor, and she recalled that word her mother had used to explain him away – figment. 'You are nothing but a figment of my imagination!'

'Eh?' Brendan was at first confused by the girl's reply, then realised what she had said, and threw a tantrum. 'I will lay such a curse on you, you – you little ginger, freckle-faced fustylug!'

Ellen was agape at the insults, and lay there, propped up in bed on one elbow with her hair in disarray and her mouth wide open.

Brendan loomed loftily over the girl and shook his fist at her. 'Figment am I? Well, this figment is going to lay such a curse on you and your mammy and daddy! You pinch-faced little pipsqueak!'

'You're a figment! Go away and stay away!' Ellen's face went pink with rage as she creamed at the living question mark, and he seemed both shocked and saddened. He backed away from the bed and a second after he had melted into the shadows, the bedroom door flew open and in came Mrs Jones with the light of the landing shining behind her. She switched on the bedroom light and saw her daughter, sitting up in bed, her face quite flushed, and the little girl was pointing to the space between the wardrobe and the wall – to that corner Brendan always came from. Without looking at that corner – because she was afraid of what she might see there - Rose led the girl out of the room and took Ellen to stay in her bed for the remainder of that morning.

When Ellen told her mum how Brendan had threatened to curse the family because she had called him a figment, Rose seemed very worried. Sure enough, the family had all sorts of bad luck. Money vanished into thin air and they all broke out in measles-like spots. Mr Jones was afflicted with a constant ringing noise in his ears that would start at

8am and suddenly stop at 7pm, and his wife sneezed whenever she ate anything. Just before dawn each morning the family would hear what sounded like heavy feet, running across the rooftops of their home, and even the old neighbour Graham heard this, but tried to explain it away as magpies running across the slates. 'Those magpies must have army boots on,' Mr Jones told his neighbour. Ellen knew all this was Brendan's spiteful work, and she really intended to clobber him with something if he showed up in her room again. Three days later, the girl's parents and a visiting auntie heard Ellen having a blazing row with her 'imaginary friend' one night, followed by a loud bang which shook the house and caused a fall of flaky dry ceiling paint in the living room. Ellen then came down wielding a garden rake and proudly announced: "He's gone at last!"

That summer, the family went to meet up with relatives in Lydiate at the ancient Scotch Piper Inn, and the Joneses weren't there long when Ellen tugged her mum's elbow and pointed to a rather strange tall bald man in a smart sharply-cut shamrock-green suit standing at the bar. 'It's him - Brendan!' Ellen whispered, and she'd gone pale.

'Oh don't start all that again!' Rose rolled her eyes and then chatted to her sister-in-law.

Brendan now had two large tufts of white hair on either side of his head to hide his huge ears.

Ellen went over and asked him why he was here.

'To woo Rose, lassie,' he said with a grin. 'Faint heart never won a fair lady.'

'Dad! He's the leprechaun who's after mum!' Ellen yelled to her father, who was bringing a tray of pints, crisps and peanuts to the table, and he returned an embarrassed and annoyed look.

But suddenly an old blind regular drinker named Bobby shouted: "What's that? It's one of *them*! Get it away from me!' and struck Brendan with his walking stick, and the entity masquerading as a human shouted something in protest – and vanished into thin air – this time for good.

'Did you see that?' Rose asked her husband? 'That man – just vanished.'

There were gasps of awe all around the bar.

The blind man said: 'Has he gone? They scare me!'

Ellen asked him how he knew about the leprechaun, and Bobby said: 'Has he gone though, girl?'

'Yes, he's gone alright – he vanished,' she said excitedly.

'They call themselves all sorts,' Bobby said, enigmatically. 'Leprechauns, Martians, ghosts, but they're no good, and they don't belong here.'

'Who are "they"?' Mr Jones said from his table, all intrigued.

'You'd never believe me,' Bobby replied, turning his face in the general direction of Mr Jones.

'Try me,' Ellen's father said, coming over to Bobby's little table.

The blind man started to speak absolute gibberish – words no one could understand – gobbledygook was the only word for the language he was speaking, or perhaps double-Dutch.

Ellen drew away from the blind man as he foamed at the mouth. He seemed to be having a fit of some sort, but then as people went to his aid, Bobby stood up, shrugged and shook his head. His white stick clicked away as he headed for the door.

'Is he okay?' Mrs Jones asked, and a drinker, aged about fifty-five, sixty perhaps, came over to the Joneses and said, 'Yeah, he's okay. Bobby has a talent, psychic like, and whenever he tries to talk about these things, whatever they are, it's like something stops him. It's very strange. He'll be okay.'

'What do you mean, "these things"?' Mr Jones was curious to know, and so was his wife and Ellen and a few visiting drinkers at the pub.

When the man tried to explain, his head began to turn sharply left and right, as if he was suffering from torticollis spasms. 'See what I mean?' the man said, pointing to his head as it jerked about. 'They always stop us.'

This freaked the Joneses and their relatives so much that they left the pub and went to a restaurant, where they all agreed it was better if Brendan was never mentioned again, and thankfully, the "leprechaun" who lusted for Ellen's mother was not heard from again, but who knows? He - or one of his countrymen - might just visit *you* one night.

Over the years in my strange line of work I have noticed how a lot of people are creeped out by three particular things – dolls, clowns and the ventriloquist's dummy, and I have quite a few eerie tales about the latter; here are just two of them. In 1964, an amazing young up and coming ventriloquist named Dennis Spicer who had many Liverpool showbiz friends like crooner Michael Holliday, and comedians Ted Ray, Jimmy Tarbuck and Ken Dodd - who knew Dennis very well as he was at the time with Forrester George, the same talent agency as the ventriloquist) and often shared the bill with him. One day, Spicer arrived late at a TV studio dressing room where Ted Ray and comedy writer Barry Cryer were waiting to go on air with him. Spicer opened a big trunk and put his beloved doll, named Jimmy Green, on a hook on the dressing room wall, then said he was going the toilet. In Spicer's absence, Ted Ray couldn't help having a root through the ventriloquist's trunk, which contained all of the props and gimmicks as well as other, smaller dolls. Ted then decided, 'We shouldn't be doing this!' and closed the trunk, and when Dennis Spicer came back into the dressing room, the doll hanging on the hook eerily said: 'He's had a look in your case, Dennis!'

Ted Ray and Barry Cryer were quite unnerved by this because it actually sounded as if the words had come from "Jimmy Green", such was Spicer's talent. The 29-year-old ventriloquist was a huge hit in America on the *Ed Sullivan Show* and in early November 1964 he was featured in the Royal Variety Performance with a corgi dog dummy, and the Queen later told Spicer she really enjoyed his act, especially the corgi jokes. Then sadly, on 15 November that year, Dennis Spicer was killed instantly in a two-car collision while driving down the A1, homeward from a charity show. One of the policemen arriving at the scene found Spicer's mangled body among the smashed and twisted wreckage, and also a little pair of shoes were seen in the debris. Then a motorist who had stopped to help heard high-pitched screams from the crushed boot of the car. It was naturally assumed that a child was trapped in there, but when the boot was opened, they found a badly damaged ventriloquist's doll with its mouth wide open and its arms raised, shielding its eyes. It was as if the thing had been alive when the car had crashed, and the policeman and member of the public were quite taken aback by this.

In March 1982, at a flat on Garston's Clarendon Road, a young lady named Rita Randallson was watching a TV variety show called *Starburst*, and among the guests (which featured Pete Price, Joe Longthorne, Elaine Paige and the Nolans), there was a ventriloquist named Ken Wood. Rita told her boyfriend Neil that there was an old ventriloquist's doll in the attic of her mum's house on nearby Island Road, and later that night she went and brought it to Neil's flat. The doll and its little tuxedo were a bit dusty but in good condition, and Neil persuaded Rita to sell the dummy via the *Liverpool Echo*'s "items for sale" column for £150. Rita said she'd drop off the ad at the Echo offices in town during her work lunch-break tomorrow, but that night around 10.50pm she received a chilling telephone call at her house. A caller with a high-pitched childlike voice said: 'I'd rather you didn't sell me, Rita, because you might die horribly if you do.'

'Who is this?' Rita asked. She listened and heard no heavy breathing, and no other sounds at the other end of the line, just a clock ticking, so the caller obviously hadn't hung up yet. Then Rita recalled how Neil had a real loud clock right by the telephone at his flat, and so Rita thought her boyfriend was probably playing some prank. A grinning Rita pressed her hand over the mouthpiece so Neil wouldn't hear what followed next. She passed the phone to her mum and in a whispering voice told her: 'Neil's just called me with a stupid voice, trying to scare me. Hold on to this Mum, and don't hang up till I get over there.'

'Over where?' the young lady's mother asked.

'Sssh! Neil's flat,' Rita explained. 'Just keep listening until I tell you I'm there.'

Rita left the house and began the two minute walk over to Neil's flat then let herself in with her key, but her fellah wasn't home from the pub yet, and there on an armchair, she found the ventriloquist's dummy with the telephone receiver on its lap, and from this receiver Rita could hear her mum's tinny voice asking if she was there yet.

Rita looked at the sinister doll in horror, then shouted out Neil's name, just to make sure he wasn't home. She looked in the toilet, bedroom and kitchen, but no one was about. She then got out of that flat as fast as her legs could carry her.

She bumped into Neil in the street outside. He had just come from the Palatine pub on Island Road, and he could see his girlfriend was in a right state. 'Come in and tell me from the beginning,' Neil suggested in a slurred voice, but Rita certainly had no intention of going back into the flat with that doll there, and she dashed off to her mother's house. Rita would have nothing further to do with that ventriloquist's dummy, and Neil sold it to a second hand shop for £45 in the end. Its present whereabouts are unknown.

COMING THROUGH THE RYE

This terrifying incident happened many years ago in the late 1990s. A Liverpool couple in their early thirties we shall call Jayne and Adam (not their real names), moved into a former farmhouse in a remote part of Knowsley. Adam had bought the house after a win on the Lottery, and had often seen the place on his way to work on the train when he commuted from Aintree. The couple quickly settled into the house but soon found themselves faced with an unforeseen problem which was taking the shine of their luxurious new home. The problem presented itself on the second month at the house...

'What's wrong?' Jayne asked, in the darkness.

'It's stress,' Adam claimed, full of guilt. 'It's funny...'

'Don't you fancy me any more?' Jayne asked, laying back as she spoke softly to his ashen face, just visible from a reflected rectangle of moonlight on the bedroom wall.

He rested on his right elbow, then tried to lay beside her, but she pulled him back to her and hugged him and kissed him and tried to get him all going again, but it was no use.

'What's wrong?' she said again, and he said nothing.

He touched her face and kissed her cheek and lips came into contact with a tear. 'Oh don't start...' he was saying when she reached out and turned on the bedside lamp and its glare revealed the whole ugly truth in her eyes. He looked non-interested, bored almost, and tired.

'Adam, it's not normal,' she told him, and the yellow-golden light from the ostentatious bedside lamp's embroidered shade made her tears sparkle. 'Couples make love, not excuses.'

'I told you it's stress!' he bawled and slammed his fist down on his pillow then buried his face in that pillow as if he was seeking some sort of sanctuary from all this.

'You said that last time,' she recalled, wiping the tears with the backs of her index and middle fingers. 'What are you stressed about?'

'It's just with getting all this – ' Adam turned and held out his palms as if he was going to catch something. 'All this came so fast, the big win and this new environment.'

Jayne sat up and shot an exaggerated puzzled look at him. 'Oh shut up – you are *complaining* because you won all that money on the Lottery? That's the best excuse I have ever heard!'

He got out the bed and stood there, naked, and yelled at her. 'What do you mean – excuse? Everything has got to be an excuse with you! You never believe me, do you? You always make out I'm lying – no matter what I say! I'm not even allowed to have a few off-days!'

'A few? Ha!' Jayne threw back her head and then turned to look away from him – towards the moonlit window.

'Well alright then! You're always saying I'm not

being straight with you – that I'm lying or making excuses as you call them – here's why I can't perform: it's getting boring!'

'Excuse me?' She presented a face that clearly showed the deep hurt, despite the mask of humour she'd put on.

'Boring!' Adam shouted, and his face went red form this wrath that was being let out from him at last. He spelt out the word: 'B-o-r-i-n-g!'

'I can spell, dickhead!' she screamed back at him then swore at him and took refuge under the duvet so only her tied-back pony tail was showing. 'Adam sat on the edge of his side of the bed, and looked at the floor. He'd said it now, and felt so guilty. He wanted to say he was sorry but he just couldn't for some deep repressed reason.

The mattress wobbled; it was Jayne coming up, not for air, but to address the accusation. 'Are you really getting bored?'

Adam muttered something that passed as "Yeah" and Jayne said, 'Oh well, you'll have to call it a day then and find someone else to get your fire all going.'

She waited for him to say "No, no, I don't want anyone else" – but he said nothing. This really creased her heart.

He turned and looked at her. He had reddened eyes – the nearest Adam came to spilling tears. In a choked-up voice he said: 'Bastard money! Haven't had a bit of luck since I won that money.'

'It's nothing to do with the money,' Jayne replied, and began to cry.

'Jayne, listen, when I said it was getting boring I didn't mean I was getting bored of you. You're not a sex object, you're my girl.'

'You're back-pedalling now because you feel shitty,' was Jayne's opinion.

'No, look, if you made me goulash every night and I said I was fed up with it, you wouldn't get a cob on – you'd just start cooking something else, wouldn't you?'

There came a very faint, barely audible response from under the duvet, where their sex-life was now dead and buried. 'You said I was boring.'

'Didn't say *you* was boring, I said *it* was boring. Stop being a martyr!' Adam could feel his heart palpitating with the stress of it all; unnecessary stress in his mind.

The mattress started shaking slightly. Jayne was crying.

He pulled the duvet clean off her and she lay there in the foetal position, curled up, her tear-soaked face hidden in her hands.

'I love you,' he told her, 'no matter what. We'll get through this.'

She muttered something incomprehensible as she sobbed and he said, 'What?' and hugged her, and she tried to pull herself away but he wouldn't let her. He waited until the crying subsided and then offered a solution which seemed audacious at first, but then it made her smile, and then giggle.

'Are you serious?' she asked, and sat up and hugged him.

'Yes, I am, well I'm not serious about sex, its just take it or leave it, and people make too much of it,' he rambled.

'Oh shut up, you love it,' she said, and asked him what he intended to do.

'I think we should have a go at role-play, like dress

up as characters,' he said, and blushed slightly.

'You're serious, aren't you?' Jayne asked him. ''Where are we going to get costumes to dress up in?'

'There's a place opened down town in Liverpool called Lili Bizarre – a fancy dress hire place,' Adam informed her.

'And what do you want me to dress up as?' Jayne was curious to know.

Adam's face was visibly burning a shade of powder pink. 'I dunno – what would you want *me* to dress up as? A Roman soldier?'

'No, that's corny, mmm let me see…' Jayne lay back on the pillows and fantasised away.

'A manga character?' Adam blurted out.

'A what?'

'A Japanese comic book character. They er…'

'You want me to get done up as a comic book character?' The corner of Jayne's mouth curled up and her nostrils flared – a well-recognised indication she did not approve of his suggestion.

'Or maybe Marie Antoinette – ' Adam's eyes swivelled about as he visualised some historically-based fantasy.

'Mm, I could be her, I suppose, but you'd have to dress up as King Louis,' Jayne reasoned.

'Nah, I hate all those frilly collars and cuffs,' Adam rejected the idea.

'Maybe you could be Robin Hood,' Jayne pictured Adam in the Lincoln green outfit but then quickly dismissed the idea.

'I'm not wearing tights,' he said with such seriousness in his voice.

'You like Batman though, don't you?' Jayne recalled

all of the Batman comics Adam was always reading, and he always dragged her to the cinema to see the latest blockbuster about the caped crusader.

'Yeah, I'd be okay with that,' he said with a self-conscious smirk, then added: 'Don't want you being Cat Woman though – I'd rather you were Marie Antoinette.'

The woman at Lili Bizarre was very helpful, and soon had the costumes sorted out for Adam's non-existent "Fancy Dress do".

That night it was a revelation for the couple. It was fun and it was stimulating and perhaps it was psychodrama – to use the parlance of the behaviourist – but Jayne and Adam rediscovered one another, both sexually and also personally. The experiment was very therapeutic on many levels, and they regained a lot of the lost feelings – a lot of the old magic that had somehow evaporated in the five years they'd been together. Each fell fast asleep smugly and utterly satisfied in each other's arms that morning around half-past four.

The week afterwards, Jayne was Wonder Woman and Adam was Tarzan of the Apes, and he even swung from a rope on the oak tree in the back garden in nothing but his loin cloth.

A few days after this, Adam had to go and visit a very ill auntie, and he told Jayne to stay at home because he knew she had a terrible phobia of hospitals, and even the smell of a particular industrial disinfectant used in those places could turn her stomach. He did promise he would return by 9pm, and what's more, he said he would be dressed as someone very 'fetching' – and how Jayne had belly-laughed when he used that old word. She in turn, planned to dress up as Dorothy from the *Wizard of Oz*.

She ate her tea on her own, and wanted to call Adam so badly but thought it unwise to; he'd want to sit and comfort his aunt in a peaceful environment. Jayne watched a bit of TV but missed her partner sorely – even more so now that they had found one another again. She suddenly remembered something. She was due to take her pill - *the* Pill – and she could not find her tray of pills anywhere. Perhaps this was a sign, she wondered; perhaps it was about time she and Adam had a child. She rooted about in the drawers of her bedside cabinet and in the drawers and cupboards in the kitchen but could not find the Cilest pills anywhere. She came to the conclusion that she had accidentally thrown them out with the rubbish and she didn't fancy delving down a dustbin – especially now that the night was drawing in. She drew the blinds and curled up on the sofa with a book, but every few pages she'd glance at the clock.

It was a bit chilly so she turned the central heating up a notch and found the warmth soporific. She began to doze off, but then she heard a click – but she wasn't sure if it had been a real noise or merely an imaginary sound inside her head. She heard the slow padding of feet in the hallway – and it sounded just like Adam coming in.

The door of the living room opened slowly – and in came – a weird scarecrow!

It gave Jayne a start at first, but then she realised Adam had found out about her Dorothy costume, and he had become the Scarecrow. 'Glad you didn't choose the Tin Man, it'd be a nightmare getting yourself into the buff!'

The scarecrow walked towards her – and this did not seem to be the way Adam normally walked. Couples notice simple things like that; the way the other moves, the way they make gestures and pose themselves; little idiosyncratic things people outside the relationship never pick up. Those sloping shoulders weren't Adam's either – his shoulders were broader.

Jayne froze in terror. This was a stranger, and he was wearing a dark brown hood of some sort with just two large eyeholes, and a frowning slit in that hood represented the mouth. He had straw protruding from all around his collar, and a shirt made of sewn-together squares of coarse yellow, purple and green fabric – like some patchwork quilt. The straw protruded from his wrists, all around the black leather gloves, and he wore faded, torn and greasy jeans, and where these jeans were stuffed into his scuffed and muddy wellingtons, there was more amber strands sticking out, giving the illusion that this figure had innards of straw.

His gloved hand reached behind to his lower back, where a long carving knife hung in a home-made leather sheath.

'My boyfriend's coming back any minute now,' Jayne gasped and her words were almost inaudible. Her teeth had chattered while speaking.

The scarecrow spoke in a long bumpkin type of drawl – an old dialect of Lancashire perhaps, and promised disembowelment and assured Jayne he'd make her eat faeces before he cut her head clean off and then bisected her. But first he was going to have his way with her, he told her, and said this would happen if she was alive or dead. If she didn't cry out she'd live for a while, but if she tried to run or cry for help, then she'd soon be 'carved-up meat'. He walked so slowly towards his terrified victim and she started to cry. She begged him to go away, but he said, 'No, I'm not goin' away lass,' and laughed. He stopped a few times and made rude thrusting gestures with the knife.

'Who are you?' Jayne asked, and almost threw up with fear.

'I am the Augury Man of old, who sheds the lady's blood on the May Stone so the crops may come!' he said in a strange melodic voice. Then he started to sing a bizarre song as he unzipped himself: 'Coming through the Rye, Coming through the Rye. Jack and Gye, out in the Rye, found a little boy with one black eye. Hey, says Jack, let's hit him on the head, No say's Gye, let's buy the lad some bread, you buy one load and I'll buy two, and we'll raise him up as other folk do!'

Jayne sobbed. 'Please don't hurt me, please go away.'

'I'll go away after I've done you,' the maniac dressed as a scarecrow assured her and made upward thrusts through the air with the big carving knife.

'Oh please Lord, help me,' Jayne prayed with a tremor in her voice.

He started singing again and he was just six feet away. He halted. 'Coming through the Rye! The little girl must die, take her womb and –'

The door opened and Adam came into the room. He took one look at the weirdly-dressed stranger brandishing the knife and picked up the expensive Hoop-back Windsor chair, and he took a swing at the eerie hooded man. The chair caught his raised arm and sent the knife to the other end of the room – with one of the gloves. The figure turned, and Adam brought the chair down hard on him. It splintered upon impact.

Jayne managed to let out a scream which ripped the air at last.

When she and Adam looked at the carpet, all they saw was the smashed remains of the £100 chair – and empty clothes. Adam picked the dark brown hood up, and then looked at the rest of the clothes of the intruder lying flat against the carpet. It was surreal and baffling.

'Where is he? Where's he gone?' Jayne asked over and over again as she held onto Adam's arm. He pulled her away from the sofa and lit every light in the living room and hallway, and then he went back to the patchwork clothes and greasy jeans and picked them up. The clothes were put in a black plastic bin bag and the knife was put in a drawer that was afterwards locked. Jayne urged Adam to call the police.

'To tell them what, exactly, eh?' Adam queried with an annoyed look. 'To tell them a ghost tried to rape and murder you?'

That evening the couple drove to the house of Jayne's family in Bootle, and as they set out from the farmhouse they saw a weird sight that really unnerved them. In a cornfield to the right they saw the silhouetted form of the Augury Man, lumbering along through the waist-high stalks and somehow leaning forward at almost a forty-five-degree angle, almost as if he was leaning into a gale force wind, yet the night was calm and windless. Adam knew full well that he had put the uncanny costume of that scarecrow straw man in the bin and the knife – which he could clearly see in the gloved hand of the figure – was supposed to be in a locked drawer. Jayne urged Adam to step on the accelerator and her boyfriend quickly complied with her wishes. He took one last glimpse of the evil being in his rear view mirror and estimated that it was heading in the direction of Ormskirk.

Within two days the couple had left that farmhouse, never to return, and they temporarily moved to a flat in the city centre of Liverpool. They have no idea who or what the "Augury" Man is (augury is an ancient word pertaining to divination to foresee the future), nor do Jayne and Adam know the meaning of the entity's eerie song: *Coming Through the Rye* – a traditional ancient song (altered and falsely claimed by the Scottish poet Robert Burns at one point in history) with a meaning that's long been lost in the mists of time. The Augury Man's reference to shedding blood on a May Stone sounds as if he is referring to some archaic blood-letting ritual to ensure a successful crop – but all of this conjecture does not explain how a seemingly solid flesh and blood psychopath vanished into thin air to leave his clothes behind, only to reappear afterwards in a field.

HAUNTED PEOPLE

Most ghosts haunt places, and the locations often have something to do with the troubled earthbound spirit and how it ended its life in this world, but I have found that some of the most frightening hauntings are not of places, but of people, and here are just a few of these people-centred hauntings.

They met in the late summer of 1972, sheltering from a summer downpour in the doorway of Timpsons shoe shop on Bold Street. He – Eric – had taken sidelong glances at the petite blonde and thought she looked a bit like Toni Arthur, the Bohemian presenter of the children's afternoon programme *Play Away*, and she – Janis – had thought Eric looked like Mike McGear out of the group Scaffold. There was small talk and chit-chat and they ended up in the Newington pub where they discussed their unusual ambitions. Janis was a cleaner at the university who was studying part-time to hopefully become an occupational therapist at the HQ Hospital of the International Grenfell Association in St Anthony in Newfoundland. 'If I get that job, my patients will include Native Indians and Eskimos from Northern Labrador,' Janis proudly told Eric, and he sipped his bitter then self-consciously told her how he'd like to become a gamekeeper in Africa. But for now, he was a

Hackney cabby. Both single and in their early twenties, the couple started dating, and when they first made love weeks later, Eric got out the bed afterwards and said he had to go home to look after his sick mum – but Janis knew somehow that he was fibbing, and naturally felt used, and worried if she'd said or done something off-putting. When Eric did stay over he never once had a wink of shut eye, and drank coffee all night to stay awake, and when Janis asked him why he never slept in their bed, the weird truth came out.

'You're not going to believe this Jan, but I swear it's true. Ever since I was about five, a thing – I don't know how to describe it; I call it "HeeShee" because I don't know if it's male or female – well, er, it haunts my dreams.'

Janis returned a very puzzled look.

Eric sighed and looked at the ceiling. He tried again. 'You're into psychology so psychoanalyse away, but here goes. My last two girlfriends were attacked by this thing, because the HeeShee is very possessive towards me. It goes into the dreams of whoever I sleep with and tries to kill them in their sleep. Shall I just call it a day now, because you're looking at me as if I'm nuts.'

'No, please, tell me more, I don't think that at all,' Janis held his hand firmly. Eric was tearful as he went on, explaining how the entity had probably killed his last girlfriend who had died from "natural causes" next to him in bed. She had started thrashing about in bed that awful night, and seemed to be choking as she gripped her throat. Eric had tried to pull her eyelids open but her eyes were white and had rolled back. He poured water on her and shook her and shouted at her, but she died without waking.

'Can you just try sleeping here once?' she asked the cabby, and he shook his head, saying, 'I'm not risking it – I love you. This bastard thing is a curse, it is, and no one believes me.'

A fortnight later they celebrated Eric's birthday and went back to Janis's flat quite drunk, and Eric dozed off on the sofa bed in his girlfriend's arms, and she soon nodded off too. Sure enough, she dreamt a bizarre hooded clown-like figure in a black robe was trying to throttle her, but she punched him, and shouted: 'Stay away from Eric, he's mine!' and the weird entity screeched back: 'I don't give up on Eric that easy! He's mine!'

Eric tried to separate "HeeShee" and Janis in the shared dream, but the surreal being knocked Janis to the ground. Janis got to her feet in this unearthly dream and laid into the creepy dream invader and began to spout lines from the Bible. HeeShee screamed at the words and swore at Eric, then shouted "I'll find another friend!" before vanishing into a kaleidoscopic jumble of images. He returned two further times a week later in Janis's dreams, disguised as a cat on the first occasion. In that dream the cat grew to the size of a lion and its face became that of the androgynous being, but once again, Janis began to cite the Holy scripture of the Bible and the entity shrivelled up and vanished. On the second occasion when it infiltrated the dream of Janis, it was a huge spider with the screeching distinctive voice of the dream invader, but again she quoted Scripture, and also the Lord's Prayer, and the weird persistent being finally gave up. Such 'dream demons' (for want of a better term) are apparently very common, and I have written about these types of entities before, such as the sinister "Mr Devlin" who attacked the unconscious minds of two young women in the Edge Lane area of Liverpool in the 1920s (and that story was called "The Man of Her Dreams").

I have no idea what species of creature HeeShee - stalker of the sleeping word – is, but the inner space of the mind is just as unexplored as outer space, and we really do need a Copernicus of psychology.

I wonder whose dreams HeeShee haunts now? Hopefully not *your* ones.

Back pain costs the country almost six billion pounds a year in diagnosis and medical treatment, and at any one time, about forty percent of the population will be suffering from backache-related problems. Backache itself isn't a disease, of course, but a symptom that something has gone awry in the body, and its causes can often be very difficult to identify, as we shall see in the following strange tale.

One afternoon in June, 1963, a 69-year-old West Derby woman named Edna Friday was looking for her uncle Ronald's coin collection up in the attic when she found an old walnut box about the size of a shoe box, with brass fleur-de-lys hinges. Edna opened the box and saw it contained old receipts dating back to Edwardian times, a few chess pieces, a bottle of laudanum and curiously, another box, which was tied up with laces and secured with some sort of sealing wax. She brought this box down to the living room and read the old yellowed note stuck to the rosewood and parquetry box, which was about 9 inches long, five inches across, and five inches deep. The note said: 'Do not open and do not dispose of or burn'. There were five little brass swastikas inlaid in the lid of the sealed box, and Edna recalled how the crooked cross had nothing to do with the Nazi party; the swastika symbol is lost in the obscurity of prehistory – and as well as being found all over the world, from the cultures of Native American Indians to the ancient Greeks, the cross is also found all over India, where it is a good luck symbol. Edna's Uncle Ronald had brought this intriguing box back from Khajuraho in Northern India, where he had helped an archaeologist to excavate in the 1890s. As she read the note, Edna's lazy 12-year-old grandson, Billy, called at her house on his way home from school, on the cadge for sweet money as usual.

Edna let him in, and as she was in the kitchen, getting some lemonade and cakes for Billy, the boy took out his penknife and cut the shoelaces which bound the box with the swastikas on. He found nothing inside the rosewood container, just a sweet smell like incense. The meddlesome lad then accidentally dropped the old box. Edna was furious at Billy for opening her uncle's box, and she bent down to pick it up – and found herself stuck. Her back had gone. 'Don't just stand there, softlad, help me up!' Edna said, unable to even lift her face to her clumsy grandchild. Billy didn't reply. There was a long pause, and then the lad said, 'Gran, there's two thingies on your back.'

Then Edna howled in agony as she felt sharp pains in her lower back. It just felt like two hot needles being inserted. Billy let out a yelp and ran out the house after seeing what was inflicting the back pain – two little doll-sized men in red, each with horns and tails were standing on Edna's back as she knelt there on all fours. The imp-like beings were cruelly inserting what looked like hatpins or needles into Edna's back. The pensioner almost passed out from the excruciating pain, and somehow managed to pick herself up off the floor. When Billy returned to his Gran's house with his big sister, Janet, the little sadistic imps were nowhere to be seen and Billy's description of them was not taken serious. Edna's backache became worse, and at night she would feel the hot needles in her spine again, and would end up crying herself to sleep. Back specialists and physiotherapists blamed sciatica, spondylosis, and a prolapsed disc, but X rays showed nothing. One evening as Edna lay face down on her bed, she saw upon the wall the eerie shadows of two little figures on her back, cast by the bedside lamp, and screamed.

The shadows of the creepy little men were thrusting long pins of some sort into Edna's back, and she thought she was just having some nightmare at first. No dream could be this painful though, Edna reasoned, and she prayed for help. She said the Lord's Prayer out loud and the shadows vanished. What on earth were those creatures? Edna got to her feet in agony and turned on the main light. Then she recalled the box with the swastikas Billy had opened and she went to get it from a cupboard in the kitchen, then placed the box on the open fire. An emission of fern-green smoke came from the burning box, followed by strange elongated ruby-red flames. Edna thought she could hear faint high-pitched cries come from the burning rosewood. After this, she never suffered from backache again. Edna told an elderly neighbour named

Alf Harrington about the spooky little figures, and half expected him to disbelieve her, but old Mr Harrington had been stationed in India in his army days, and said he knew of a fakir in Calcutta who sold various boxes and containers that were alleged to contain imps that could inflict all sorts of harm if they were released. Some of the boxes the fakir sold were very similar to the rosewood box Billy had unwittingly opened, and Harrington recalled a weird incident which occurred when a friend of his – a sailor from the Dingle named Corrigan – bought a teak cigarette barrel from the fakir which was said to contain a real-life genie named either Jinell or Janell. This genie was said to stimulate one of the chakras in the body which would make the sailor virile and sexually energetic. Edna blushed when Mr Harrington reeled off this story in a matter-of-fact style. 'But Corrigan was consumed by this genie, like, and ended up raping a woman in Italy and was nearly castrated,' Harrington recalled. 'And the fakir also had things called "pain imps" which attacked the person who let them out of their box, and they would inflict all sorts of aches and pains which would eventually wear the victim down until he expired. No doctors could ever get to the bottom of the victim's symptoms, but a few psychic people could sometimes see the imps.'

What Mr Harrington says is true, and many fakirs (though not all of them, as many are gifted charlatans) can create these imps and genies with the power of the mind, and such entities that are born of the mind are known as tulpas – thought forms which coalesce from concentrated thought to become tangible beings with minds of their own. Once a "magician" or fakir creates a tulpa, he has to keep it under his control or the tulpa will try and dominate him and sometimes even attempt to kill its creator. The esoteric procedures for creating such tulpas were once a closely-guarded secret, but nowadays, since the advent of the ubiquitous internet, the techniques for making tulpas have been revealed online, if you know where to look. The story of the "pain imps" reminds me of another odd tale that came my way some years ago from a reader named Lisa Jackson. In the 1970s, when Lisa was a child, her parents, David and Jenny, went to live in a beautiful cottage near Ormskirk. David had had a small win on the Pools and couldn't believe his eyes when he saw the cottage was up for sale for just £29,000. David had always wanted to live in a rural setting in such a cottage, and was only too eager to sign on the dotted line after the transaction had taken place at the estate agent's office. Jenny, his wife, set about decorating the old quaint dwelling with her sister Jane, and David and his brothers fixed the roof of the cottage then set about clearing the acres of weed around his new home. A small mound about five feet in height and six feet in length was unearthed by the clearing of the overgrown weeds, and finding it unsightly, David and his brothers dug into the mound and found all sorts of strange items; little axe-heads, copper cups as big as thimbles and tiny bits of pottery. David's oldest brother Peter thought he had been stung on the back of his right hand during the attempted levelling of the mound, but could see no stinger or any discoloration of the skin where he felt a smarting sensation. Within the hour, the fingers and thumb of Peter's right hand had become swollen and red, and if he even tried to move his digits he almost passed out with the pain. Another brother of David suddenly suffered what he felt was a slipped disc. He locked in place as he bent down to pick up a sod of earth, and could not straighten up. A cousin was enlisted to help David Jackson finish the levelling of the mound, and this man, who was only 32, suffered a stroke which left him paralysed down one side of his body for almost six months. David's wife and her sister were convinced something supernatural was going on in the field, and that malevolent forces had not taken kindly to strangers destroying that mound. Lisa, the couple's 5-year-old daughter, was obviously not told about the suspected witchcraft going on, but one night, the child woke up in her bed and saw "three little men" about two feet in height, standing on the counterpane of Lisa's bed near to her feet. In a weird high-pitched voice, one of the shadowy figures told Lisa they'd kill her father unless he left their "hill". The three diminutive figures then vanished. The girl told her mum and dad what had happened and they said she'd merely had a bad dream, but as the work went on to flatten the mound, bizarre dangerous mishaps took place. Two experienced hired labourers with pick-axes were simultaneously struck down with crippling backache, and became so incapacitated by their agonizing conditions, they were taken straight to hospital, but despite various X Rays and in-depth examinations of the mens' backs, the cause of their suffering remained unknown, and the backaches suddenly ceased in both subjects after a fortnight had elapsed.

David asked his wife and sister-in-law Jane to help him clear the mound, but all three of them came down with a strange skin infection which was diagnosed as Impetigo – a contagious condition usually associated with children, and yet Lisa had not been affected by the unsightly infection. Then David, wife and Jane and her sister Jennifer were all crippled at bedtime with strange cramps in their legs. Then David's oldest brother, Peter, went to the doctor with his swollen hand again, and this time the physician saw what he thought was a splinter under the skin of Peter's thumb. The GP extracted the object and was astounded to see that it was a tiny greenish piece of wood with one end shaped like an arrow. As soon as this bizarre object was removed, the swelling in Peter's hand died down. These arrows of unknown origin are known in the world of the occult and country folklore as "Elf-shot" – sinister arrow-headed projectiles, thought to be fired at humans and animals by elves and their kind, usually to inflict all sorts of conditions – some of them lethal – in their targets. The word "stroke" which we use for a sudden paralytic seizure comes directly from the term faery stroke – which was supposed to be caused by a bolt or Elf-shot fired by the "Little People" to cause paralysis and sometimes death in humans and animals.

Needless to say, David Jackson decided to leave the mound well alone, and after some very strange goings-on at the cottage which lasted for two years, he gave up his dream of a life in the country and moved back to Liverpool with his wife and daughter. I believe an old woman – regarded by the locals as rather "New Agey" - who acknowledges the faeries of Ormskirk - now lives in the said cottage and has not come to any paranormal harm whatsoever.

We now continue our quest for haunted people. Let us move from the sphere of pastoral faeries and malevolent sprites and head back to the city – to a flat on Lark Lane, just a stone's throw from Sefton Park, in the spring of 1979. Bill and Mandy Carver were both aged 25, and after living at home for years, they had now found the combined financial resources to rent a flat virtually anywhere they liked. Mandy worked for a travel agency in the city centre and Bill had a fairly stable job in retail, working for the outfitters Burtons to be exact. Not so long ago they had both been in bad relationships, but after meeting one another two years ago, they realised they were made for one another. Upon this mild spring night at around 11.40pm, the couple kissed and said goodnight to one another before falling sound asleep in their king-sized bed. But around one in the morning, something had awakened Mandy. She lay there in the darkness for a moment – and then she heard the sound that had recalled her from the pleasant world of dreams – a sobbing lady.

The crying seemed to be coming from the street, so Mandy slipped out the bed and carefully tiptoed to the window. She placed her face close to the net curtains and saw nothing but an empty street and a few parked cars below.

Bill woke up, and sensing the empty space and lack of body heat beside him, he opened his tired eyes and looked at the silhouette at the window. 'What are you doing?' he asked.

Mandy rushed back to the bed, got in and told him about the crying female she had heard a minute or so ago.

'It'll be someone passing by,' Bill suggested in a far away dreamy voice. 'Sound really travels at night,' he added, then started to snore.

Mandy felt like turning away from Bill to go to sleep – towards the window, where the moon was now partly visible among the clouds. She closed her eyes in this chosen comfortable position and drifted off.

She had not been asleep two minutes when she heard the crying woman again.

Mandy jumped, startled, and sat up in bed, because this time it seemed as if the crier was in the bedroom – but there was no one there – just strands of moonlight on the carpeted floor, and an old wardrobe at the end of the room.

'Bill,' Mandy gently shook her partner awake and told him about the crying sounds, and how the noise seemed to originate in the bedroom.

'Oh go to sleep for goodness sake, Mandy,' he growled, 'you've been dreaming. I never heard anything.'

'I wasn't dreaming it, I distinctly heard it,' Mandy assured him, but was greeted by a deep prolonged snore. She settled down and tried to sleep, but for the next fifteen minutes (and she timed this by her bedside clock), Mandy heard the invisible woman crying her eyes out. As the baffling sobs petered out, Mandy got out the bed and turned on the main light in the room. Bill was furious, and said she was hearing things and told her to switch the light off. This she did, and she found it hard to get back to sleep because she wondered if the room was haunted. Somehow, Mandy managed to fall asleep, and in the morning over breakfast, Bill asked her what she had heard and apologised for shouting at her, but he had been very tired and had been scared of oversleeping in case he lost his job. Mandy told him she had heard a woman crying somewhere close between one and two in the morning. Once again, Bill offered a mundane explanation to the sounds: 'It's probably been some girl going home from a club after having a row with her fellah, and she might have decided to go back to him, which is why you heard her again later on as she walked past again.'

'No, there was something – well, something *odd* about this,' Mandy recalled the eerie echoing sound to the crying.

'You mean like a ghost?' Bill extrapolated with a sneer.

'Maybe, yes,' Mandy admitted her suspicions. 'The house this flat's in is pretty old – Victorian I'd say.'

'Ah, I don't believe in all that mumbo jumbo,' Bill sipped his cup of tea and glanced at his watch. 'Come on, we better get a move on in *this* world, it's nearly half-eight.'

Bill dropped Mandy off on Bold Street and drove on to Burtons, and that morning, during elevenses, Mandy managed to have a quick chat about the 'crying ghost' with Maureen, an older work colleague at the travel agency. She thought she'd be as sceptical as Bill, but Maureen was quite open-minded. 'We've got one in our place,' she said, all matter of fact.

'What, you mean – a ghost?' Mandy whispered, rather shocked.

Maureen nodded and stirred her coffee. 'We live in an old house on Aigburth Road, not that far from you. We hadn't been in the place a week when I saw this thing one night. He'd gone to the pub at eight o'clock sharp, and I was sitting reading in front of this open fire with the dog sprawled out at my feet. I was made up with this fire because all I'd known was a gas fire. Anyway, the dog, Kelly – she's a Welsh Springer Spaniel, suddenly got up off the carpet and looked at the corner of the room and started to growl, and her ears went up, and her fur went up as well. I couldn't see what she was looking at, and I said to her, "Ah, what's up, Kel," and then I saw this – face. A face in the wallpaper pattern. We hadn't got round to decorating yet and still had this horrible old-fashioned dark paper on the walls, and the face was sort of hidden in the pattern, so she had been staring at me and I hadn't even seen her at first, but when I did, I ran out the room. I walked the streets in shock, and realised Kelly was still with me. I went to the pub, and told my fellah what I'd seen and he seemed really embarrassed by me saying all this in front of his mates. He acted all macho at first and said "Oh, Go home, it was probably your mum," but he eventually realised I was deadly serious and he came home with me, and we both saw her – like a sort of silhouette – looking out the living room window. And he went: "Who's that?" and I told him; I said, "That's the ghost, I haven't got any mates around," and you should have seen him – he was terrified, and kept delaying going into the house.'

'And whose ghost is it?' Mandy wanted to know.

Maureen shrugged. 'We see her now and then out the corner of our eyes, but she stays low key now. The dog looks up at the corner where she saw her the first time, but the wallpaper's gone now – we redecorated the place. So, yeah, I do believe you might have heard a ghost, Mand, but there's nothing to be scared of.'

Maureen's ghost story only served to make Mandy afraid of the phantom crier, and that night, she hugged Bill in bed, dreading the sounds of the spooky sobs, but thankfully she heard nothing. However, on the following evening, this time at 10.10pm, Mandy was sitting on a sofa with Bill, watching a film, when she heard the melancholic woman again. She asked Bill if he could hear it – and he said he couldn't. Mandy persuaded her partner to turn the volume down on the telly, but still he could hear nothing. This really scared Mandy, for now she thought she was suffering from some mental illness, as she was literally hearing things. The crying sounds plagued Mandy for weeks, and in the end, Bill said he'd had enough. Mandy thought he was going to leave her, but instead, Bill said he had been looking at a house in St Helens that was cheaper to rent than the flat they were in. The couple moved to the semi-detached house, but two days after they have moved into their new home, Mandy trembled when she heard the same sobbing noises she had heard at the Lark Lane flat. On this occasion the time was 11.50 pm. Mandy started to cry and Bill made things worse by telling her she should go to see her doctor. Mandy panicked, and believed she was going slowly mad. She ended up sleeping with headphones on that were plugged into a radio, but still she would hear the accursed weeper. Then one Sunday afternoon, Bill decided to take Mandy to Chester for a day out, and at this stage, he was so afraid of seeing his partner committed to a psychiatric unit. He held her hand on the train down to Chester, and during the journey,

Mandy clearly heard the crying woman again, and she turned to Bill and smiled faintly, trying to ignore the sound, but he said to her: 'It's okay, I can hear that as well.'

The two of them turned to see who was crying behind them, and Mandy saw to her astonishment, that the woman who was crying loudly – and attracting the attention of many other passengers on the train – was her old friend from her schooldays - Joan Maudle. Mandy and Joan had been best friends from way back - from their days in the infants in fact, but had sadly lost touch after leaving school. Mandy went to see why Joan was crying, and when her old friend saw the familiar face through the tears, she embraced Mandy and gave her a real bear hug. It turned out that for the past few months, Joan's boyfriend had been emotionally and sexually abusing her. I can't put into print just what he did to Joan, but he was so depraved he ended up almost making Joan suicidal. It soon became apparent what had happened, for when Mandy told Joan about all those nights she had been haunted by the sounds of a woman crying, Joan told her she had been hearing her old friend crying for help as she sat alone in her living room after the abusive episodes. It had to be some sort of telepathy – a crying out for help which was somehow picked up by Mandy. This seemed to be the case, because after the chance meeting with Joan on the train to Chester, Mandy never heard the ghostly sobs again.

THE KARMA GANG MYSTERY

This strange story came my way in response to a timeslip incident I reported on the radio a few years ago. A retired policeman named Roger Owen telephoned the receptionist at BBC Radio Merseyside and asked to talk to me. Roger's contact details were taken down and I duly telephoned him. He didn't like talking on the phone about this matter, he said, and so we met up at a café on Bold Street, where Roger told me of a number of weird incidents that had taken place in Litherland in May 1964. This is the gist of what he told me.

Chelsea Road, Litherland, 1964. The jigger that cut through that road into Kilburn Street is alleygated now, but it was in that handy shortcut of an entry where Owen, a green rookie police constable and a hard-boiled sergeant came upon the semi-conscious body of a yob named Dean on a Whit Saturday night that year. Dean gradually regained his senses, and tried to get to his feet, for he wanted to go home. He wouldn't say who'd given him a hiding, and Sergeant Breeney wanted to know 'the gen', and took great delight in questioning the notorious stocky blood-soaked delinquent about his attacker. 'Tell me who you had a run-in with, lad,' Breeney asked softly, 'you don't have to name names. Was it that gang from Bootle? Or was it that shower from Moore Street?'

'It was girls, mister!' a little snotty-nosed boy with a basin hair-cut said, somewhere behind PC Owen, startling the young constable. Dean told the little ragamuffin to 'button it' but the sergeant gave the lad a boiled sweet and said, 'Go 'ed lad, tell us what happened.'

The kid said three 'big girls' in funny clothes battered Dean, and that "this girl with like all coloured hair, like paint in her hair or sumfin' gave him a haymaker and then kept hittin' him with a big long pole…"

Dean, obviously humiliated by the bizarre revelation butted in, 'It wasn't a pole, it was a golf club – a putter or driver or something.'

The policemen grinned widely at each other. 'A bleedin' bunch of judies with golf clubs jumped you?' Breeney recoiled in amused disbelief. And then Owen followed a trail of blood spots round the corner of the alleyway and saw something glowing on the wall. In some sort of luminous spray paint, the glowing graffiti read: K@rm@ G@ng. In 1964, the "@" (at sign, also called *arobase*) was a symbol commonly found mostly in the staid ledgers of accountants and businessmen to stand for "at the rate of". The symbol was not as widely known as it is now because the "@" forms part of every email address on the planet, and this use of the at sign came about around 1971 when US programmer Ray Tomlinson first used the symbol in an email address. Since then of course, the symbol is also used at the start of any Twitter user name. The use of the symbol in the intriguing message on the back alley wall seems a bit of an anachronism to say the least, and is more in keeping with contemporary graffiti street-art.

The little boy looked at the luminous letters on the wall and said "a girl with a white face and a blue mouth did that, and chased me and spat at me but I ran away."

'A girl with a *blue* mouth?' PC Owen jotted down the boys words and grinned. 'You're not having me on are you, son?'

'No, mister, and she had a big club as well,' the boy told the young constable as he struggled to put into words what had happened.

'He means a baseball bat!' Dean shouted to PC Owen.

'Why would these girls jump you?' Sergeant Breeney asked Dean. 'Had you been trying have a bit of how's your father with them, eh?'

'I'd never seen them before in me life,' Dean touched a bloody ear and felt his ribs, and the police sergeant had him taken to hospital. Owen jotted down the strange graffiti in his notebook. Later that evening, back at the station, Owen asked Sergeant Breeney who he thought the girls were.

'Probably some kids who have watched too much telly larking about,' he reckoned over a cup of tea. 'The telly puts all these daft ideas into their heads, it does.'

'I remember all this ten years ago with the Davy Crockett craze,' said an old overweight and round-faced policeman on desk duty, 'all the kids were running round in coonskin caps, toting plastic Kentucky rifles. Something's kicked these girls off – the Beatles probably.'

More reports of the weird female trio started to come in, and Breeney and Owen investigated an attack on Alpha Road, just 220 yards from the first assault, next to a corner pub (possibly the Pacific Hotel). Two 17-year-old Mods , Paul and Bernie, had been attacked by the outlandish-looking girls and left with fractured arms and legs. Paul had suffered a broken nose - inflicted by 'a bird, about six foot, green lips and a polka dot scarf. She wore black leather gloves with the fingers cut out, and I didn't want to wallop her back, being a judy like,' Paul explained. His brother's Lambretta had been wrecked by the three girls, and there was a reference to the golf club weapon again and multi-coloured hair. This time PC Owen received a tip off from a middle-aged woman who swore the girl with the rainbow hairdo lived at a local address on Hartwell Street. She was aged fifteen. Owen later confronted the girl and discovered she had a cast-iron alibi: she'd been babysitting in Bootle on the night of the attack on the Mods. The "Karma Gang" was at large for a week or so then was seen no more, and there's probably a rational explanation if you dig deep enough; it could have all been one huge prank by three girls who had dressed up in fancy dress, but somehow I personally have the feeling that a timeslip might be the key to this odd case. I'm probably way off the mark, but is it possible that some three-girl street gang from the future were able to ambush archaic yobbos through some time portal? If this was the case, it would certainly explain the use of the "at sign" in the graffiti and the way the sprayed message glowed in the dark. If this *is* the case, then perhaps that suspect – the babysitter on Hartwell street – was the great-grandmother of the futuristic gang-leader!

STRANGE WARNINGS

Sometimes, death gives a warning of his approach. I honestly don't know who or what issues the eerie premonitions, but heed the following accounts because – Heaven forbid – such a strange warning may come *your* way at some point in your life…

One mild May afternoon in 1995, 47-year-old Eric Lewis of Childwall went to pick his son up from school, and upon reaching the busy junction where the roads of Wellington, Picton, Rathbone and the Wavertree High Street meet, he found the lights on red. Eric switched on his car radio, then glanced up, and saw something that will haunt him to his dying day. A tall hooded figure (well over six feet) in some sort of monk's robe stood there on the road ahead, and it was not only jet black, it looked as if it had a faint aura of darkness around it. A chorus of car horns sounded behind Eric because the lights had changed to green, but he was too scared to drive forward. Eric couldn't see the face of the entity, just its back, and he froze in terror. All of a sudden, a bus came hurtling from the right – from Rathbone Road – and it seemed to hit the hooded figure. The bus mounted the kerb, tore across the pavement, and the lantern hanging over the entrance of the nearby pub was taken clean off by the vehicle. When the bus had passed by, there was no sign of the reaper-like figure. Had Eric paid attention to the impatient motorists behind him, he would have driven forward and been instantly killed by the bus that had gone through the lights for some unknown reason. All the way to the school, Eric thought about the sinister hooded man, and decided it had been a warning, perhaps from death itself. He still doesn't know why he was spared, and to this day he always avoids the junction where he saw the creepy apparition.

We could say these warnings are the work of angels, but that doesn't always apply, for some bad people have had the Devil's own luck. Hitler's neck was saved on too many occasions by such strange premonitions. The Fuhrer had an uncanny feeling that he'd die if he did not get out of a beer cellar in Munich shortly after the outbreak of WWII. Not long after he left the political meeting in the cellar a bomb left to kill him went off, and eight of the dictator's comrades died. Dozens more at the subterranean gathering received life-changing injuries in the explosion. This is just one of a plethora of life-saving premonitions Hitler had. Surely, if an angel had intervened to save the Austrian's life on those occasions, it had to be one of the Fallen Ones belonging to Lucifer.

Here in Liverpool, on a foggy evening in October 1952, a hardened criminal from Knotty Ash named George went into the Globe pub on Cases Street (near to the eastern entrance of Clayton Square). In a few days George was going to London to 'do a bit of business' with a few acquaintances, but something uncanny happened which changed his travel plans that evening. A strange old tramp in old-fashioned clothes came into the pub off the foggy streets of Liverpool and kept gazing at George, who thought his eyes were scary. The man asked for – and was given - a glass of water, and then he went to a corner and chalked the word "EUSTON" – with the T in the word shaped like a cross – on the darts scoreboard. He walked out the Globe and George felt there was something very unearthly about the chap, and so out of curiosity he tried to follow him, but the man literally vanished on setting foot outside the pub. George looked into the cold swirling fog, and he suddenly had a very bad feeling about the "message" the man had chalked on the scoreboard and so he cancelled the trip to London. The train he would have been coming home from left Euston on the morning of 8 October and became involved in a horrific crash involving two other trains at Harrow and Wealdstone. 112 people died in the crash - including the driver of one of the doomed trains – a man named Albert Perkins, who George actually knew, because he lived by him up in Knotty Ash. Around 340 were seriously injured in addition to the 112 who perished in one of the worst train crashes in British history. George never saw that old tramp again, and wondered whether the man had simply been mentally unbalanced – or had he warned George about the forthcoming carnage on the rail tracks that evening by chalking the name of the station – Euston – where George would have boarded the train to a horrific death? Most of the passengers who had been in the carriage where George would have sat were crushed to pulp, and the others, including several young women, were trapped under the wreckage and literally roasted in the ensuing blaze in front of the traumatised locals who had been unable to help them. The screams of these victims were said to have been heard several miles away. George shuddered when he read these morbid details about the crash in the newspapers, and he wondered why innocent people had suffered such an agonising and terrifying death when a worthless criminal like himself had been spared, apparently by some strange warning.

A strange – and very gruesome – number of warnings have taken place at a certain house in the Bootle area over the years. The first of these terrifying incidents took place in 1975 when a single mother and her 9-month-old baby moved into one of the four flats in the haunted house. Kimberley, the 23-year-old mum, had just got her little daughter Tracy asleep one evening around 9pm when she heard someone crying and moaning outside in the communal landing (which was on the first floor). Kimberley opened the door a few inches and peeped out, and she beheld a sight that was the stuff of nightmares. A woman with a typical 1940s hairstyle stood there, clutching the banister rail with her left hand, and she had a gaping raw red hole where her left eye should have been, but this was nothing compared to the sickening state of the rest of her body and what was hanging out of it. The woman had shards of glass sticking out of her neck and breasts, and her night-gown was blood-soaked and ripped and tattered so that her body was exposed from the abdomen downwards. That abdomen had a huge ripped hole in it which extended from just under the breasts down to the woman's vagina, and out of this nightmarish hole, the bodies of two blood-soaked babies (obviously twins) were dangling by an umbilical cord. The upper baby was hanging out of the stomach - along with dangling intestines – with its arms reaching out in the direction in front of the woman, and the other twin was hanging down by the woman's knees with the cord looped around its neck. There were no signs of life in either baby. The woman suddenly opened her mouth and vomited a great quantity of blood and watery liquid, and a few of the drops of this violently ejected fluid hit Kimberley's face. Kimberley screamed and slammed the door shut. Her baby was startled from its short-lived slumbers by the screech, and began to cry. Kimberley pushed an armchair at the door to bar the entrance of the mutilated woman and her unborn babies, and she grabbed little Tracy from her cot and backed away as she heard the moaning sound outside. Fortunately the eerie lamenting and groans ceased, but Kimberley would not leave that room until the next morning, and when she did, she saw no evidence – not a single spot of blood – anywhere on the landing or the stairs. The poor woman had obviously been a ghost. The young mother had suspected as much from the outdated hairstyle of the mangled and ripped open woman – that she was a phantom – but whose phantom? She met old Mrs Murphy, who lived in the flat below her, and told her what she had seen, and Mrs Murphy, seeing how distressed Kimberley was by her experience, brought her and her baby into her own flat and made the girl an extra sweet cup of tea (which is supposed to be a way of treating shock). Mrs Murphy eventually told Kimberley that she had seen the ghost of a certain woman who had been killed in the Blitz during the Second World War. A bomb had hit the house and left the woman – who had been expecting twins – horrifically, and fatally wounded. The woman had lost her eye and the blast had ripped her open, exposing the poor unborn babes. A surgeon later stated he was amazed the woman had survived her appalling injuries for the few minutes she had. The woman had walked down the stairs and had dropped dead from shock and blood loss upon reaching the hallway, and every now and then, several tenants had heard – and some had seen – the poor bomb victim moaning and crying, and eventually collapsing with a thump in the hallway. Mrs Murphy said that every time the ghost appeared, it seemed to be an omen: 'A warning to the person who sees her,' she explained, and told how, upon the last occasion when she was seen, the man who saw her was left with a broken spine after he crashed his car and was thrown through the windshield of his car. Mrs Murphy might have been right about the ghost serving as a warning, because when Kimberley eventually went back to her flat later that day, she noticed that the central frame in her bay window had become loose with some sort of mould, and had she leaned on it, she would have gone through it and probably fallen to her death. Kimberley told the landlord about the dangerous window and he said he'd get someone to 'fix it in a week or so' but Kimberley decided to leave her flat, and as her brother was helping her to pack her stuff, the window fell out and crashed onto the street below, narrowly missing a child. I mentioned this incident on a radio programme about ghosts and several people called and correctly identified the address of the haunted house, and one caller, a woman named Marie, said she had seen the stomach-churning sight of the badly maimed and blood-soaked woman staggering down the stairs one evening around 1979. At the time, Marie had just moved into the ground floor flat in the Bootle house, and was not aware of the place being haunted. She could see something dangling from the woman in the poorly lit hallway, but did not know it was the woman's unborn babies. Marie *did* sense that the figure descending the stairs was not a flesh and blood person, and she turned and ran out of the house and refused to go back, even to pick up her stuff, and her brothers had to go and get her belongings. On the day Marie left the house, her boyfriend, who was working on a building site in Germany, was decapitated in an horrific accident when a cable on a piece of machinery snapped. Another caller named Robert did not see the ghost but heard it on two occasions, and on the first occasion, which was just before Christmas in 1990, he almost died after contracting meningitis, and when he heard the weird moaning and sobbing sounds a few years later, he went to visit his mother to tell her of the ghostly sounds, and was later involved in an accident in a factory which left him without the tip of his little finger. He believed that the ghostly moans had been some omen. As far as I know, the ghost of that unfortunate wartime victim has not been seen or heard from since. At the time of writing, the haunted house is occupied and is now subdivided into two flats.

Here's another case of a strange warning.

One frosty morning in Edwardian times, a sweet-toothed raven-haired Welshman named John Vaughan called into Mrs Norris's cake shop on Renshaw Street. Vaughan was a 25-year-old reporter with the *Liverpool*

Echo, and lived off nearby Berry Street. Like clockwork each morning Mr Vaughan left for work at 8.15am, and usually called into the confectioners on Renshaw Street to grab a box of cakes for his elevenses, and upon this morning, the Welshman noticed 60-year-old Mrs Norris was not her usual chirpy self – she seemed rather glum, and so he asked her what the matter was. 'Something is bothering me, Mr Vaughan, and I'm probably being very silly, but superstition has always been my weakness.'

'Superstition?' Vaughan asked as Mrs Norris tied the box of cakes with string. The confectioner tried to smile, and then told him straight. 'I believe I was visited by an angel yesterday afternoon,' she said, and blushed slightly.

'An *angel?*' Vaughan asked with a trace of a smile on his lips.

'Yes, an angel, and no, he didn't have a pair of wings before you ask,' said Mrs Norris all defensively. She continued: 'He told me someone had sent him to warn me, and his eyes, oh, I have never seen eyes like them.'

'Sent to warn you about what, Mrs Norris?' the hard-boiled journalist enquired, finding the woman's claim far-fetched yet intriguing.

'I don't know,' Mrs Norris told him, 'but he said I must not come into this shop on Monday morning or I'll lose my life – and then he – well, he just went. He faded away.'

'I don't understand what you mean – faded away?' the reporter asked, for he was fascinated by this story, but thought his editor would probably dismiss it.

Mrs Norris was quite clear on how the mysterious visitor had departed. 'He faded away, Mr Vaughan, vanished before my eyes, as he stood right where you are now.'

'Did he look into your eyes and say anything as he vanished?' Vaughan asked, handing Mrs Norris a shilling.

She shook her head, and the reporter said: 'Stage magicians have been known to hypnotise people –'

'Good morning Mr Vaughan,' the confectioner interposed huffishly, and she turned and went into the back of the shop.

On the morning of Monday 22 January 1906, at 8.15, John Vaughan called at the cake shop on Renshaw Street, but found it locked. He realised Mrs Norris had heeded her 'angel' and he smiled and walked to the offices of his newspaper. Vaughan had only covered fifty yards when he heard a mighty crash behind him followed by terrible screams. He turned to see a green tramcar which had left the rails on the bend from Leece Street into Renshaw Street, and it had overturned and smashed into the cake shop. Vaughan ran to the scene of the crash and saw around seventy passengers crawling out of smashed windows. The tram was leaning at 45 degrees against the cake shop, and it was ready to slide down onto two old men who had been thrown onto the pavement in the impact. Vaughan dragged the men clear just in time as the tram smashed down onto the pavement. It was a miracle no passengers were killed, and stranger still many of those passengers said they'd had strange dreams warning them not to get on the tram the night before. To her dying day, Mrs Norris believed the tall stranger with the peculiar eyes who warned her to stay away from her cake shop that January was some sort of angel.

Always obey your premonitions.

Not all supernatural warnings are visual – some are olfactory – they subtly signal the approach of death and danger with certain scents and aromas, and this phenomenon is known in the world of the occult as the "Smell of Death". Folklore says that the Angel of Death sometimes presents a unique scent similar to that of the May blossom, and there are many references to this dating back hundreds of years. It is said that the Great Plague of London had the smell of a mellow apple, and when this scent invaded a street, people would lock their doors and put up the shutters, for Death was doing his rounds. I myself have smelt what could be the scent of death on several occasions in places where people have soon afterwards died, and have always found the fatal fragrance reminiscent of hawthorn (which ironically is the traditional repellent for vampires). Many times I have visited people in their hospital beds and have become alarmed when I have detected that smell, because, without a single exception, that mysterious paranormal perfume has been detected shortly before the death of the bedbound patient – and many others have witnessed this. A nurse I interviewed many years ago at one of our well-known hospitals first noticed the Smell of Death when she first began to attend patients at a certain ward in the hospital. The nurse – Judy – told me how a young man who had shattered the bones of his legs after crashing his motorcycle had been operated on, and later left in a peaceful corner of the ward. She really got on with the patient and saw him make a speedy recovery, but a few days before he was due to be discharged from the hospital, Judy thought she could smell something sweet around his bed, and at first she thought it was some aftershave. She then recalled how she had smelt that same sweet aroma when she had nursed her grandmother in her sickbed at her home in Tuebrook. Judy's mother had smelt the sickly sweet aroma too and had told her that it was a bad omen. Within the hour of detecting that scent, Judy's Gran suddenly passed away. Now Judy could smell it around this young man who seemed to be making a steady recovery. His progress chart said his bones were mending and that he had responded very well to treatment – but then the patient suddenly died from a blood clot. The body was taken away and the smell remained for a few hours, then faded away. This was to be merely the first instance of many – of patients who seemed to be doing fine – only for some cruel unforeseen danger to arise after that devious pleasant scent became noticeable. Seasoned matrons and hard-boiled doctors and one surgeon have all mentioned this phenomenon to me, but I am at a loss to explain it, unless, as the superstitious people of long ago asserted – the Angel of Death really does have a sweet scent.

LIVERPOOL LEY LINES

Throughout June to November 2009 I received quite a few telephone calls, letters and emails when I was presenting a regular slot about the paranormal on BBC Radio Merseyside, and the subject of the calls and correspondence was a mysterious laser-like beam of greenish light seen over Gateacre Park Drive, Escor Road, Well Lane, and also over a section of the M62 Motorway. The beam was radiating in a horizontal position about a hundred feet or more from the ground. A few of these reports were mentioned in the radio station's news bulletins, and the Northern Lights were blamed, as well as "chain lightning", UFOs and even someone messing about with a laser pointer. I didn't notice the geographical pattern of the ghostly beam at first, but in July, I got more reports, from a milkman, postman, a bakery worker on his way to work at 5am, and a policeman who was on duty at 4am. Then came other reports of lights as far afield as Bidston Hill, Birkenhead, Kirkby, Speke, Walton, Childwall and Woolton. I was very intrigued by more and more reports of a strange flickering searchlight-type of beam that had been seen over the East Lancs, the M57, and Croxteth Hall Country Park. A school caretaker had seen the beam appearing and vanishing about 200 feet over West Derby Golf Club and the same night, weird lights were seen flashing over Knowsley Community College. Around this time, I and other researchers into paranormal phenomena were also receiving reports of "The Hum" – an irritating very low frequency sound that has been heard in these parts (and right across the country for that matter) for decades. A woman in Gateacre Park Drive had told me how she and her husband had been suffering from chronic insomnia because of the dreaded Hum, which even seemed to be affecting the behaviour of her elderly cat – normally a very calm and placid feline – who would run around in a panic when the low frequency invaded his home. Just a few doors away from this couple, a family had reported hearing ghostly faint echoing voices speaking in an unknown language all hours at night. Only then did all of the strange goings-on start to make some sense. I noted the reports on an ordnance survey map and was very intrigued to see that all of the locations of paranormal activity prescribed a line which stretched over ten miles from Camp Hill – an ancient Iron Age fort in Woolton – to St Chad's – a church built on a hallowed pre-Christian site that predates the Norman Conquest. In other words, I seem to have stumbled upon a ley line – a mysterious alignment between two ancient sites, said to have been created by the same mysterious peoples who constructed Stonehenge and erected the thousands of other enigmatic standing stones found across Britain and parts of Western Europe. I wondered if other locations could reveal other possible ley lines, and consulted my files. I marked all of the various incidents of a supernatural nature I'd investigated on a huge detailed map and discovered that another ley line seemed to run from All Saints – probably the oldest surviving church in Liverpool (and like St Chads, built by the church fathers on a site revered by "pagans") – for just over six miles, to St Chads in Kirkby. More discoveries followed which shocked me. The ley line from All Saints goes north to St Chads, but also south to Speke Hall, in a perfect line, and from St Chads, the ley line stretches to another ancient site – the hilltop where, in the days of the Druids, people worshipped something archaeologists are still in the dark about. That revered hilltop is now the site of Walton Church (also known as the Church on the Hill in times past). For over a thousand years a church has stood on this sacred hilltop, and a Saxon cross used to crown it in days of yore. The ley line then runs straight as a laser for six miles to the pagan capital of North West England – Bidston Hill, the scene of a host of supernatural activity over the centuries and the site of ancient carvings of a cat-headed goddess and other arcane symbols. If we then trace the ley line back to Speke Hall (a Tudor mansion built on another historical site) we have a complete perfect isosceles triangle. All of the points on this possible ley line coincide with hauntings, mysterious humming sounds, timeslips, phantom voices, electrical interference (such as street lamps flickering on and off and mobile phones dropping out of their networks), and of course, the ley line seems to manifest itself as the "beam" that has been seen over Gateacre, Childwall, parts of Knowsley and other places in its path. It's as if some ancient beacon of energy is being occasionally activated and transmitted to and from the crest of Camp Hill, to All Saints, St Chads, Walton Church, Bidston Hill and Speke Hall (a place exceedingly well-known for its ghosts). One of my hobbies is electronics and on 3 May 2014 I and a fellow researcher went up Camp Hill with various paraphernalia, including a device I made myself from a few electronic components (a field-effect transistor, battery and a LED indicator) to detect electrical fields. In essence the device was a very sensitive electroscope. Ironically, minutes after my arrival on Camp Hill I was struck by a bolt of lightning in front of witnesses, and there wasn't a cloud in the sky, and no thunder followed, just a loud crack and a sizzling noise. The bolt went through my right hand and left me with a minor burn. Everyone present felt the air bristling with a static charge before this incident. I'll put the circuit diagram and notes for building the field detector on my site – www.slemen.com – soon, and you can try this experiment for yourself. I am not trying to delude you or myself into believing a ley line exists which runs around the North West; I am merely exploring possibilities, but I would still caution you to remain open-minded, unlike many nowadays who blindly believe in certain mediums etc. In 2010, a person got in touch with me to tell how, one evening in August of that year, he was driving along the M62 when he saw flashes of light which seemed to cross from left to right. Then his car – which was only a year old – stalled for no apparent reason. I mentioned this on a programme on BBC Radio Merseyside and discovered other vehicles has recently stalled on that same stretch of the motorway – and our hypothetical ley line runs straight through this "black spot" on the M62. Incidentally, that same year in November, birdwatchers saw a V formation of geese (possibly migrating) as they passed over Camp Hill in Woolton, when suddenly the birds seemed to hit an invisible barrier in the sky, and some fell, apparently stunned, but recovered in time before they hit the ground. It was as if the geese had flown into an unseen force field, one of the ornithologists told me. Many who witnessed this strange incident mentioned a peculiar smell of ozone that was present in the atmosphere at the time, as if there had just been a thunderstorm.

At a house on Inchcape Road in 2013, there was a spate of poltergeist activity which terrified a family. A radio was smashed against a wall, and a TV was wrenched from its wall bracket. That same week, a poltergeist was disrupting the home of an elderly couple on Walsingham Road by shaking a fridge till it toppled over and blowing the lighting circuit. Just a fortnight before this I had investigated a humming sound which had made a house vibrate to its foundations on Barnham Drive, Childwall. All of these 'hauntings' lie exactly on the apparent ley line which runs from All Saints. The same projected ley line, incidentally, runs straight through the house on Childwall Valley Road where the infamous murder of schoolgirl Lesley Hobbs took place in the 1960s.

In 2013 I received several emails from people in Kirkby who had seen a shaft of light, as straight as a laser, but some five to six feet in thickness, traced through a mist over the Westvale area. Two men in their twenties returning from a nightclub saw this beam from the corner of James Holt Avenue and Richard Hesketh Drive, and they estimated the beams stretched as far as the local municipal golf course. The beam was bright and seemed to sparkle, but was only seen for about 20 seconds. These beams in the sky have been seen all over the world for centuries and are often explained away as chain lightning, auroras, and even shooting stars, but the ones seen in the skies of Knowsley, parts of Liverpool, and also Wirral, seem to manifest in a very intriguing pattern which I have studied for some time. This pattern is, as I mentioned earlier in this chapter, triangular in nature, and the beams link many ancient sites in a manner which leads me to believe that a hithero undiscovered ley line could be behind the eerie shafts of light.

If a ley line is indeed running through this region, what energy is being transmitted along it and who is responsible for creating it? The honest answer to both of these questions is simply, I do not know. There are people who believe in a mysterious form of energy known as "Telluric power" which is generated by the Earth itself, and perhaps the wizards of old, such as the legendary Merlin, knew how to tap into this power and used it to heal, harm and even conjure up ghosts. I would imagine that the peoples who created the ley lines were the same ones responsible for building Stonehenge and the extensive network of baffling megalithic standing stones which cover the British Isles, perhaps as the Ancients' answer to a type of National Grid power lattice. I really do think archaeologists have underestimated the technology of ancient humans. If you are interested in this subject, obtain a detailed map of our neck of the woods, and note down the many ancient wells, churches and sandstone relics such as the Calderstones - six stones which once covered the tomb of a Neolithic chief. The tomb was a mound situated at the junction of Druids

Cross Lane and Menlove Avenue, and the Calderstones are now on display in a greenhouse in Calderstones Park (and amongst the marks carved on the ancient stones, some are relatively very recent, and the engraved initials "JL" are clearly visible on one stone – and this might be of particular interest to Beatles fans, as John Lennon lived very close to these stones). Some years ago I accompanied a dowser across Liverpool who claimed a ley line of immense power ran from Bidston Hill, across the Mersey, straight through the Liver Buildings, through Mathew Street and onto the site of a suspected plague pit on Copperas Hill (beneath the postal sorting office there). A neutral witness accompanied the dowser and me on a trip to Bromborough, where, the dowser claimed, 'lines of magnetic force' were radiating from the "Anglo-Viking Preaching Cross" in the churchyard of St Barnabas. This renovated cross dates back to about 900 AD. The neutral witness was quite sceptical of the dowser's claim about the magnetism, and produced a compass to see the effect of these supposed lines of force, and sure enough, the compass started to spin, but how a sandstone cross was possible to generate a magnetic field was not explained. Should any of you find strange alignments other ley-hunters have missed, please tell me about them (via tom@slemen.com).

Incidentally, here's another mystery which seems to tie in with ley lines and beams of unknown energy lighting up the skies of Merseyside and Knowsley. Over the years I have had quite a few reports - particularly from Knowsley and North Liverpool - of a strange unexplained phenomenon known as a "false dawn" whereby the skies suddenly lighten as if the sun is about to come up, only to darken again. These reports were mentioned briefly in local newspaper articles the size of postage stamps, and the meteorological experts and astronomers were quick to blame the Northern Lights at first – even though most reports put the night-time glows in the southern skies, and then the blame was put on the zodiacal light – a faint luminance caused by rays from the un-risen sun reflecting off dust in the solar system. Another lame explanation hinted that the bogus daybreaks were the work of the *gegenschein* – a German astronomical term meaning "counter-glow" – again, caused by light from our sun bouncing off interplanetary and meteoric dust out in space. I am only an amateur astronomer, but even I know that both the zodiacal light and gegenschein are exceedingly faint, and we would have to turn off the streetlamps of our light-polluted cities to notice these ghostly glows in the sky. The false dawns seen by people across Kirkby, Prescot, Halewood, Croxteth, Whiston Huyton, and parts of Liverpool between January 1970 and October 2004 were bright as the pre-dawn sky, and one housewife in Huyton told me how she and a relative sat in their garden at one o'clock one warm morning in May 1977 and were able to read newsprint by the strange light in the southern sky. By 2.15 am the sky had gone pitch-black gain. I have received many emails and letters about this phenomenon over the years, including a report from a man named Gary, who worked in a Prescot filling station from the 1990s to 2010. Gary clearly recalls how, one morning at 1.20 am in October 2004, just before Halloween, he was talking to a group of taxi drivers who were filling their fuel tanks when the skies became almost as bright as daytime. This unearthly effect lasted until just before 2 am when the night returned quite abruptly. One of the cabbies phoned his brother Des in Liverpool to tell him about the sudden daylight and Des told him how birds were singing in Sefton Park as if morning had arrived. A housewife named Mary in Westvale, Kirkby was also a witness to the bizarre premature 'daybreak'. Mary had left her bed to get a drink of water and thought she had overslept, for she could clearly see the patio through the kitchen window, but upon casting a bleary eye at the clock on the wall, she was amazed to see that it was only around 1.30am.

JOHN GOODWILL OF HUYTON

Full moons appearing on February 14 – Valentine's Day – are rather rare, but there was one in the sky in 2014 as I wrote this. A local reader named Valerie recalls a full moon looming in the sky on the night of 14 February 1968, and this small detail sticks in her memory because of a terrifying string of incidents which took place on a night we would usually associate with romance. She was living in the Woolfall Heath area of Huyton at the time, and was 22 years of age. In December 1967 at a pub in Liverpool city centre, she met a rather debonair Jason King look-alike named Martin, who owned a yellow jaguar and lived on Roby Road in a rather posh-looking cottage. The two seemed compatible enough at first, but by February 1968 the cracks were beginning to show in the relationship, for Martin was what we would now term as a control freak. He didn't like Valerie wearing mini skirts, or any skirts for that matter with a hemline above her knee caps, and then there was Martin's insistence that Valerie should brush with a particular brand of smoker's tooth powder, because he had noticed the slight yellowish discolouration of her frontal teeth. Furthermore, Martin was always correcting Valerie; her grammar was constantly scrutinised, and her pronunciation of 'book', 'look' and 'cook' in particular. Valerie's mother didn't like the sound of this prospective son-in-law one bit, and nicknamed him Lord Muck. Valerie had a feeling Martin was going to propose at a secluded country pub near Ormskirk on Valentine's Night, and a friend of the girl had even seen Martin looking in the windows of a jewellers. Valerie's mum said she had never heard of anyone going down on bended knee less than six weeks after meeting, and she asked her daughter if she really wanted to spend the rest of her life with someone with a high opinion of himself who had a compulsion to exert control over her as well as constantly correcting her. Valerie said she was going to test Martin by deliberately wearing a short skirt on the night of their Valentine date, and, what's more, she'd make sure she smoked a ciggie in his beloved Jaguar car. Well, the night of the date arrived, and Martin picked up Valerie from her home in Woolfall Heath. 'I cannot believe you, Valerie,' he said with a sulking expression as he drove down Cartmel Road.

'You can't believe *what?*' Valerie asked, feigning puzzlement.

'I can't believe you are wearing a dress that's almost short enough to be classed as a belt!' Martin replied, squeezing the steering wheel with his black leather driving gloves. 'And smoking in the car,' he added, winding the driver side window down. 'It's as if you're purposely doing this to irritate me.'

Valerie blew a smoke ring and grinned, and Martin

accelerated and turned onto Liverpool Road, heading south. Valerie queried his route: 'Where are you going?'

'Home, to get a can of air freshener. I despise the stench of tobacco in my car!' was the abrupt answer.

By the time they got to Church Road, the couple were having a full-blown slanging match, and Valerie got out of the Jaguar and slammed the door after swearing at Martin, who reacted by speeding off. Valerie looked around and saw she was near the gates of St Bartholomew's Church. A full moon hung in the sky and the cold February night air was laden with an eerie silence. Not a car passed by, and Valerie stood there, finishing a cigarette as she got her bearings. She would have to turn around, walk up Church Road, and keep walking. Then she'd go up Twig Lane and cross over Liverpool Road to reach her home on Cartmel Road – and she was in high heels. As Valerie was about to walk off, she saw a light shining to her right, coming from the direction of the church graveyard, and the young lady turned to see what it was. At first she thought someone was shining a torch at her, but then she noticed the illumination was coming from a globe of bluish-white light about the size of a football. It grew in brightness as it flitted towards Valerie, and suddenly, this sphere of light faded and in its place there now stood a very bizarre-looking figure: a man who looked like a cavalier from the days of the English Civil War. He had on a floppy wide-brimmed hat with a light-coloured feather in it, and his hair was black and curly and long - shoulder-length in fact. The weird stranger had a van dyke beard and a pair of black piercing eyes that gave an impression of insanity. Under a long satin brocaded knee-length coat he wore a slashed padded doublet jacket, white frilly lace collar and matching cuffs, and while his left hand rested on the hilt of a fancy and fearsome looking sword, his right hand was brandishing some sort of flintlock pistol, and the barrel was aimed at the night sky.

Valerie went weak as she realised she was looking at an actual ghost, and more out of nerves than curiosity, she said: 'Who are you?'

The uncanny-looking Cavalier shouted a word that sounded like "Skookum", and then he looked at Valerie's shoes as he put the pistol in his belt. His dark eyes swivelled upwards as he scanned her legs and dress, and then he looked at her face. 'The Devil grill ye in your own grease,' the ghost said, and Valerie found herself trying to run away up Church Road in her heels. She heard the cavalier shouting something to her, but she wouldn't look back, and she started to pray.

She then thought she heard the creepy apparition shout out something that sounded like "hot pudding for supper!"

Valerie almost sprained her ankle in the heels as she hurried along, and she was so afraid, she was unable to glance back to see if the ghost was still there. Then there was a loud beep, and Valerie jumped with fright. It was a repentant Martin in his jaguar, cruising slowly alongside her. He shouted to her and told her to get in the car but Valerie just continued walking. She looked back now that Martin was here, and saw that the cavalier was gone. 'Stop being a nitwit and get in!' Martin bawled, and when Valerie did get in the car, Martin said: 'Who was that man you were talking to by the church?'

Valerie was so glad Martin had seen him, but her boyfriend had seen the ghost from far off as he drove up the road, and by the time he had reached Valerie the shadowy figure had gone. When Valerie told Martin he had been a ghost, her boyfriend said there were 'no such things as ghosties' and that it had probably been someone going to some Valentine's Day fancy dress party. Valerie told Martin about the huge orb of light and Martin shook his head and said light played very strange tricks at night. Valerie was just so glad to be with someone and she and Martin went for a meal and a drink at a tavern near Ormskirk, and Martin proposed, as Valerie had expected. She turned him down, and said it was all too soon. At first Martin was heartbroken but soon realised he was being hasty. Valerie met a friend at the tavern and she invited Valerie and her boyfriend to a party in Huyton which went on till six in the morning. During that party, someone found a ouija board, and twelve tipsy people placed their fingers on the base of an upturned wine glass. Martin and Valerie did not participate in the ouija session, and neither Valerie nor Martin had breathed a word about the ghostly encounter outside St Bartholomew's. The sliding wineglass began to spell out a word: G-O-O-D-W-I-L-L. "Goodwill?" asked one of the sitters. A serious man in his early twenties asked out loud: "Is this your name?" and something thumped the table hard. The glass then skated about on the tabletop and picked out the letters: J-O-H-N.

"John Goodwill... Is that your name?" asked a girl who looked a little scared.

A child's scream pierced the tense air - it came from the throat of a little 5-year-old girl who had sneaked out of her bed upon hearing the racket downstairs at the house. The girl's mother picked the child up but the daughter kicked and shrieked, and claimed that a "scary man" was in the room. The mother - and a sympathetic Valerie - went upstairs with the frightened child, whose name was Michelle.

Michelle said the man had been looking over the shoulders of the people at the table as they shoved the glass about, and when Michelle described the ghost, Valerie went cold, because that child gave a description of a man in a big floppy hat with a feather in it, and when she had calmed down a bit, she even sketched the ghost, and that drawing looked just like a cavalier. Valerie left the party with Martin and for weeks had the unsettling impression that the cavalier was following her. Valerie and Martin married in the following year and moved to Chester, where Valerie felt as if she had finally shaken off the ghost. I have searched parish records and various historical archives and as of yet, have found no one named John Goodwill - but I'll keep looking.

BROUGHT TO BOOK

I try my best to classify the ghost stories and mysteries I investigate into specific groups, such as poltergeist hauntings, possessions, timeslips and so on, but still some stories resist all attempts at classification and explanation. Here's just one of these occult oddities from my files.

For legal reasons I have changed names and places in this strange story, but everything else is true – but unexplained. In April 1984 at a certain library on Merseyside, a 30-something librarian we shall call Declan Mayvoreen was dividing his thoughts between the vagaries of the Dewey Decimal book classification system and his girlfriend Andrea's request for a 1.3GS Nissan Cherry. He had promised Andrea he'd get her that car for her 30th birthday – but he had already frittered a sizeable amount of the £4,600 he'd loaned from the bank on his gambling. Andrea's birthday was in a fortnight. Declan asked his workmate Steve Morrice for a loan but was turned down flatly. Declan was rather disappointed by Steve's refusal to lend him money because he always seemed to be loaded, and there were rumours at the library that Steve had inherited a fortune and really had no need to work. Steve said he was skint and yet Declan later heard that Steve was buying himself one of those newfangled home computers, and they didn't come cheap.

Then out the blue a mysterious golden answer to

Declan's predicament presented itself. The head librarian Mr Rogers told Declan to bin twenty-six dusty old volumes from the storage room, and Declan begrudgingly carried the purple mildewed books to the skip in the library's backyard. As each tome was dumped, Declan noticed they were each stamped with a gold letter of the alphabet on their spines, and he opened Volume M – and saw the unusual surname of his workmate – Morrice – at the top of a paragraph. The text read: 'Morrice, Steve, librarian. Habitual burglar. Deliberately ran over girlfriend's cat in January 1978 after she broke engagement off. Morrice had two-year affair with neighbour's wife [and her full name was given] (1981-82). Secretly slashed tyres of work colleague Don Harding's car over football argument, 1983.'

Declan couldn't believe his eyes. Who had written this? Who had discovered all this about Steve? He felt confused. He recalled that Don Harding – a fellow librarian who now worked in another part of the city – had indeed had his tyres slashed last year, but surely no one as placid and as laid-back as Steve Morrice would have done it? What a strange thing to find in a book, Declan thought. He flipped through the pages and saw that there were hundreds of more surnames written in bold with all their secret sins detailed – every skeleton in every cupboard! Should I tell Mr Rogers what I've just found? Declan wondered, then pondered the possibility that the head librarian had known about these books and wanted to get rid of them because they were like the logbooks of every single dirty secret of every soul in the city. No, surely he'd have kept them and hidden them if he had known the dangerous material they contained.

Declan retrieved the volumes from the skip and hid them in his locker. He took the M volume to a café on his lunch break – and tremblingly flipped through the pages until he found his *own* surname. He went cold when he saw the long entry pertaining to his darkest secrets – secrets that could ruin him. Declan read the eerie printed words which listed such misdemeanours as the time, when he was nineteen, when he stole a bundle of ten and one-pound notes from his grandmother's purse, the day after she had died…and – oh Lord no! Declan broke into a cold sweat, because there was a well-worded mention of the time when he had hid in his mother's wardrobe when he was thirteen, meaning to jump out on her, but instead she had come into the bedroom with a man who had come to fix the boiler, and Declan had not only watched them…

'Hiya Dec!' The new librarian, 18-year-old Lucy Bates, plonked herself down at Declan's table and asked what he was reading, and his heart pounded. He felt a spasm in his mouth pull his bottom lip to one side, and he slammed the book shut and made a feeble excuse to leave. 'I've just remembered something, I think I forgot to lock my car door,' he mumbled.

'Oh,' Lucy said, puzzled at the way he blundered into a waitress as he hurried away from the table clutching the old book.

That evening Declan sat engrossed in his study at home, perusing some of the most shocking, sickening, and occasionally funny secrets of the local populace. Declan's thoughts once again turned to the author of this encyclopaedia of evildoers. Who on earth had compiled this incredible damning dossier? Surely he had to be some agent working for an intelligence service? No, that didn't add up somehow. This was a blackmailer's dream! People in all positions from dustmen to doctors – everyone – had all of their hidden vices and criminal history logged here by some all-seeing recording demon. What were the 26 books doing in a dusty old storage room anyway? Mystery upon mystery. 'Well, this will be my ticket to fortune and power,' Declan whispered, and he poured himself some Jim Beam. He wrote a menacing letter to Steve Morrice, warning him he had proof of his burglaries, photographs of the adulterous affair, the slashing of a friend's car tyres, etc, with instructions as to where to leave the £200 for the blackmailer. What would he call himself? Who would this super-blackmailer be? Declan had little imagination to dream up some menacing supervillain name that would role off the tongue. So he decided on "Nosy Parker", and giggled. Then Declan planned to blackmail everyone! He drank an awful lot of whiskey, and every now and then he would hear Andrea's far-off voice asking him if he was coming to bed.

'Not yet, love!' he shouted back several times.

The librarian with the ultimate trump card – well, he had a whole suit of such cards – felt invincible now. He staggered round his study, talking to himself, swearing in a low voice so he wouldn't be heard by his girlfriend. 'That bastard Morrice,' he murmured, opening the door which led into the garden. 'Morrice will be the first to feel the wrath of the Nosy Parker. No wonder he was always loaded, robbing bastard.

Who'd have thought that hypocrite was a burglar,

eh?'

He looked up at the full moon and lifted his glass in a toast to his new career: the master-blackmailer of Liverpool. 'And that arsehole of a bank manager who wouldn't give snow in winter, Bernie Wartzer – I bet there's plenty on him!' Declan turned and went back to the desk and went off into a dreamworld of vengeance and bitterness as he sat in the padded chair. 'Wartzer...let's see what we have on him,' he chuckled, and reached for the W volume, but then he froze as if a thousand cogs had seized in his body, and he actually heard himself snore once – and then oblivion. All that whiskey had cocooned him in a warmth and sleepy smugness.

'Declan, come on!' said a voice which sounded as if it was underwater.

Andrea shook him awake, and she told him they'd been burgled. Declan had left the door in his study wide open. The burglar or burglars had come in from the garden as he was dead to the world from a sweet overdose of Jim Beam.

'What?' Declan felt as if his head was made from concrete, and he tried to lift it and his hands searched for the precious books. 'What?' he cried loudly.

The 26 books were gone and not much else; just a little cigarette lighter built into a miniature wooden clog – a tourist novelty from Amsterdam, given to him by his mum.

'No, no,' Declan kept saying as he looked around his study. He looked at the shelves and saw that the books were indeed nowhere to be seen, and he felt a sense of mounting panic, and it rose up from his bowels and went to his throat. He searched the garden but the books were not there and he searched every room in the house, over and over until he could face the fact that the 26 books were gone. He cried, and Andrea thought he was having a breakdown. 'They were just books,' she told him, 'they could have taken your cashbox in the bedroom.'

'Just books,' Declan mimicked Andrea's squeaky voice and she glared in response to the cruel impersonation. 'These were not *just* books, they were – ' Declan almost told her what had been lost, but closed his eyes and suddenly remembered the blackmail letter he had written for Steve Morrice, and he looked on the desk among the various papers there but could not find it. Never mind, he would write another one and quote those dark secrets he could recall from volume M; that'd make him a few bob.

Declan talked of the burglary at work later that day, but never mentioned the vast treasury of secrets that had been stolen, and a curious thing happened.

Steve Morrice had a peculiar 'knowing' look – a sinister twinkle in his eye. Declan was not imagining this – he was not being paranoid – he suddenly knew who the burglar had been who had taken those priceless books. And sure enough, the next day, a brown manila envelope arrived at Declan's home, and it told of the money he had taken out of his dead grandmother's purse, the disgusting acts of voyeurism in his mother's wardrobe, and some very serious crimes Declan had committed not so long ago. All Nosy Parker wanted was £300 'every now and then' - left in a certain place - and Declan's unsavoury past would stay buried...

GATEACRE'S GHOSTLY COACH

The ancient district of Gateacre is not only one of the most important historical areas of the North West (with around a hundred listed buildings), it is also one of the most haunted regions, and I speak from many years of investigation into the supernatural. The very origins of the place-name Gateacre is cloaked in mystery; some local historians believe the name means "the way to the field", as gate is an archaic word from Middle English meaning way, and "acre" may refer to the vast grazing fields that once existed where Gateacre Brow is now located. Alternatively, the etymological origins of Gateacre could be derived from the Anglo-Saxon for "God's Acre" – "Gottesacker". I'm not sure where the name came from, but there's one thing I do know – Gateacre is a village of ghosts, timeslips, doppelgangers, Faeries, – and dare I even say it – of witches too. There are enough paranormal mysteries in Gateacre to fill a volume the size of a telephone book – and all the time I hear of new ones. In the autumn of 2013, for example, I investigated several reports of a phantom black coach drawn by two horses, driven by a man in a top hat. This vehicle, which seems to date back to Victorian or Edwardian times, has been encountered by people from all walks of life, and a few unlucky witnesses in vehicles have even passed *through* the apparition. In early November 2013 a woman we shall call Jane, had to make a trip to a sick relative in the dead of night, and so she telephoned for a private cab which took her from her home on Stapleford Road to the house of her ill aunt, who lives off Acrefield Road. The journey was a little over sixteen hundred yards, but as Jane was being driven up Belle Vale Road, the driver of the cab remarked on the strange ground mist covering the area (just before St Stephen's Church), when suddenly, something terrifying took place. Two horses appeared in the middle of the road, and then a coach materialised behind them, and the cab driver and Jane could see a lamp of some sort on this old fashioned vehicle. The cabby braked and uttered a profanity out of shock, but the horses thundered towards his vehicle, and the driver gripped the steering wheel and braced himself for the impact. Jane let out a scream as the horse-drawn carriage hit the cab – and went straight through it. Jane felt an ice-cold blast of air go through the interior of the private cab, and the driver later said he had felt his stomach turn over when something passed through him. He pulled over by St Stephen's, got out the vehicle, and looked back to see a vague outline of the phantom coach moving off silently down Belle Vale Road. Jane had to remind him that she was in a rush to get to her sick auntie, but all the way to Acrefield Road the cabby talked non-stop about the very close encounter. I have collected many similar accounts of the ghostly coach and it seems to come from Beaconsfield Road, close to the site of the former Strawberry Field orphanage. The earliest record of the coach seems to be about 1930, but it's possible that the four-wheeled apparition was seen long before that. A policeman named Norman once told me that he and a colleague had almost collided with the coach one morning in 1997 when their patrol car was travelling along Woolton Hill Road. The time was about 3.15 am and the coach was speeding from the Blackwood Avenue end of Woolton Hill Road. Thinking the coach was solid, Norman swerved to avoid it and then tried to chase after it but it faded away into nothing as it trundled along Gateacre Brow. 'We never mentioned this incident to a single soul – to anybody - at the time for obvious reasons,' Norman told me. A retired postman also told me how he saw the coach around 7.30am one foggy morning around March 20th 1968 as it flew past him on Childwall Valley Road, heading towards Caldway Drive, where he lost sight of it in the morning mists. An older colleague of the postman said he had seen the same coach years before travelling at a phenomenal speed down Netherley Road, towards Tarbock Green, and he had even heard the driver of the coach cracking his whip as the carriage went by. The older postman did, however, frighten his younger colleague by saying that bad luck was supposed to befall those who saw - or even heard - the "Black Coach". However, the young postman's luck seemed to improve after the spooky encounter – he won a small fortune on "Red Alligator" in the Grand National a week later and in the following month he also won a holiday in Spain when he entered a competition run by a national newspaper!

When I mentioned the phantom coach in the *Gateacre Journal* an elderly woman named Margaret contacted me to tell of a very frightening encounter with a woman in black who came out of what seems to have been the spectral coach. This encounter happened one Christmas Eve in the early 1960s when snow had fallen. Margaret was a mother of three in her thirties at the time and held no belief in ghosts or any aspect of the supernatural. It was 10.40pm and Margaret and her husband James were enjoying a sherry as they watched the seasonal television programmes (with the volume turned down low in case the children's slumbers were disturbed). All of the children's wrapped presents were ready to be laid on their beds in the wee small hours, and as the snow fell outside the semi-detached house, a lovely peaceful atmosphere seemed to descend too. Margaret heard what she described as the dull clip clop of horse hooves outside somewhere and she went to the window, and through the feathery flakes of snow she saw an old-fashioned horse-drawn coach approach with a single twinkling golden light on it. James was called to the window to see the strange sight and by now the coach had pulled up at the gateposts of Margaret's home, and the couple could see the two dark horses and the carriage quite clearly. Margaret could even see the exhaled breath of the animals. A man in a top hat appeared at one side of the carriage and stooped to pull down fold-out steps from under the door of the vehicle. He opened the door and helped a eerie woman in black down onto the snow-covered pavement. The woman wore a huge hood and Margaret and James could just about see her pale face within this hood, and they naturally felt very uneasy by the appearance of this outdated lady and the stark black coach, the driver and the two horses. The woman walked straight through the closed wrought-iron gate – and seemed to glide up the path leading to the front door of the couple's house. Margaret and James were understandably shaken by this, and Margaret clung on to her husband and trembled. The couple didn't utter a word, and were both in shock.

Then came the sound of something moving in the hallway. The ghostly lady in black had somehow entered the house through a locked door just as she had passed through the closed gate outside, and now she was moving along the hallway with a faint rustle of fabric. The door to the living room opened steadily – and in came the alarming apparition. Margaret hid behind her stunned and frightened husband. The woman's face within the hood looked as white as the freshly fallen snow outside, but her large sorrowful eyes were dark and tinged with redness. The apparition was clearly levitating off the carpet by a few inches, and seemed to be about five feet and five inches in height. No feet could be seen beneath the long flowing black gown. James also noticed that the ghost cast no shadow. The figure turned right and seemed to float back the way she came, out into the hallway, and moments later the couple saw her black stark form gliding up the path. She passed through the closed gate, and the man in the topper opened the door of the carriage for the ethereal lady, and she went into the vehicle with a fluidic motion. The trembling couple then watched the coach move off silently towards Gateacre Brow. When Margaret and James went outside, they saw no footprints in the snow on the pathway to the gate and when they also inspected the pavement and road outside their house, they saw no tracks or rut marks made by the wheels of the carriage in the snow. The couple went back into the house, and Margaret took her grandmother's old Holy Bible out a biscuit tin and left it on the telephone table in the hallway as some form of protection in case the lady in black returned – but the ghost never did. The couple never got much sleep that night, and at 6.30am, most of the children were up and playing with their Christmas presents. The identity of the lady in black is unknown, and although Margaret's house dates back to Victorian times, she – and I – have found no references or reports of a ghostly lady being seen at that address. Hopefully, we may know more about the apparition one day.

MORE SHADOW ENTITIES

In 2006, two Liverpool men in their thirties came to Benidorm looking for work – and found it. Terry secured a well-paid job as a bricklayer with a mixed workforce of Spanish, Geordie, German and Polish tradesmen, and Larry landed a job as a bouncer at a club. Both men started in the winter months when tourists are thin on the ground in Spain, but now the summer had started in earnest and Benidorm was heaving. Larry was somehow making so much money as a one-man self-appointed bouncer-management agency, he had moved into the Gran Hotel Bali while the builders were putting the finishing touches to a beautiful little villa he'd put a deposit on in Playa De Levante. It was becoming rare for the two Scousers to meet up because they were now living miles apart and led hectic lives, but one night in August (the hottest month in Benidorm) of that year, with the temperatures reaching 78 degrees Fahrenheit, Larry and Terry met at a quiet pub at Calle Gerona, and had just sat down when a female voice behind Terry said: "De dónde eres?" Terry turned to see Leah, a girl he'd had a crush on in his college days back in Liverpool. She was working as a nanny in Benidorm and this was one of her rare nights off. Terry and Leah caught up on each other's lives and by two in the morning they were thoroughly drunk, and the couple went to stay at Larry's villa in Playa De Levante. Larry was very proud of the villa, but when Leah saw the place, she became very nervous and said she'd have to get back to her employer's home. Terry wouldn't have it and he begged her to stay at the villa, and Leah reluctantly acquiesced – and stipulated that there would be no "hanky panky". Terry laughed and said he was too intoxicated to do anything anyway, and half an hour after they went to the villa the couple were snoring in each other's arms – but then at 4am, Terry awakened to music playing somewhere. Larry knocked on the wall of his bedroom and told Terry to keep the noise down.

'I haven't got any music playing!' Terry shouted back, and listened; the tune sounded rather familiar; it was a song he hadn't heard in years: *Another Night* by the dance group Real McCoy, a mid-1990s hit from ten years ago. Then suddenly, a faint greenish-yellow circle of light shone from nowhere onto the bedroom wall, and a silhouette of a peculiar elongated man in a trilby with a walking came appeared – and danced in quite a weird manner to the dated music. Terry shook Leah awake and she saw the dancing shadow-man too – and then the bedroom door barged open and an irate Larry told his friend to "switch off that radio". The ghostly spotlight on the wall faded upon Larry's abrupt entrance and the silhouetted dancer instantly vanished. Everyone went back to sleep, but at five that morning, Leah woke up and said someone was sitting on her feet. Terry opened a bleary eye – and saw the shadow-man was back – and was now sitting on the end of the bed. The sun had already risen upon this summer morning and so Terry could now see the ghost clearly – and it was pure silhouette with no other features to it. The same song - *Another Night* - played again, and the balcony doors flew open. The silhouette ran and jumped over the balcony as a male scream ripped the air. Leah screamed, thinking she was witnessing a suicide, but when Terry went and looked over the balcony, he saw no one below. Leah was so shaken by the experience she and Terry left the villa and went to a café for an early breakfast. Leah said she had been nervous about coming to Larry's villa because a man who committed suicide – by jumping off the balcony in 1995 – was said to haunt the place. He'd been a local singer and dancer, and because of the haunting, the villa became hard to let. Leah had not realised she had seen a ghost until Terry had told her that he could see no body beneath the balcony. Larry left the villa when he heard about the ghost, and it's still empty. What's intriguing about the Benidorm ghost is the way it appeared as a silhouette; these supernatural beings – known as shadow people – are being increasingly reported across the world, and there are many of them in the Merseyside area in particular. I have included many accounts of these peculiar and sinister two-dimensional beings in my previous books, but here are just a few more accounts of these creepy silhouetted entities.

Just a stone's throw from the Rocket Pub, on Glendevon Road in the Childwall area of Liverpool, there is a semi-detached house where a very unusual and baleful image is seen with some regularity on the wall and ceiling of a bedroom: the silhouette of a huge hand with long tapering fingers some five feet in length. I first heard about this ominous phantasm in the early 1990s when I was writing a series of articles on local ghosts for the now defunct *Merseymart* newspaper. A reader named Mary told me about the uncanny projection of the hand being seen when she lived at the house where the silhouette is seen, back in the 1950s. When Mary was about ten years of age, she saw the hand stretched out on the ceiling of her bedroom one night around 11pm, just after she had gone to bed. There was a little bit of light coming into the room from a street lamp, and by this faint illumination, the little girl watched spellbound as the hand moved about on the ceiling. Mary looked around the room at first, wondering if someone was playing a joke, but she soon realised no prankster was about, and she became a bit scared. She left her bed and went downstairs and told her mum and her grandmother (the child's father worked nights in a factory in Speke). When Mary and the elders came into the bedroom and the light was switched on, there was no sign of the oversized hand. Of course, as is almost always the case in these matters where minors witness something supernatural, Mary wasn't believed, but her mother and Nan didn't accuse the child of lying; they thought she'd had a nightmare which had overlapped into Mary's waking world. The next evening though, again at around 11pm, Mary was lying in bed, having some difficulty getting to sleep. She was trying to push the memory of the strange hand out of her mind, and she could hear the faint sound coming from the TV set down in the living room. She began to drift off – when some movement to the left of her field of vision startled her. The girl turned her head and looked at the left wall, and there, lengthwise upon the vertically striped wallpaper, was the hand, with the fingers pointed upwards and this time the thumb was bent. The hand made a waving gesture, and almost immediately, Mary slid her right leg from under the blankets and placed her little bare foot firmly on the linoleum floor. She got out of bed and headed for the bedroom door to the right, but, quicker than her eye could really perceive, the hand slid along the walls and went to the door, which it now appeared on. This really scared Mary. It was as if the hand was trying to bar her exit.

Mary backed away from the door, stumbled over one of her dolls on the floor, and fell backwards, landing on her bottom. She let out a scream and started to cry, and she heard the volume of the TV set downstairs being lowered, and then came the hurried rhythmical thumps of the girl's mother as her slippered feet came up the stairs, followed by the slower measured pad of Nan's feet. The bedroom door opened and the ceiling light in the room came on and Mary's mother found the girl sitting on the floor, in tears. She asked her daughter what had happened and Mary told her about the hand which had tried to stop her from running away. Once again the women thought the girl had simply had a nightmare, but on this occasion, Mary's Nan stayed behind in the bedroom and sat stroking her grand-daughter's head as she lay in bed. About fifteen minutes later, Mary watched her Nan switch off the light, then stand in the doorway of the bedroom with the light from the landing lamp shining behind her.

'You have a good sleep and dream of nice things, Mary,' the child's grandmother said, but just as she was about to leave, she saw something flit across the ceiling, followed by a terrible scream from her grandchild. The shadow of a huge hand had appeared on the ceiling. This time an adult was witnessing the unexplained two-dimensional form which had been haunting Mary. The girl's Nan stood there in shock, gazing at the hand on the ceiling, watching it start to make a fist which shook, and suddenly, Mary ran blindly into her knee as she made her escape from the room. Child and grandmother hurried down to the living room and soon they were both telling Mary's mother of the strange manifestation on the ceiling. The three females remained in the parlour for almost an hour before Mary's mother sneaked up the stairs and peeped her head around the door of Mary's bedroom. She could see nothing. She switched on the light and saw something very surreal and frightening that is unexplained to this day. An old wardrobe, measuring about seven feet in height, had been turned completely upside down in the corner of the room, so that it was resting on its head. Cobwebs and the skeleton of a dead mouse were visible on the exposed upturned base of the wardrobe. It would have taken some force to invert that heavy wardrobe, and yet no one in the house had heard anything. This really spooked Mary's mother and she never told her daughter what had happened and let her sleep with her that night. There were further glimpses of the eldritch hand for about a week or so, and then it wasn't seen until the next residents moved into the house on Glendevon Road in the 1960s. During this period, the hand was seen during the daytime as well, and again it was only seen in that particular bedroom that had once been Mary's but now the bedroom belonged to a 15-year-old boy named John, and he was more fascinated than frightened by the spooky hand. Also, during the three years the family lived at the house, all five members saw it – and furthermore, they all often heard what sounded like a choir singing an unintelligible hymn in a very creepy manner. No furniture was upended or moved during this time, but John had the feeling the hand was trying to communicate something to him through some sort of sign-language, and although he sensed the thing was not good or Godly, it didn't seem to be evil either, just weird. John felt as if the thing was frustrated by some language barrier, and every now and then he would watch it emerge from what seemed to be a slit in the corner of the room. The boy's dog seemed fascinated by the apparition but never barked at it. John asked the hand: 'Who are you?' and it would always touch its third finger with its thumb in reply, and John also noticed how sometimes the silent shadow would change from being a right one to a left hand. The lad's younger sisters were terrified of the hand and John's parents didn't even seem to be that curious about the entity. They would just smile and act as if it was an everyday thing. When the family left to move to a house in St Helens, John was heartbroken because he knew the thing – whatever it was – would not be able to follow him - and it never did.

I occasionally receive correspondence about the shadow hand of Glendevon Road, and I am informed it still makes an appearance from time to time, but just what this thing is, remains unknown. Why does it take on the form of a hand? Why does it haunt that particular house? There are so many questions and sadly no answers at all at the moment to throw any light on this mystifying ghostly form.

Not all shadow entities are seen on walls or ceilings.

Many of them can appear flat, as if they have been cut out of black card, but they are seen in the middle of a room or in an open space outdoors. In a certain well-known supermarket in Liverpool, staff working all hours in the morning to stack shelves and clean the floors of the aisles have encountered the scary jet-black silhouette of what seems to be a man in a finely cut suit, standing watching them as they work. He is always seen between the hours of 3.30 am and 5 am, and for some obscure reason the ghost seems mostly active on Wednesdays. No one has identified the entity but some think it's a manager who supervised the houseware section of the supermarket. A 19-year-old named Allison was stacking shelves one morning around 4.30am when she had the very unsettling feeling that someone was behind her, watching her. The girl turned and saw the silhouetted ghost starkly contrasted against the white background of a sign advertising milk. Allison dropped a jar of mayonnaise in shock and hurried away to tell a work colleague, and when she looked back several times at the apparition, she saw to her horror that it was coming in her direction ever so slowly. The lighting in this part of the supermarket then dimmed for some reason, heightening the creepy atmosphere even more. Allison came very close to handing in her notice at the supermarket after this creepy encounter, but two workmates told her that the ghost was harmless and that they had seen it on many occasions, apparently observing them from a distance as they worked the graveyard shift. The ghost hasn't been seen as regularly as it used to be (unlike in 2012 when it was very active indeed), but it is still occasionally seen, the most recent appearance being Monday, 5 May 2014. I was shown an alleged photograph of the ghost, taken by one of the supermarket staff on her iPhone, and the entity just looks like a slightly blurred image of a black cardboard cut out of a man of about six feet in height standing in a deserted supermarket aisle. Footage of the ghost is also said to exist, captured by the supermarket's closed-circuit TV camera system, but I cannot look at it because the senior manager of the store doesn't want any adverse publicity. I told him that interest in ghosts is at an all-time high now and he'd probably get more customers if he advertised the fact that the supermarket had a resident ghost, but the manager was not convinced.

Many years ago another shadow being – the silhouetted figure of a woman with a bun in her hair who also wore a skirt that went just below her knees, was greatly feared by the children of a tenement named Sidney Gardens in Edge Hill, south Liverpool, in the 1960s. This eerie living shadow was unusual because it spoke, and screamed. The apparition was always seen during the dusky nights of autumn between seven and eight o'clock, running along the top landing on the eastern side of the tenement. Kids would dive out of 'her' way as she screamed and ran silently along, and then she would say something unintelligible, throw her head back – and then jump backwards over the wall of the landing to fall about a hundred feet, but the shadow always vanished before it reached the pavement and roadway below. No one knows the identity of this ghost, and Sidney Gardens has long gone now, but a former resident of the tenement told me that the entity was possibly the earthbound spirit of a demented woman who threw herself off the top landing after her husband left her in the 1960s.

THE HANGING
BRIDES AND GROOMS

One of the most chilling and baffling supernatural mysteries was first reported to me in 2010. A cleaner in her forties named Chrissy at a certain hotel in the Edge Lane area told me, how, during preparations for the celebrations to mark the Queen's Silver Jubilee in June 1977 (close to the monarch's official birthday), something happened one morning which almost resulted in the cleaner having a nervous breakdown. Chrissy turned up at the hotel around 6am to start her usual early shift, which routinely ended by nine. Chrissy walked into the foyer and was surprised to find it in darkness. The lighting in the reception area was normally always on but usually kept a bit dimmer at this time in the morning, yet on this occasion it was pitch black in the foyer, and when Chrissy groped about for the light-switch, she failed to locate it. 'Where the bleedin' hell's it gone?' she remembered saying in an annoyed tone as her hand searched for the switch. As she searched, the cleaner became aware of a rhythmical swishing sound nearby, and wondered what on earth it was.

All of a sudden, a yellowish light flared up on the right side of the foyer, and this illumination looked like a flickering flame in a frosted-glass or ground-glass globe. The light from this old fashioned naked-flame lamp revealed a scene which shocked Chrissy so much it left her gasping for breath in one of the worst asthma attacks she had ever experienced.

Instead of the foyer being there, the unfamiliar vintage gas lamp revealed a vast room of about fifty feet square – possibly more – and suspended from the ceiling of this unidentified hall, there were about twenty or more people – all couples dressed as brides and bridegrooms *hanging* by ropes with nooses around their necks. The rhythmic sounds Chrissy had heard before the light went on were the polished shoes of a hanged man scuffing against the white cloth spread out on a table as he swung to and fro. This man was a bridegroom in a finely cut suit, and what made this shocking spectacle even more macabre was the fact that he was holding hands with a young lady in her beautiful bridal dress and veil, and she too had been hanged - and so had the other (possibly nine) couples who were dangling by ropes. Some of the hanged couples were turning slowly in circles as they hung there while others were kicking their legs and making awful choking sounds. Chrissy can't recall what the ropes were attached to on the ceiling – whether the ropes were strung from hooks or perhaps one of the many unlit chandeliers she vaguely recalled being up there. What Chrissy does recall is turning around, running out of the structurally altered foyer and trying – unsuccessfully to scream. Chrissy ran out of the hotel and kept running until she managed to flag down a police car on Edge Lane. She couldn't speak because she was in such shock, and the two policemen who got out of the patrol car tried to calm her down, as they were used to treating members of the public suffering from shock. Chrissy managed to get out the words: 'Hotel…down there…people hanging…horrible!' And then she burst into tears and suffered a chronic asthma attack . One of the policemen took her into the car and radioed for an ambulance to treat her and possibly the people the cleaner claimed to be hanged. The other police constable ran to the hotel, but found the place as it had normally been, with the foyer dimly lit and nothing amiss. He rang the bell and a receptionist with bleary eyes appeared to confirm that nothing out the ordinary had been seen in the last half hour when she had crossed the foyer to unlock the door for the arrival of the cleaner – who she had not seen yet.

When Chrissy had recovered from her asthma episode she gave a detailed account of what she had seen and the police told her they had found no hanging people or any evidence of ropes or anything sinister at the hotel. The incident was eventually put down to stress, even though Chrissy was not at all stressed at the time. Then the mystery deepened, because Chrissy contacted me at a radio station where I had been talking about haunted hotels, and when I repeated her story to the producer of the radio programme, he told me not to mention the mass hanging at all, as many of the listeners, who tuned into the afternoon programme might be upset. I thought this was ridiculous, as there were worst stories being reported on the news bulletins of the station, but I complied with the producer's wishes and said a certain cleaner had seen something which seemed to involve a timeslip at a certain hotel in the Edge Lane area. Three people called the station and not only identified the hotel, they each said that they too had seen the people hanging in a hall at that hotel. It transpired, after many in-depth interviews with these people, that they did not know one another, and did not know the cleaner

Chrissy, so there was no possibility of any collusion between them and Chrissy. The first person to telephone the station was a 66-year-old man named Graham who had worked as a chef at the hotel in the early 1990s, long after Chrissy had give up her cleaning job there. Graham told me that one morning, around 1.30am, he and two members of the kitchen staff had been having a sherry after providing their services to a three-hour banquet (for a well-known charity club) had which had just come to an end. Graham was literally putting his feet up after working so hard all night, and his assistants, 22-year-old Camilla and 24-year-old Sean were, like Graham, sipping a sherry and talking about the trials and tribulations of the banquet when Camilla suddenly said: 'What was that?'

'What was *what?*' Sean asked her.

'I just heard a woman scream,' Camilla replied and she got up from the long table and went to a large serving hatch and opened it. She could see nothing but a darkened hall where three tables were still covered with plates, glasses bowls, bottles and ashtrays – the aftermath of the big banquet.

Then all three of them heard a strange echoing sound, like a group of people all speaking at the same time, and Graham said: 'That's coming from the foyer. Have some of the guests returned?'

Sean left the kitchen, went down an L-shaped corridor which led out onto a passage which brought him to the foyer area, but instead of seeing the foyer, Sean saw something which chilled him to the bone. He saw a dozen or more people – men and women - hanging by their necks from ropes, and as he looked on in horror, he saw more of these people – who were all dressed in old-fashioned clothes, jumping off tables at the far end of the unidentified room – and they had nooses around their necks. Sean saw that most of the women wore white bridal gowns, and the two nearest to him had veils on. The assistant cook ran as fast as his legs could carry him back to the kitchen, and collided with Graham and Camilla, who had also gone to see where the odd noises had come from. Sean blabbed out: 'People are hanging themselves in there!'

Graham and Camilla went with him and saw the same thing Sean had just described. Camilla let out a scream and as she did the whole scene changed in an instant to the foyer they were all familiar with. They all looked at one another in shock and disbelief, and Graham called for the receptionist on the intercom and told her that he and his assistants had just had a very strange experience. The receptionist, a woman in her early forties named Jane, returned a puzzled look. Graham told her about the couples hanging themselves, and Jane said: 'What? In here?'

'Yes, in here, as clear as day,' Graham replied, 'we all saw them.'

Jane then admitted that, on several occasions, always in the wee small hours of the morning, she and several guests over the years, had heard voices in the foyer which sounded like a crowd of people talking excitedly in an echo chamber.

'That's what we heard just before we saw them,' Camilla told the receptionist.

Camilla's father then turned up to take his daughter home, and Sean was only too glad to leave when his taxi arrived at the hotel to take him home to West Derby. Graham stayed on for a bit to see if there were more ghostly goings-on, but saw and heard nothing out of the ordinary. He was a chef at the hotel until 1995 when he left to become a chef at another well-known hotel in the city centre. He never had any further psychic experiences and has now retired. Graham has no idea what he and two other witnesses saw that night, and I later introduced him to Chrissy, plus two other people who saw the ghastly mirage from the past at the hotel concerned. These two other people were Bryan, who worked at the haunted hotel from 1997 to 2001, and Jan, who worked at the hotel from 2008 to 2010. In December 1998, Bryan, who worked in the hotel kitchen, was cleaning up the hall after a Christmas works do, and at one point, which he puts at about twenty minutes past midnight, he went to the toilet, which is quite near to the foyer, but found the reception area pitch black. 'Have the lights gone?' he shouted, and noticed the place was silent and also very cold all of a sudden. Bryan took his keys out of his pocket and fumbled to switch on a small LED keyring torch, and by the light of this torch he saw two women in white long dresses, hanging side by side with huge nooses around their necks. 'Jesus!' Bryan shouted in shock, and backed away, and he felt something heavy against his back, and what's more, this thing moved, as if it was *suspended*. Bryan shone the torch at it and saw it was a man in a black suit, and his feet were dangling about four feet off the ground. The man's eyes were bulging and the same type of large noose could be seen around his neck. His head looked as if it was almost resting sideways on his right shoulder; in other words, this man had been hanged and the noose had broken his neck. Bryan ran blindly into the darkness and could see nothing he could identify. None of the hotel's usual doorways or fittings was there; it just seemed to be a cold uncarpeted hall, and his footsteps echoed. He thought he saw rows of round tables covered with pale cloth, and then, all of a sudden, a wall-mounted lamp at the far end of the hall lit up, and Bryan could see 'dozens' of bodies hanging by their necks to his left, and they were the bodies of men - in black or brownish suits - and women in long white dresses. Bryan saw double doors to his right and headed towards them, wanting to get out of the place. 'I thought someone had murdered these people in the hotel,' Bryan told me when I interviewed him at his Wirral home. 'The supernatural interpretation didn't come until I approached the double doors.'

As Bryan tried to push open the doors, he suddenly found himself in the car park of the hotel. He turned around and saw a brick wall behind him, and yet he had just come from that direction a heartbeat ago. He walked back into the hotel and decided to tell no one of his bizarre and frightening experience, but he did tell his father when he got home and his dad opined that the thing had been some form of timeslip, but the question still remained: who were the hanged people? What appalling circumstances could have possibly led to a mass suicide – all by couples who looked as if they were married or ready to tie the knot (no pun intended)?

Jan worked at the hotel as a receptionist from February 2008 to December 2010, and one night in August 2009 at around 11.40 pm she had to summon an ambulance for a guest who had suffered a cardiac arrest. The guest was given CPR by the paramedics and taken to Broadgreen Hospital, and after the drama of the night, Jane went to read a magazine in the small office behind the reception area. A cook named Anthony brought her a coffee at around twenty minutes to one, then left the hotel. Around five to one that morning, Jan distinctly heard a female scream somewhere nearby, and she checked the reception area, the staff toilet, the dining hall, but saw no one about. Around 1.10 am, Jan heard the same scream again, and this time she went into the reception area, and her account from then on stands in very close agreement to the previous accounts in this strange haunting. The foyer was pitch-black. Jan looked back at the office and saw the light was still on in there, so she thought a fuse had blown which only affected the foyer lighting circuit. She tried the light switch in the foyer just to be sure – but couldn't find it – then Jan looked around and saw that she could no longer see the light from her office. She reached out, thinking her hands would feel the counter of the reception but instead she blundered into a table which hit her thighs. The temperature now dropped and for a moment, Jan thought she was outside. Jan could hear her heels tapping on what sounded like bare floorboards – even though the foyer was of course, carpeted throughout. A light source came on behind her, and when the receptionist turned, she saw a globe of light which seemed to be on a wall. Knowing there were no such quaint lamps in the hotel, this confused the receptionist, and she again tried to return to her office, but as her eyes became accustomed to the dim light, she suddenly noticed 'about seven or eight bodies, hanging there. 'They reminded me of marionettes, of puppets,' Jan told me, 'They were lifeless and in silhouette. Then I realised they were actual people, and that they'd been hanged.'

Jan screamed, and immediately the black cold spacious room or hall was replaced in an instant with the warm carpeted reception area and gone was that table which had barred her way to the office. Jan had nightmares for a long time about the hanging people. She could see that some were men and others were ladies, but they were mostly in silhouette because of the position of the wall lamp. Jan was so scared that night, she telephoned a friend who lived close to the hotel and she spent the night with Jan. There were no further strange goings-on or any other bizarre phenomena that night.

I have looked into the history of the hotel, and so far, I can find no reports of any Victorian or Edwardian suicide cults, but of course, you never know what went on in those days, as scandals were often hushed up when the well-heeled members of society were involved. If I find any information which throws light on this strange haunting, I will of course, publish it in my newspaper columns and I will certainly lay the details down in any future books.

THE AMNESIAC

Many years back a friend and I were asked to investigate alleged poltergeist activity at a certain private hospital in the North West. A specialist and several nurses had seen flowers uprooted and scattered across a lawn and one nurse had felt something ice cold stroke her face as she walked along the path next to the lawn. I investigated and kept a watch on the area where the activity had taken place and saw nothing, nor did any of the electronic equipment I carried pick up anything. On the second day of the vigil, a nurse pushed a man in a wheelchair towards me. This man had suffered a stroke six months before which made his speech slurred, but I could understand every word he spoke, and he asked to see me because of a bizarre incident which had happened back in the 1970s. We will call the man Chris because he asked me not to identify him for reasons that will soon become clear. From 1971 to 1995, Chris had been a psychiatrist at a certain mental hospital in the North West, and in 1973, a young lady of about eighteen was brought to him. She had been found wandering the streets of Liverpool without any clothes and seemed very confused. She had no identification on her and had apparently lost her memory. She could not remember her name nor where she had lived, but she seemed to have a faint

Liverpool accent. Detectives circulated pictures of the girl in the press, assuming someone would recognise the young woman and even interviewed shopkeepers and pub landlords on the street where the girl had been found wandering, but it seemed as if no one in the area knew her. Dental records were consulted and the girl – nicknamed "Tuesday" by one of the investigating detectives because of the day she was found upon – even had her fingerprints taken but she had no criminal record. Chris had studied hypnosis and the police asked him if it would be possible to plumb the depths of Tuesday's memory to unlock the secret of her identity. Chris said hypnosis was not some magical power, and some people simply couldn't be hypnotised at all. He said he would question the girl first and see if he could perhaps jog her memory by playing pop songs that teenagers of her age group would listen to. This approach never worked. Tuesday would put her hands to her ears and squeeze her eyes shut as if she regarded the pop music as a racket. Chris gave the girl a huge drawing pad and a felt tip pen to see if she would draw something – some object that would provide him with a clue to the identity of this young amnesiac. The girl drew a candle for some reason, just a simple rectangle with a single line for a wick and a simple tear-shaped flame. Chris asked her what it was. 'A candle,' Tuesday told him.

A few days later at the hospital, the girl had to be restrained after apparently having a nightmare. She had fallen asleep in the afternoon, and had awakened about ten minutes later in a state of abject terror. When she finally calmed down, Chris asked the girl what the nightmare had been about. The girl said she had seen people screaming in a fire, and the faces of some of these people melted and fell off their skulls with the intense heat. Chris wondered – had Tuesday survived a horrific house fire and had she possibly seen her family burnt to death? If so, had the horror caused a breakdown and had her mind protected her from the images of the deaths by repressing the memories of the tragedy? Checks were made by the police, and it was found that no such fires had occurred anywhere in Liverpool in recent months. The girl suffered from more nightmares which were even more terrifying than the first one. She dreamt an old naked woman was being urinated on by three grotesque green-skinned men with pot-bellies, and after their deplorable treatment towards the old lady, they tied her to a post, then one of them produced a poker with a glowing bright orange tip and pushed it through the old lady's right ear. The elderly woman's screams were deafening, and the three weird lime-green men laughed. The poker was shoved further into the pensioner's ear and suddenly it emerged from her other ear, and a spray of smoke billowed up from the exit wound in the left ear. The old woman's head fell forward, and hung limp as she became unconscious with the horrific pain, and then the surreal and frightening green men began to hit her with black metal instruments that resembled ice picks, and at this point, Tuesday awoke in a sweat and found herself paralysed for a moment. She thought she could still smell the burnt flesh of the old woman, and then she began to scream. The girl had further nightmares I dare not ever put into print because they describe bizarre acts and depraved, horrific actions that would sicken even the most ardent horror fan.

Chris told a senior colleague named Alec about the amnesiac's disturbing and graphically violent nightmares, and Alec said the girl obviously had serious issues which indicated that she had perhaps been physically abused, perhaps by a violent parent or step-parent in the past. Tuesday's nightmares became so regular, the girl ended up sedated.

And then, about a month after the girl had been brought to the hospital, she asked to see Chris. He visited her at her bedside and a screen was put around her because she wanted to tell him something very private. What Tuesday told Chris was initially taken as a disturbed fantasy, and no one can criticise Chris for thinking this, given the horrendous nightmares his enigmatic patient had described to him in the past. Tuesday said her name was Elizabeth, and gave a certain – and rather rare surname. She told Chris that she had died around 1900 after murdering two children left in her care. She had killed the children just to see what killing someone was like, and had afterwards regretted it, but soon had the urge to kill again. She had then become very ill a few weeks after the double murder – and she recalled gazing at a candle by her sickbed and watching it grow dimmer as she died. She remembered gasping for breath and asking for more light, but then it went all dark. She had died, and then she had gone straight to Hell.

Chris tried to evaluate this twisted fantasy the girl was coming out with, and told her to continue. 'Elizabeth' described Hell in terrifying details, and said that as far as the eye could see, there were naked people being tortured and humiliated as well as downright slaughtered, but some were put aside for special torture schemes, and from time to time, some of the damned and condemned managed to hide and even escape. The worst fate was the Pit, but the girl was almost sick when she explained what fate awaited those in this abyss. 'Hell is not below in the earth,' the girl told him with chilling authority in her voice, 'but somewhere very close by, and it's hard to get there and it's even harder to escape from.'

'You're telling me you've escaped from Hell?' Chris asked, wondering what this Hell and the Pit were representing in the girl's distressed psyche. Was there a classical Freudian interpretation to this sinister scenario?

'Well they know I got away, and they're coming to bring me back,' Tuesday, or Elizabeth – or whatever her name really was – became very nervous and started to cry. 'You don't believe me do you?'

'Yes, I believe that *you* believe this, but look, just calm down just a minute – ' Chris forced a smile and tried to reassure her and allay her anxiety but he wasn't fooling anybody – he was a bit afraid of all this talk about the infernal regions, and this actually surprised him.

'I can feel them pulling me back, and I found out before that I don't even have a heartbeat and I can't find my pulse,' the girl told him and wiped tears from her reddened eyes. She grabbed her tummy with her hands and cried out. 'They're pulling me back!'

'Tell me about the children you think you killed…' Chris was saying, and he raised his hand and pushed it through a gap in the screen and frantically beckoned a nurse.

'Go on, find my pulse – and try and listen to my

heart!' she lunged forward on her bed and her small fist struck her bosom. 'You won't hear a thing!'

A male nurse came around the screen, and Chris said to him: 'Can you just take Tuesday's pulse? I want to reassure her - '

'My name's not Tuesday you blockhead! I told you! It's Elizabeth!' the girl bawled.

The male nurse told her to calm down and then he felt for a pulse at her wrist, but returned a perplexed and embarrassing expression to the psychiatrist. 'I can't find anything,' he mumbled, and he tried again as the girl sobbed. 'Keep still, miss!' the nurse became irritated by her erratic behaviour. 'No, nothing,' the nurse said, turning a worried face to Chris.

The girl let out a terrible scream and sat upright in the bed as if she had just been shot in the solar plexus. She gripped her abdomen and her eyes bulged, and she vomited all down the front of her nightdress. 'Help me,' she groaned.

And then she was simply not there.

Chris looked at the empty bed, then back at the nurse, but that nurse was transfixed – his wide scared and confused eyes looked at the impression left by the patient in the pillow. He stood up and pulled the blanket back, almost as if he expected her to be hiding beneath it, and he saw a yellowish-brown mess of semi-solid faeces and a spreading pale amber urine stain.

'Where did she go?' the nurse asked over and over, and he even looked under the bed.

Chris and the nurse told a detective what had happened, and that detective just stared back into Chris's face and after a pause, he said: 'You've fucking lost her?'

'No, look, I know this sounds unbelievable – ' Chris attempted to get the unearthly truth across to a man who only dealt with logic and hard evidence, but the ways of the Occult show a frank disregard for the rudimentary laws of our little world.

'Oh it *does* sound *very* unbelievable, sir,' the detective interrupted, and looked the male nurse up and down. 'And I think you and this fellah here must have been on some of your own drugs.'

'What a downright silly thing to say! We saw her disappear in front of our eyes,' the nurse said, raising his voice in anger because of the disgraceful way he was being talked to.

The detective lit a cigarette and continued: 'I'll be honest with you two now and tell you both that this looks very bad for you and this hospital – losing a patient…'

'I give up,' Chris told the policeman and hid his face in his hands. 'We've told you the truth – we can't take this any further. I don't know what to say – nothing like this has ever happened to me before.'

'Oh we *will* take it further, I can assure you of that,' the doubting detective assured the two men before him, and then he set about launching an enquiry and formulating ridiculous conspiracy theories which all came to nothing. The search for 'Tuesday' was eventually called off and placed in that catch-all file for such insoluble 'crimes' – the missing persons folder.

I have looked for Elizabeth with the unusual surname in the archives, and although I have found one person of that name who lived in Aigburth in late Victorian times, she was not – as far as I can tell –

involved in any double child murder, but you never know – some murderers kill and get away with it – well at least as far as the justice of *this* world is concerned. The Elizabeth I found died from influenza, aged 17, so perhaps she is indeed the girl who allegedly escaped from that fabled place of eternal damnation, some seventy-odd years after her earthly death. Does Hell exist? Well hopefully, the reader has led a spotless life and he or she will never find out whether Hell exists from first-hand experience one day…

NOT YET

If anyone had a heart as cold as interstellar space, it was John Remayne – or so they said, "they" being the people who only saw him drinking hard most evenings and Saturday afternoons at Liverpool's oldest pub, Ye Hole in Ye Wall on Hackins Hey, somewhere off Dale Street. Those very few who really knew the hard man glimpsed a different interior from the mythical one. It was now 1980 and the times were changing, probably for the worse, but Remayne still wore his blue suede shoes and sported his thick voluminous hair (now with strands of tinsel grey) in a well-slicked quiff, but below the forelock the seams were splitting. He was 56 but looked much older, because he had carried a guilty weight in his heart for 31 years, and no one knew just what this crime had been. There were daft rumours about involvement with the Krays and even the Great Train Robbery crew, but no one really knew the score. Some thought it was odd how John Remayne had stopped drinking in his old haunts – the White Star down by the Cavern and the Prince Arthur up in Walton, as if he was avoiding someone from his past perhaps. The most curious beings in this world are cats and Scousers, and many a local drinker tried to pry out the truth by plying Remayne with his favourite poison – 'black and tan' – but not one could even scratch the surface. Then one day a square-shouldered American of military bearing named Joe McGill came into the Ye

Hole, and it turned out that he had once been Remayne's rival in love, and the whole truth came out and McGill kept saying "No hard feelings though, bud," and actually got Remayne pie-eyed. The former Burtonwood serviceman was eventually sent packing by some harsh words from Remayne, who then cryptically sobbed: 'All our bleedin' yesterdays! Stupid Yank, reminiscing like that - it'll bring her out of the woodwork now! Stupid sentimental big-mouthed Yank.'

And on the following day, on a Saturday afternoon, Remayne was in the White Star, and a beautiful pallid girl with raven glossy hair piled up in a bun and the most striking baby-blue eyes came in. She wore a smart tweed jacket, a black pencil skirt and stilettos – and she went to Remayne and softly called his name as he was drinking. 'John, you promised me that you'd come with me,' she said in a low sweet-sounding voice.

He slowly put the glass down on the bar counter, then turned as all the drinkers looked on; surely she was his daughter? The clientele wondered.

Now they both had tears in their eyes; a man in his late fifties and girl who looked barely out of her teens.

'I know,' John told her, 'I'm sorry.'

'Come on, come with me now, please John,' she said and tears rolled from those blazing blue eyes.

'Not yet,' he said, sounding choked, and people began to notice that the young lady had no reflection in the pub mirrors. Before anyone could realise the significance of this eerie fact, she vanished. She was literally gone in a moment, and John Remayne and all eyes in the room were staring at the place where she had been.

Long ago, John had fought for that girl's love, and had won her from that Yank McGill in an actual old-fashioned duel with guns at dawn and all that, and McGill almost died and lost an awful lot of blood, but true to the unwritten rules of honour, the American never grassed on John.

No two people had ever been so close as John and Maria, and they were soon engaged, but Maria became ill. It was cancer. She was given months to live and said she wasn't scared of death – just of being without 'her John' for all eternity, and so he promised Maria he'd go with her when her time came, and even had all the pills ready for that day, but to his eternal shame couldn't go through with it when she had died in his arms. Not long after her death, Maria's love remained so strong towards John that she even managed to return from beyond the grave, and began to visit him and always she would beg him to join her in the next world.

He hid in the pubs among the living and drank hard to numb his aching guilt-ridden heart, but still she visited, and he would always say: "Not yet, my love.'

One evening in the middle of the 1980s, they say that John Remayne was drinking in the White Star in Rainford Gardens, when in walked Maria, on the very anniversary of her death, and she pleaded with him to come with her, and many of those present were either bemused or disgusted at the idea of a woman so young crying for a man so old – but then Remayne put down his drinking glass, said goodbye to the barman, and turned to take the hand of the girl. Maria was seen to hug him, and they embraced for a while as people laughed and some joked about the age difference. The couple then went outside, and about five minutes later, two young men came rushing into the pub and said an old man was lying in the street outside. They had asked him if he was alright but there was no reaction whatsoever. A first-aider hurried outside and felt for a carotid pulse, but there was none, and an ambulance was called but it was too late; John Remayne had passed away.

THE GREAT MORSE CODE MYSTERY

Early in 2014, Jeff, a forty-year-old man who has lived in Wirral since 2010, began to hear some strange noises in his head. It all started one night in January when he went to bed at his semi-detached home on Moreton's Harvest Lane. Jeff read a book as his wife Sarah watched a movie on Netflix on her iPad with her earphones plugged in so the sound wouldn't disturb Jeff should he drop off. As Jeff sat propped up in bed with three pillows at his back, he became aware of a strange electronic sound in his right ear. It sounded like Morse Code. He asked Sarah if the film she was watching had anything to do with Morse Code and she shook her head, puzzled. 'Can you hear that?' he asked Sarah, who paused the film, shot an annoyed look at him and took off her earphones. She could hear nothing beyond two cats fighting in the distance. After about thirty minutes the bleeps in Jeff's ear stopped abruptly. He heard it on and off over the next few months, always between one and two in the morning. Sarah badgered her husband to see a doctor, thinking he had tinnitus. The doctor said the course of Erythromycin Jeff had been prescribed for a gum condition might have affected his ears – a well-reported side effect of the antibiotic. Tests were carried out which eliminated tinnitus, and Jeff was told he might be hearing things because of stress. Jeff told a friend named Doug about the weird Morse Code, and Doug, being a radio ham who still had a CB radio from the Eighties, knew Morse Code well, and told Jeff to try and write down the dots and dashes the next time he heard them, and Jeff attempted this with a writing pad. When Doug finally decoded the message, he said it was the following cryptic sentence repeated 5 times:, "2065 AD Test, do you receive? Crimea". Has someone in the year 2065 found a way to transmit messages into the past? Or did someone with a powerful transmitter in the vicinity of Jeff's home somehow broadcast a high-frequency signal directly into Jeff's ear? The answer was never discovered, because Jeff stopped hearing the accursed bleeps in April 2014.

The Moreton Morse Code Mystery is not unique. Over the years I have had dozens of reports from people who have been plagued with strange Morse Code-like bleeps in their head, and some reports go back to the 1960s – like the one from Priscilla James. In 1969, Priscilla was 22, and lived in Everton. One June night she went to bed around half-past eleven and was just about to doze off when she heard a succession of electronic beeping sounds of differing durations. She sat up in bed and listened, and realised with a sense of mounting panic that the sounds could still be heard when she plugged her ears with her index fingers. After suffering from some insomnia because of these strange auditory intrusions, she went to her doctor and he sent her to the Ear Nose and Throat hospital on Myrtle Street, where a specialist could not diagnose the odd sounds. Priscilla's older brother Paddy was in the merchant navy and was also a radio ham who had once talked to fellow radio rig enthusiast King Hussein of Jordan on his short-wave transceiver from the attic of his Everton house. Paddy was an expert on Morse Code and one evening Priscilla dictated the dots and dashes she could hear to Paddy, and he said one message was "Answer me" followed by an unknown Morse Code letter. 35 years later, that 'unknown letter' turned out to be the "at sign" (@), officially added to the Morse Code in 2004 so radio operators across the globe could email one another. The 1969 message then, when it was later re-examined, seems to have contained an email address; but who on earth would be sending emails in 1969? Priscilla heard no more bleeps after July 1970.

In 2010, Bob, a man in the Walton Hall area of the city, telephoned me on air on the Billy Butler Show on Radio Merseyside to tell me how he and every member of his family had been hearing More Code in their heads, always at night, for about three months. Bob and his family went to their doctor who gave them all a clean bill of health. A mobile phone mast miles away was suspected of generating the signals but the signals from such phone masts are simply too high in frequency to be heard by humans. A paranormal investigator stayed at the house for three days, and he too heard the faint high-pitched dots and dashes of what was unmistakably More Code, but he could never tape the sounds; it was as if the only apparatus that could detect them was the human brain. There was a case many years ago of a man who had a metal wire put in his dentures to strengthen them after they broke, and this wire acted as an antenna and pulled in a medium wave broadcast of BBC Radio Two. But the More Code heard by Bob and his Family seemed to be affecting their brain's hearing centres or possibly their inner ears, and the only waves that can produce that affect are microwaves, but who would be sending More Code, which is an archaic, way out of date code, in this age of digital hi-tech communications? The matter has still not been resolved, but after the radio show had ended, I was inundated with dozens of similar stories from listeners who had also heard the accursed Morse-like Code, and some of them had endured it for over a decade. If you have heard these sounds, email me: tom@slemen.com and let me know about it.

SPEKE'S SPECTRES

'Speke', my old history teacher Mr Clarke, used to tell me, 'is a unique place-name found nowhere else in England outside of Liverpool'. This error finds its way into a surprising number of local history books, but way back when I was in short trousers, I told Mr Clarke I had found a Bramford Speke down in Devon. He wasn't at all pleased by my find in my little atlas book but everyone in class loved me for showing him up. Speke is still unique though; its town was the creation of visionary Sir Lancelot Keay, the City Architect, who was also the Director of Housing in Liverpool between 1925 and 1948, but of course, the district of Speke is ancient and referred to in the Domesday Book and no one is really sure about the origins of its name; it could be derived from the Anglo-Saxon word "spic" which means bacon, because there was once a sizeable swine field in the area, but somehow I don't buy that, and think the real origin of Speke's name has now been lost in the mists of time. Speke's greatest tourist attraction – and possibly Liverpool's for that matter – is the beautiful Elizabethan manor house Speke Hall, which I have written about many times in my books. It is a wonderful atmospheric place of ghosts and timeslips, and well worth a visit even if you're not into the paranormal. Speke has quite a few ghosts besides the ones that reside in Speke Hall, and these are the subject of this chapter.

The momentary lustful indiscretion took place that

Saturday night in October 1977 at the Pez Espada club on Liverpool's Temple Street. While an intoxicated husband named Alan went to the gents, his friend Lionel leaned forward and passionately kissed Alan's wife, Melanie. The husband was the 35-year-old shopwalker of a well-known Liverpool retail store, a dead ringer for Goodies member Tim Brooke-Taylor, and his 25-year-old wife Melanie was – in her own words – 'a leggy beanpole' Marti Caine lookalike. Lionel, the adulterous friend of Alan, was a 50-year-old baldy postman - and neighbour of the couple on Dam Wood Road in Speke.

'Gawd, I really fancy you Mel,' Lionel's words were muffled by the violently pressing lips during the fervid full-on kiss, and Melanie's hands ran around his scalp as clubbers cringed, sneered and tutted. The kiss broke off almost a minute later, and a few seconds later Alan came back from the loo and asked his wife if she wanted to dance.

'Nah, Al, I'm friggin' knackered,' she told him and looked at mesmerised Lionel from under her heavy blue eye-shadowed lids.

Alan swore in the amplified din as the DJ spun a single of Baccara's *Yes Sir I Can Boogie* and people took to the floor. As Alan, in his Ferrari-red penny-collar shirt and bottle-green flares, danced with a stunning statuesque brunette who towered over him in silver platforms, Lionel was whispering sweet nothings into the ear of Melanie. She whispered back into his ear as she kissed him. She wanted him to stay over at hers tonight, on the sofa, and the minute Alan dropped off (as he always did when he'd had too many lagers) she would come downstairs and have some fun on the sofa – and maybe the kitchen table – that was the plan.

The three friends were riding home in a rickety Hackney by three that morning, and throughout the journey, Alan kept insisting that Lionel should stay over with him and Mel. 'I'll do a big fry-up supper for us,' Alan promised, his eyes crossing at one point, 'sausages, black pudding, beans, tomatoes and fried bread.' Then he slumped sideways towards the door of the cab and with the side of his face pressed against the side window he fell sound asleep as Melanie and Lionel kissed. The cabby smiled and shook his head as he watched the all-too-familiar scene in his rear-view mirror.

Alan came to at his house and went up to bed with Melanie, and she winked at her secret lover. Lionel lay back on the sofa, and Melanie came down with blankets and a pillow, saying Alan was 'throwing his heart up' but that she'd be down soon, but Alan must have been much sicker than Melanie thought because she never reappeared, and Lionel fell asleep waiting.

He awoke around 4am – and felt something on his chest; he thought it was Melanie at first, but when his eyes adjusted to the semi-darkness he saw that it was someone, or *something* swathed in a white robe of some sort; it looked like a woman's delicate build and this person was sitting on his chest, facing away from Lionel, with her legs (which were also cocooned in that white fabric) parallel to his. A raspy vaguely female voice came from the white hood of the creepy figure: 'This one is not for you. You are cursed to die, and will burn three times, and the last fire shall consume you for eternity in Hell.'

Lionel felt faint with fear. Surely this was a

nightmare and he was still asleep? No, he could feel his heart racing, and this was simply too real to be a bad dream.

He then heard a scuffle behind the curtains.

The hood of the unearthly woman twisted to present a skeletal face behind some white veil. 'Go home, adulterer,' she said, then cackled, and vanished, and as she disappeared, the weight on his chest went with her.

Lionel got up off the sofa, went into the hallway, and lunged straight for the front door, but it wouldn't open. In blind panic he had not realised the bolt was on. He was that scared he opened a small long window to the side of the front door and climbed through it, then legged it to his house, which was only thirty-odd yards away. When he got home, he bolted the door, turned the lights on in the hall, kitchen and living room and poured himself a large scotch. He leaned on the mantelpiece and looked at his trembling hand as it held the glass. That thing had been a ghost, he told himself, and it had told him he'd burn three times. 'Why?' he said to himself, 'What have I done to deserve a fate like that?'

Could someone have spiked my drink? He wondered? And then he decided against that possibility. He'd heard about ghosts and the like but had never really believed in all that stuff, but the thing that had been sitting on him tonight had been the real thing. 'Why tell me things like that?' he said after a sip of the whiskey, 'I haven't done anything. I'll go and see a priest.'

A breeze pushed the ajar door a few inches and Lionel felt his heart jump. 'This is all her fault,' he hissed, thinking of Melanie, 'throwing herself at me!

I'm a free agent, a single man, so why would I go after her? She's married.' He said, trying to convince himself that he was just some victim of her seductive ways. He hardly slept a wink that morning, and kept seeing that ghastly skull-face behind the fine pale veil, and he went round that Sunday morning at 11am to let Melanie know that the affair was over – but when he called, Melanie and Alan were up and having breakfast. Mealnie seemed worried and invited him in.

'Have the police been to yours yet?' Alan asked Lionel as he sat at the breakfast table with a sickly pallid face.

'Eh?' Lionel was taken aback by the question.

'Where did you go this morning?' Melanie asked, and looked pretty annoyed.

Alan thought quickly on his feet. 'I didn't feel well, and I didn't want to throw up all over your sofa so I went home – why? And what are you talking about, the police?'

Some psycho with a knife broke in here this morning,' Alan told him with a very grave expression, and clutched Melanie's hand.

'What?' Lionel recoiled.

'He climbed through the window in there, in the lounge,' said Alan, nodding to the doorway at the lounge. 'Used the knife to somehow lift the catch. He could have slit your throat as you slept if you hadn't gone home.'

'You're having me on,' Lionel gasped, not even meaning what he said, and he suddenly remembered the noise he had heard behind the curtain when that thing had been sitting on him.

'I'm deadly serious mate,' Alan's voice deepened.

'For some reason he never went upstairs to us – thank God - and never took anything, but he must have put the bolt on the front door after you went. You sure you never heard anything when you were here?'

Lionel didn't answer, because he suddenly realised with immense relief that the ghost had not been talking to him this morning – it had been addressing the maniac with the knife.

'Lionel? Did you hear anything?' Melanie reiterated her husband's unanswered question.

Lionel looked at her, startled as he came back to the present. 'No – no, not a thing. Never saw anyone about either when I went home. Odd.' Lionel realised he would have killed him only for the intervention of that "ghoul". The prowling knifeman, I am told, was never brought to secular justice, but later died in a house fire, was afterwards cremated, and, perhaps, as the unknown ghost predicted; he is now continually roasting in the eternal fires of Hell.

Less than half a mile to the north-east of the last haunted house, there is another haunted residence – a bungalow, on Elloway Road, an L-shaped road of about 330 yards (or 301 metres or so for the metrically minded), and this ghost is, like the one documented on Dam Wood Road, rather hard to explain. In 2002, a couple we shall call Don and Linda – both in their mid forties, were inseparable. They went everywhere together and most who knew them regarded the couple as a real-life Darby and Joan, as soulmates and so on. In October 2002, Don lost his job and the only work he could find was as a watchman at a factory, and so he'd leave his little home on Elloway Road around 9pm and embark on a twenty minute drive to the factory at Widnes, where he would stay on duty to about 7am. These hours were obviously unsociable and neither Don nor Linda wanted to be apart, but they needed the money (and Linda had been looking for a job since being made redundant five months before), and they were always on the phone to one another during the long watches of the night anyway, so Linda didn't feel as lonely as she thought she'd be. Things were going okay for a few days, then one night around 11pm, Linda had just finished having a fifteen minute chat with her husband, and was ready to settle down with a book, when she saw a light out the corner of her right eye. At first she thought it was the headlights of a car outside, but when she looked over towards the window, she saw that the light was not only inside the room, it was in the form of what seemed to be a globe about the size of a grapefruit, she estimated. As Linda watched the ball of bluish-white light in astonishment, it grew rapidly and changed from a globe to a sort of rugby-ball shape (an ovoid), and then it stretched even more, and Linda now started to panic. The glowing form of a man in a pointed hat came into focus as if someone was adjusting the lens on a projector, only this figure was definitely three-dimensional, and although it was glowing slightly, it seemed solid. However, Linda recalls seeing the window blinds through the entity, but only just. The strange man who stood in the bedroom looked like something out the medieval era. He wore what looked like some pointed balaclava with a long stern face in it, and his eyes were jet black and really penetrating. The tunic he wore was of a faint lime-green almost, and something about it reminded Linda of Robin Hood, especially the odd dark blue tights the man had on. She could not see his feet though.

When this uncanny apparition walked towards the bed, he pointed at Linda and in an accent she had never heard before, he said rather loudly: 'I want to tell you something!'

Linda screamed, threw the book at the creepy manifestation, but whether it hit him or went straight through him Linda does not know, because she threw it and almost instantaneously threw herself out the bed. She closed the door behind her and stood in the hallway, where she switched on the light and wondered if she had been seeing things. She even pinched herself to see if she was dreaming, and confirming to herself that she was not dreaming, she opened the bedroom door quickly and looked in – and he was still there, looking very angry now as he stood on the side of the bed where the door is. Linda slammed the door and in her bare feet, ran to her friend Carol's house around the corner on Alder Wood Avenue. Carol was alarmed to see Linda in such a state – in her bare feet too – on her doorstep, and asked her what the matter was, because Linda was out of breath, clutching her bosom (because she had shooting pains in her heart, she said) and almost in tears. Carol's 10-year-old daughter Carly stood behind her mum, wondering what was going on. Linda staggered into the house and told Carol about the weird ghost which had appeared in her bedroom, and Carol told her daughter to make a cup of tea for Linda as she sat her friend down on an armchair. Linda regained her breath and described the materialisation of the sinister phantom and told Carol how it had said it wanted to tell her something. Carol didn't know what to think; she knew Linda was a very level-headed down to earth woman, and she had worked with her at a school ten years back and had always found her as a truthful person, never prone to tell fibs. Carol did know however, that Linda was very clingy with her husband Don, and she wondered if her nerves had got the better of her when he was away on nights. Young Carly diligently brought not only some hot sweet tea to Linda, but also a saucer of Jammie Dodgers, but Linda had lost her appetite from the shock of encountering the weird-looking spirit. 'I know I wasn't seeing things, Carol,' she told her friend, 'because it was real – it was real as her,' she said, pointing to Carly, then she realised that open talk of the ghost might scare the minor, so she silently mouthed to Carol: 'Shall we talk in there?' nodding to the kitchen.

'Nah, she isn't scared of all that stuff,' Carol said with a grin as she threw her arm around her grinning daughter's shoulder, 'she loves ghosts and witches and all that.'

'I'd have loved to have seen it,' Carly said, and she went and brought a drawing book and asked Linda if she could sketch the ghost.

'No, Carly, let Linda recover, she's had a shock,' Carol told her manic daughter, and Linda tried to smile at the disappointed child.

'You've never seen anything like that in that bungalow before have you?' Carol asked.

'No, not in all the years me and Don have lived there,' Linda confirmed. 'Oh God, I've left my mobile in the house too,' Linda realised, and her cup began to rattle on the saucer as her hand trembled. 'Say Don calls? He'll think something has happened.'

'Use my phone if you want, Lin,' Carol suggested, and picked her iPhone up off the coffee table.

Linda shook her head. 'I don't even know his number, Carol, it's mad isn't it? He puts all the numbers in me phone.'

'Was he see-through or did he look like he was solid?' Carly asked, and held a pen, poised to take down Linda's reply in the drawing book, but her mum told her to be quiet.

'I'd better be getting back, Carol,' Linda said, a few minutes later, 'I didn't lock the door.'

'You look the same size shoe as me, Lin, a six,' Carol gazed down at her friend's bare feet.

'Yeah, I am,' she said and grinned, and looked at her dirty soles.

Carol gave her a pair of slippers, and she and her daughter accompanied Linda back to the bungalow. When they went inside, all three saw a brief glowing light in the hallway suddenly fade away. 'Did you see that, then?' Carly exclaimed, and seemed a little afraid as she hesitated to go into the hall. Her mother though, hurried in and looked around, then beckoned for Linda to come inside her home. Nothing was out of place in the bungalow – only the paperback which Linda had launched at the ghost. It was now on the bedside cabinet, as if it had been placed there. Carol and Carly stayed with Linda for almost an hour, and during their stay, Don called – and was told about the ghost.

'You winding me up?' he asked, and Linda said she

was not pulling his leg. Don told her he wanted to jack in his job and get a day job, and he asked Linda what the ghost looked like, and she told him and also related the strange message it was going to impart before she threw the book at it.

'Look love, why don't you stay over at my sister's?' Don suggested. He was referring to his sister Julie, who lived five miles away in Huyton. Linda said she'd be okay and that she probably wouldn't see the thing again. Carol asked her if she'd feel better staying with her for the night but Linda said she'd be okay, and would sleep on the sofa. Carol suggested something to make her feel a bit better: 'I'll phone you on the hour if you want, Lin, and see if you're okay if you want.'

'Nah, its okay Carol, I'll be alright, honest,' Linda assured her. 'Thanks for offering though.'

Carly started to offer some advice. 'If he does come back, make the sign of the cross and then just – '

'Okay Carly, shut up,' Carol said, and glared at her enthusiastic daughter. She smiled at her friend and warmly told her: 'If you need me Lin, just phone, any time of the night.'

As soon as the mother and daughter had left, Linda switched on the telly, the radio, and put the lights on in the hallway and living room. She even decided to do her washing, and felt even safer with the washing machine rumbling in the background. She kept her bedroom door firmly shut, and every half hour Don was either texting or calling her. When he came home a bit earlier than normal that morning – about 6.50 am, Linda was so glad to see him, and he went straight into the bedroom and asked exactly where the ghost had appeared and she went through it all again – how it started to materialise as a globe, then went oval and became longer vertically until it formed the body of a man who looked like something out the days of the Sheriff of Nottingham.

'And are you sure you didn't doze off, love?' Don asked. 'I've done that and thought I have heard you shouting me and all kinds.'

Linda nodded and closed her eyes then looked in the direction of the window. 'Don, I swear on my life and yours, I didn't hallucinate him – he was there, before God he was. I went out the room, looked in again, and he was still there.'

A week went by, and then Don had some good news: he was allowed to have a week off, and that meant they could both go to bed at the same time and sleep at night now like everyone else, at least for seven days. Then, on 30 October – the night before Halloween (and also known as Devil's Night and Mischief Night), something incredible happened. The couple were sitting up watching telly in their bedroom as they held hands. A light appeared in front of the Venetian blinds to the right – and right away, Linda knew it was that thing coming back. Don swore and said, 'What's that?'

As before, a globe of white light with a blue halo hovered there, about five feet from the carpeted floor of the bedroom, and as the couple watched, it expanded – much quicker than on the last occasion – and immediately it stretched to form the tall figure of a man in archaic clothes; the pointed velvet balaclava, the pale green tunic and tights that made the wearer look as if he had just stepped out the Middle Ages, and on this occasion, the feet could be seen – and they were long pointed footwear, 'Like something out of *Blackadder*,' according to Don.

Linda screamed and tried to get out the side of the bed but Don had hold of her little fist in a tight grip, and he seemed terrified. He swore in a way Linda had never heard before, and he picked up the alarm clock from the bedside cabinet and threw it into the face of the ghost, but not only did the clock go straight through his face, it created a hole in his pale face for a moment, and then the features reformed, coming back together in a very disfigured manner. Linda somehow summoned up strength she normally didn't possess, and she dragged Don across the bed as the terrifying glowing visitor lunged forward.

'I want to tell you something!' he cried at the couple, and his face only seemed to have one black beady eye and a thin down-turned mouth. The nose and other eye looked vaporous and indistinct. Then Linda noticed he was reaching for a huge dagger in a sheath attached to a thick leathern girdle around his waist, and she cried out: 'He's got a knife!'

As she pulled Don out of the room, Linda tripped on a mat and fell, and Don fell onto her, winding her. He managed to get to his feet and closed the bedroom door hard, and then, as he picked up a crying Linda, they both heard loud raps on the door – and to Linda it sounded as if the supernatural visitant was stabbing the door with that dagger. She let out a scream, and she and Don were soon outside. They wandered from their home in shock, both barefooted in their night clothes, and Don looked back to see the faint glow of the TV in the bedroom on the window blinds of the bungalow. They walked to Carol's and now Linda's friend knew for sure that the ghost was real and not imagined, for Don looked terrified, and an ambulance was called for when he experienced sharp shooting pains across his chest. Don was taken into hospital and kept overnight, and this time, Linda had to stay with Carol, and she kept crying. On the following bright sunny but crisply cold morning, Linda went back to her bungalow with Carol and Carly, and upon entering the place, they heard a loud hissing sound coming from the bedroom. The TV had been wrenched off the wall and lay partly damaged on the floor with white noise blaring from its speakers and a picture of static snow on its LCD screen. As the bungalow had been unlocked all night, no one knew if someone off the street had walked into the place and tried to rob the TV but had perhaps dropped it - but that didn't seem likely. Why would anyone try and rob a television and not even switch it off, and why for that matter, would they not take other valuable items from Linda's home? Nothing else was touched. Then, as Carol switched off the damaged TV, Carly let out a scream and pointed to the corner. There stood the very figure Linda and her husband had fled from the night before. He was trying to hide between a wardrobe and the corner, and he was looking down at Carly with an expression of intense hatred. Carol grabbed Carly by the hand and ran out of the bungalow, and Linda followed hot on their heels. All three of them were nearly run down by the car of a neighbour, a man in his late twenties. They told this neighbour what had happened and he could see something had upset the trio, so he gingerly went into the bungalow, but came out about a minute later and said no one was about.

Enough was enough and Linda and Don moved from the bungalow to a house in Halewood. I gave a brief mention of the haunting on a radio programme and admitted I was baffled by the identity of the ghost. However, in the following week when I returned to the radio station, an old man was waiting for me in the reception area. His name was Alfred. Alfred told me that he was in his late seventies (and he certainly didn't look a day over sixty), and he had a very intriguing story to tell. In October 1966, when Alfred was 33, he had been visiting his aunt on Gerneth Road at the western end of the Speke housing estate one evening when a bunch of young kids ran up to him and said two men were fighting one another with knives. Alfred went with the kids to the corner of the road, where Speke Town lane meets Gerneth Road, and there were two men dressed in very odd clothes. One wore a dark balaclava with a pointed peak of the type I had mentioned on the radio, and he also wore a tunic and tights of some sort. This strangely-dressed man was locked in battle with a blond long-haired and bearded man with a tunic and brownish-looking tights, and both were trying to stab the other with daggers. They had both sustained wounds from the knives, and the sleeves of both men were tattered and bloody. As they both wrestled with one another, they backed away from the cheering children and a few older teenagers – and vanished into a hedge on the corner, and there was a pause as everyone looked on in stunned silence for a while. Then the youths examined the hedge and saw that there was no way the two battling outdated men could be in there, and the gang eventually dispersed. When Alfred eventually reached his aunt's home, he told her about the strange incident, and although she was a very old fashioned God-fearing lady, she told her nephew that such antiquated ghosts had been seen years before when the Speke housing estate was being built in the late 1930s and 1940s. The identity of these ancient ghosts is unknown, but from their attire, we can be sure that they probably predate the more common Victorian era ghosts.

We move now, just a little north of Speke, but not too far away.

In the summer of 1970, a 19-year-old girl named Michelle, of Barford Road, in Hunts Cross, got a job at a certain tea factory in Liverpool city centre, and she hadn't been working there long when she met and quickly fell in love with a delivery driver at the factory – a 21 year old man named Barry Collier, who hailed from Upton, near Widnes. Barry loved Michelle as much as she loved him, and longed to take her on dates in Wales and the Lake District, but had spent all of his savings on a moped just before he met Michelle. He dreamed of the day when he could get a decent good car so he could take Michelle out on proper dates, but she didn't mind riding pillion on the moped as long as she was with Barry. About a month into the relationship, sad news reached Barry: his favourite uncle, Humphrey had passed away at his home in Heswall, but there was a silver lining to this black cloud; Uncle Humphrey had left his yellow Triumph sports car to Barry in his will. Barry said nothing to Michelle, and decided to surprise her. He turned up at her home one Saturday evening in the sports car, and she was initially excited, but then she confessed she also had reservations about the flashy car. 'Girls out there will be throwing themselves at you when they see your new car,' she said, with a glum expression. 'Don't be daft,' Barry laughed, 'I'm a one-woman man, Michelle. Let them throw themselves! Now, let's go the pictures eh? And then we'll go to a restaurant. I've been saving a few bob, see.'

A red-headed lad named Mick who had fancied Michelle for years was very jealous of Barry's sports car, and as he came down Barford Road he said to Barry: 'You wanna watch no one scratches that car, mate. Some green people about.'

Barry and Michelle ignored him. They went to the pictures and then to an Indian restaurant on Bold Street, and at 11.30pm, Barry dropped Michelle off at her house – and her mother said she wanted to meet him. For some odd reason, Michelle was a bit self-conscious about her mother's strong Irish accent, but Barry found it endearing and really got on with her. It was almost two in the morning when Barry left, but before he went, Michelle sat with him in the car and they talked, and kissed and held hands. 'I better be going, love,' Barry said, and suddenly, the couple heard something under the car. 'What's that?' Barry asked, and wound down his side window and looked out. He looked back at Michelle with a dazed expression. 'There are little people round the car,' he said, and looked out the window again. Michelle thought there was a punchline coming, but realised he was serious. She then looked out her side of the car – and saw a weird-looking man, about a foot tall, in a silvery oyster-grey one-piece suit and a pointed cap. She screamed and wound the window up and clung on to Barry. There were pattering noises on the roof of the vehicle and all of a sudden the car lurched towards one side. The beings had burst the front right tyre! The couple sat there in terror until Michelle's mother came out and asked what was wrong with the car. When Michelle told her about the "Little People" her mother made the sign of the cross. Barry changed the tyre and looked at the engine - and noticed to his horror, that the brake cable had been cut. He had to stay in Michelle's home that morning and borrowed money from his father to have the brake cable fixed. A neighbour of Michelle later told the girl and her mother that she had seen a lad with red hair looking under the bonnet of the sports car just after Barry had gone in with Michelle to her home. This red-haired person was probably Mick, but nothing could be proved, although Barry warned him if he ever came near him or Michelle again he'd give him a hiding. Michelle's mother was very superstitious and believed those little beings who had burst the tyre had done so to stop Barry from driving off with a severed brake cable – to perhaps a fatal crash. Michelle said perhaps she had seen cats, and tried to explain the little people away, but Barry said he had definitely seen weird diminutive figures and he also had the same feeling as Michelle's mum – that those things had somehow been trying to avoid him driving off. The strange thing is that there have been sightings of fairies and elves and leprechauns - and whatever else we humans choose to call these beings – in the Hunts Cross and Speke area. In more recent times, in 2011 and 2013, there was a widely reported rumour that little men had been seen in a certain well-known supermarket just a stone's throw from Barford Road, only these entities were tiny, with estimations of their height being about two to four inches. I received a few emails, tweets and letters about these two flurries of alleged sightings, from several people in and around the Hunts Cross, Halewood and Speke areas. Long before the supermarket (where the little men were allegedly seen) was built, there was a mound on the wasteland to the north of the supermarket's present site which was said to have been an original 'fairy mound' – a hollow hill were – according to widespread beliefs among the Celtic peoples – the fairies live. To intrude upon these mounds or to damage them was said to be highly unlucky and even fatal to the transgressors, and even today, proposed new roads and highways in Ireland will be diverted around them. The one which existed to the north of the supermarket was levelled, and I believe all sorts of accidents occurred on the building site soon afterwards. If the fairy folk did save Barry's life by preventing him from driving his sabotaged car, could his girlfriend's Irish mother have somehow been an influence in the little people's actions? I have noticed such connections where Irish blood is concerned; its as if there is some affinity between the fairy folk and people who are Irish, Cornish, Welsh, or Scottish – in other words, Celtic – and that also means a high percentage of Liverpudlians too. One afternoon I was on the Billy Butler Show on Radio Merseyside when I received a call on air from an elderly member of the public – a woman named Mary who was in her early nineties – and she recalled the fairy mound in Hunts Cross, and told me how a little figure, just a few feet in height, was often seen upon the hill. This was a beautiful lady in a long white robe with jet black hair.

Mary saw her many times, both as a child and even in her twenties. People said it was bad luck to see this doll-sized ghost but Mary somehow empathised with the apparition and felt the figure was sad because she had lost something or someone. Perhaps the lady was one of the Fay – the old name for the fairies – and she was possibly sad at the way the beautiful countryside around Hunts Cross had been steadily urbanised and built upon over the years, or perhaps the Lady of the Fairies knew the mound would soon be destroyed by the 'developers'.

In the late 1950s, a newly-married couple in their twenties named Kate and Bernie moved into a house in Speke not far from Clough Road. Bernie worked for a printing firm up in Fazakerley, and one day he came home at teatime and excitedly told Kate he'd been invited to a "works function" that would either be held at Wilson Hall in Garston or another, even bigger venue in Woolton. Kate asked what he meant by a works function and Bernie impatiently told her that it was a social event put on by his employer, Mr White, and that it was to be a fancy dress party and dance ball. 'Am I invited?' Kate queried with a suspicious look, and Bernie said, 'Yes, of course you are. Thing is, you'll have to go in fancy dress though, and so will I.'

Kate found the idea amusing and as she stood at the cooker with a pan of scouse simmering away, she dreamily wondered who she'd like to go to the ball as. Bernie undid his tie and sneakily took a slice of apple pie from the larder and told his wife: 'Oh, yeah, Larry might come over tomorrow after work. He's going to the ball as either Elvis Presley or a clown.'

'So I'll finally get to meet your workmate,' Kate

remarked, then wondered out loud: 'Will he be coming in costume?'

'I can't see him getting on a bus dressed as Elvis,' Bernie laughed. 'We're just talking over costumes and that.'

Bernie then talked all through teatime about certain historical and popular character he might dress up as, and decided on Robin Hood. Kate said she was not going to the ball as Maid Marion, as Bernie suggested, but Marilyn Monroe perhaps, or a ballerina.

On the following day at 5.45pm, as Kate was busy over the stove as usual, cooking the tea for Bernie, she saw someone enter the kitchen. It was a man dressed in some sort of costume. He wore a white curly wig, a grey well-cut collarless jacket with huge buttoned cuffs from which there sprouted frilly white pleated shirt-sleeves, and he also had on a silk brocaded waistcoat and funny tight trousers that went to just below the knees, where his white stockings ran down to his buckled shoes. The stranger was holding a piece of paper which he seemed engrossed in, and Kate suddenly realised it was Larry, Bernie's good friend at work. But where was Bernie? 'You look great,' Kate complimented Larry and then asked where Bernie was. The man seemed stuck for words, and then in an odd well-spoken voice he said: 'You must warn your husband to take great care in the morn when he is on the road yonder in his vehicle.'

Kate was baffled by this, and Larry went out the kitchen and Kate followed him a few seconds later and found the hallway empty. She checked the living room and looked everywhere in the house but Larry was gone. Then Bernie came home with a short dark-haired man of about thirty, and he introduced him: 'Larry, this is Kate; Kate this is Larry!'

Kate stood there in shock. 'If this is Larry, who was that before?'

'Who was *who* before?' Bernie asked, confused and a little embarrassed.

'Honey, a man came in here before and he was dressed in old-fashioned clothes, with a little white wig on too. He said you should be careful on the road outside tomorrow – and then he vanished.'

'What are you talking about?' Bernie gave a little false laugh and looked sidelong to Larry, who seemed a bit afraid of this spooky talk.

'He was standing where Larry is standing now,' Kate pointed to the spot. 'And then he walked into the hallway and he was gone, but I didn't hear the door open or close.'

Larry didn't stay long when he heard about the alleged ghost, and Bernie sulked all night because he thought his wife had put Larry off coming round with her stupid story, but, mindful of the alleged ghost's warning, Bernie drove his firm's van carefully along the icy road the next morning, and was overtaken by a car – which skidded and went into a deep pond near Clough Road. The driver was lucky to get out of the submerged vehicle and the car was never recovered. There were old legends that stated the pond in question was bottomless, and possibly led to the river. Kate witnessed the accident from the window that morning as she watched Bernie drive off to work, and she realised that whoever that man in the old fashioned clothes had been, he had probably saved her husband's life, and for that she was exceedingly grateful. The identity of the apparition has not been determined, nor has anyone established just what that sheet of paper was that the mysterious visitor was reading. Was he some spirit guide or an angel in an outdated disguise? We can only speculate.

TIMESLIPS GALORE

We all think we are on fairly intimate terms with time, and we all think we know what it is and how it flows, until we try to seriously define it – then we come unstuck. Attempting to define "now" is a simple example of the strange slippery deceptiveness of time; we can never bottle the moment we call "now" or even measure it with any certainty, because it can be split into smaller and smaller fractions that boggle the mind. If you happen to be 32 years of age, I could technically say you're roughly a gigasecond old; that's one billion seconds, or about 31.7 years. That's one way of measuring the present duration of your life, but when we want to measure smaller durations of time, we do, of course, use the good old second, and if you're into the technical side of computers and have an interest in electronics, you'll probably know about milliseconds, microseconds and nanoseconds. But what about a yoctosecond? A yoctosecond is one septillionth of a second, and you can't even really visualise something of that type of duration; and then we have the phenomenally shorter Planck time (named after the legendary physicist Max Planck); this is the time which elapses when something travels one Planck length – possibly the shortest distance between two points that can be conceived by present science, or if you want to get technical, it's: $1.616199(97) \times 10^{-35}$ metres. To imagine how short a Planck length is, imagine a tiny little dot that measures 0.1mm across; this just within the range of your vision. Now, imagine if that tiny dot was inflated until it became the size of the observable universe (and we can see the universe in all directions for about 45.7 billion light years). Now, if our tiny little 0.1mm dot was expanded to that size, the Planck length, on this new scale would be – wait for it – 0.1mm. So, Planck time is a unit of time which equals the time taken for something to travel the incredibly tiny Planck Length – and that is as near as you can get to defining "now" – but that might change in the future as we delve deeper into the nature of reality with new measuring techniques. Some physicists think time is continuous, but there are some who believe in the "Chronon" theory – that time is not continuous but made up of tiny particles of time called Chronons which can be pictured as beads on a string, with each bead representing a tiny indivisible unit of time. Another mystery about time is its directionality – it seems to travel in one direction only, and this is known as the arrow of time. There are no known scientific laws to explain this, and if time started to reverse right now so you began to read this book backwards and watched the clock on the wall go anticlockwise, no logical laws would be violated and the laws of physics would not be contradicted at all. In such a counterclockwise world, the dead are exhumed by gravediggers, a graveside service is said in reverse by the priest, and the coffin is taken by backward-walking pallbarers to the funeral service at the church, and from there the coffined corpse eventually makes it to the mortuary, and then on to the hospital or place of death, where it revives! Smokers in such a topsy-turvy (but entirely logical) world would clean up their lungs by reverse-smoking stubs that grow into cigarettes, and most country and western songs would have a happy ending.

The altering or hindering of the flow of time was once believed to be impossible but thanks to thinkers such as Einstein and others of his cerebral calibre, we now know that time is affected by gravity. A clock ticking on the ground floor of a block of hi-rise flats will tick slower than a clock on the fifteenth floor, but we have to consult incredibly accurate atomic clocks to measure this tiny difference in time. We now know that if we could build an artificial black hole, perhaps at a safe distance from earth, just beyond the orbit of the moon, its intense gravity could be used to allow travel into the past and future.

An incredible amount of timeslip reports have been coming my way of late, and I will detail some of them in this chapter. A few years ago on the radio I appealed for witnesses to an alleged timeslip involving a bus on Allerton Road, and I did not give any of the main details out about this purported slippage in time, so I was very intrigued when a man emailed me in January 2014 to tell how he had been the driver of the vehicle concerned. One dreary grey afternoon in the late 1990s, a B10B bus with 33 passengers onboard was travelling along Allerton Road, heading for the city centre, when something spectacularly strange took place. As the bus passed a branch of Max Spielman, sunlight flooded through the windows of the bus, and the driver noticed a 'diversion' road sign, telling him the road ahead was closed. The driver was new, and unfamiliar with the route, and as he swung the bus right to turn into another lane, he couldn't believe his eyes. There were gasps of surprise from the passengers, especially the older ones, who instantly recognised the green liveried tram coming up the road towards them from Smithdown Place. Such trams had not been seen on the roads for about forty years. The driver then noticed the tramlines on Allerton Road, and one of his reference points – Sergeant Pepper's Bistro – was now some sort of roofed waiting area which resembled a glorified bus stop. Some of the passengers on that time-slipped bus contacted me at the radio station. A woman in her seventies named Peggy took in a lot of the detail that day, despite her macular condition. Peggy had known something was wrong when she saw Alldays Newsagents – a shop that she had visited in her childhood, and Peggy also noticed all the awnings – the canvas coverings over the shops we rarely see nowadays. One passenger in his twenties named Gary said the tram on a collision course with the bus was a Number 5W, and such a numbered tram did indeed run on that route, a long time ago. During the timeslip, the bus driver's radio went stone dead, but the vehicle's electrics were not affected. The driver turned the bus in a panic to get out the way of the archaic tram and went back down Allerton Road, and suddenly the sunlight faded and a drizzly grey afternoon returned. The radio in the busman's cab came back to life, and Peggy felt so sad to see that all of the old shops had vanished and new ones now stood in their places. A further fascinating incident came to light from an interview with the passenger who had experienced that magical history tour: Mike, an apprentice gasfitter in his twenties and his father Phil, said that during the timeslip, the woman sitting in front of them temporarily changed into a woman who wore clothes typical of the 1920-30s – a royal blue cloche type of hat and a furry-collared jacket. A minute later the woman seemed to fade away, and was replaced by the female bus passenger. The bus driver's colleague later told him how, one evening in November 1997, he had been driving his bus down Leece Street when he found himself sitting at the controls of a tramcar. Seconds later, the steering wheel reappeared and the driver was so shocked by the experience he took a few days off, citing chronic backache as an excuse. Einstein said that yesterday, today and tomorrow are just illusions – all time is eternally present, and I for one believe him. It would seem that time is as vast as space (and you can't have one without the other – they are a continuum) and not only is all of space out there in the universe, every point in time is as well, and that means there are points in time where the *Titanic* is just about to encounter the iceberg, and much further down the timeline, Leonardo is poised with a brush before a piece of poplar wood measuring 21 inches by 30 inches as he sets about creating the *Mona Lisa*, and so on. In the other direction on that timeline, you are kicking away in your mother's womb, and a little further along you are being buried or cremated at around 1,700 °F. If you happen to be getting murdered or you are dying in an accident at some point in time in the future, it might be in your interests to know just when these possible events will take place so you can avoid them. In the old days, seers, fortune tellers and prophets were consulted by people who worried about future outcomes, and the Church tried to stamp out any such form of divination or occult-based predictions. I recall a priest telling a woman off who had been to see a spiritualist, and I also recall a vicar advising me not to popularise Tarot Cards. The representatives of Christianity will often quote scriptures from the books of Leviticus (usually 20:27) and Deuteronomy (18:10-30) when they condemn psychics and fortune tellers. In the Bible's book of Corinthians (11:14-15) there are claims that all so-called spirits of the dead talking to mediums are actually demons. The Church views this state of affairs thus: the good dead are in Heaven living a life of unimaginable bliss, and the bad dead are suffering unending torment in Hell. I have the utmost respect for all religions and I know the people of most churches do a lot of good charity-wise and so on, but people who have lost loved ones will not always be strong enough to believe what they are told by the Church, and they will be so desperate to contact husbands, wives, sons and daughters and grandparents who have died, they will give anyone professing to be a medium a chance. And of course, I personally know of many absolute bastards who pretend to have mediumistic powers, and many of these people have attacked me (always on blogs, never in person) because I have mentioned this side of the 'Psychic Scene'. Of course, although the Church condemns people who try to contact the dead or look into the future, the Bible is ironically based largely on the testimony of prophets! The attitude of the Church towards people attempting to pierce the veil of time to look into the future is very similar to the appalling way it once treated people who tried to fathom out the nature of space with telescopes. Through his basic telescope, Galileo noted from the phases of Venus and the way the moons of Jupiter revolved around their parent planet that the sun was the centre of the solar system, and this Earth was not the centre of the universe – and the Church branded him a heretic, as it had done with that other genius who moved us a little further out of the Dark Ages – Nicolas Copernicus, who was so afraid of the Church, he only dared have his revolutionary book on the groundbreaking heliocentric theory published upon his deathbed. People were imprisoned and even burnt at the stake for criticising the Bible and questioning its statements about the earth. There are statements about the immovability of the planet earth in the Bible, in 1 Chronicles 15:30, in Psalms, and in Ecclesiastes 1:5. All these scriptures state that the earth does not move. It says in Ecclesiastes that the sun rises and the sun goes down and hastens back to the place where it rises from. Strangely enough though, in the Book of Job 26:7 it states rather accurately that the earth hangs on nothing. Because of the threat of death, torture and imprisonment from the Church, freethinkers had to be careful what they said or wrote about, and so, any hope of progress in astronomy was seriously hindered for centuries. Now we know the Earth does move – it orbits the sun, and our sun is just an unremarkable middle-aged star which is not at all perfect; it does indeed have sunspots – as Galileo saw and sketched in 1612, triggering a bitter feud with the Jesuits, who claimed the sun was perfect and had no such blemishes. And today, the Church condemns anyone dabbling not in space – but in time; it strongly disapproves of anyone experimenting with prophecy, whilst forgetting that the words of Hebrew prophets are regularly read out and quoted from the pulpit every Sunday.

Let us now move on from the prejudiced theological opposition to our attempts to peer through the mists of time, and let us look into some intriguing timeslip cases.

It was a cold February evening in 1991 when four art students studying interior design were putting the finishing touches to a very impressive mosaic in the hallway to a renovated Liverpool University building that dated back to the 1850s. Three of the students were girls, all aged 21, and their names were Dionne, Beth and Lucy. The male student, Bryan, was aged 20.

The time on the huge black-framed electric clock in the hallway was crawling towards 11.20pm, and the students were supposed to have knocked off at 8.30pm but had become caught up in their work. Lucy said she felt tired and she left at 11.30pm and headed for her flat on nearby Mulberry Street. Bryan was the next to leave, but he said he might return later in the night. This left Dionne and Beth to tackle the finishing touches of the multicoloured mosaic. They chatted about ex-boyfriends and music, and a transistor radio was providing them with a little extra company. Around midnight, Dionne was at the top of a ladder, inserting the tiny coloured glass cubes into the wall when she suddenly stopped dead. 'What's that?' she asked, and looked down at Beth, a petite blonde who was holding the ladder steady. 'What's what?' Beth asked.

'Music – listen.' Dionne thinned her eyes and angled her head as she listened.

'It's the radio,' Beth told her and smiled. Dionne shook her head and told her to turn the radio down, and when Beth did, she and her friend could clearly hear echoing music somewhere in the distance. Then it stopped.

'I think I'll call it a day, Beth,' Dionne suddenly decided, and descended that ladder awfully fast.

'Oh come on, Di,' Beth laughed, 'you don't think there's something spooky about that music do you? It's someone else's radio playing somewhere.'

But Dionne got her coat and left. Beth said she'd finish the mosaic off alone, and laughed at the idea of the place being haunted. She poured herself a coffee from a Thermos flask and turned the radio up again. At precisely 1.40am, that radio went dead, and Beth heard what sounded like the singing voices of a man and woman harmonising. They were singing *Ah, Sweet Mystery of Life*, and all of a sudden, there came a sound of a great crowd – a hubbub and sounds of laughter and clinking glasses. It was coming from behind Beth. The girl turned and looked through the wide double-doorway and saw a vast crowd of people at a party that was in full swing. The men wore tuxedos and the ladies wore beautiful dresses, and some had on twinkling tiaras. They were all in what had been an empty hall until a minute ago. Some of the partying guests were standing on tables, toasting and shouting, and all of this was unfolding under beautiful glittering chandeliers. One of the men rushed over and grabbed Beth and dragged her to his table, and she dropped her cup and saucer and yelped, but the man said: 'Come along, dear,' and he wore a monocle. He held Beth at the table as the female guests laughed at her, and then suddenly the music and singing stopped, and everyone began to cry. The faces of the guests became sickeningly pale and skeletal, and Beth screamed and ran straight out the building. She heard a man and a woman shouting something that sounded like, 'Don't run off!' and 'Come back!' but Beth ran as fast as she could and felt her legs becoming weak as she did. It was like trying to run from something terrifying in a nightmare. The girl stumbled down the large wide steps outside and skinned the palms of her hands, and instead of telephoning a security guard to tell him she had vacated the building, Beth, being in complete shock, went straight to her flat in a terrible state. She put the security chain on and looked at the four reddish marks on her upper arm where that man had grabbed her so hard. She recalled the scent of the women from that party and recalled little details of their outdated dresses and she also remembered a man eyeing her through a glinting monocle with a sinister expression which gave her nightmares for years.

I later discovered that in 1914 a grand party was held in the building where the students had been working on their mosaic, and not long after, many of the men in that party would have went off in a very enthusiastic manner to fight in World War One, and it's highly probable that most of them never returned.

Beth returned to the building with her friends after this spooky incident and told them what had happened, but never hung round the place later than 5pm, and so she experienced no further ghostly goings-on there, but many security guards – even to the present – have told me about strange scents being detected there in the wee small hours, of an alarm being triggered by something, always around 4am, and of certain security officers leaving after encountering strange orbs of light. There's a fine line between a timeslip and a 'conventional' re-enactment haunting, and this case lies somewhere in between a shift in time and the type of ghostly activity that comes from a terrible period in the past when the Nemesis of a infamous war claimed so many young lives.

Now, let us move back a little further in time to look at another timeslip.

If you know where to look in the sky tonight, you'll see a ghost – the Andromeda Galaxy, 2.5 million light years away, and if anyone on a world orbiting a star in that galaxy is observing us, they'll be seeing the people and animals of this planet as ghosts of long ago – ghosts that are two and a half million years old, in fact. The Andromedans would see peoples, animals and plants that became extinct long before the rise of the Ancient Egyptians, Greeks – and possibly the Atlanteans.

Time and space often conspire to play some similar strange tricks that we poorly educated souls label as timeslips. Here's an example of an eerie shift in time which I heard about first-hand, from the girl who found herself in the centre of a timeslip which changed her whole view of the world and the nature of reality. In the summer of 1980, a 17-year-old Toxteth girl named Suzi fell in with the wrong crowd, and began to take drugs. She became a follower of punk rock, exchanged her glossy long black hair for a spiked 'Dennis the Menace' hairstyle, and took to wearing a studded dog collar around her neck. She wore thick white foundation and heavy black eye make-up to zombify her image, and donned a torn black tee-shirt (featuring the Sex Pistol's iconic hit *God Save the Queen*), tight leather trousers and maroon Doc Martens. Someone gave her LSD, and she freaked out on a nightmarish trip and ran screaming from her Toxteth home on Bedford Street South. The girl's 68-year-old Nan Susan (whom Suzi was named after) was heartbroken by the descent of her beloved granddaughter into drug-taking, and went looking for her, but Suzi was nowhere to be seen and no one recalled setting eyes on her after she had fled the house on her bad trip. I have noticed over the years how grandparents seem to have telepathic and empathic connections with their grandsons and grand-daughters, and Susan undoubtedly had a psychic bond with her grand-daughter and just knew something terrible had happened. Susan also felt that something unearthly had happened to Suzi, and she wasn't wrong about this, either.

Three days later, Suzi was found unconscious on her doorstep. Her Nan and parents took the girl in and laid her on the sofa. She smelt of smoke and was covered in dust. When the teen recovered she told a very strange tale. After she had fled from her house suffering from weird and disturbing hallucinations because of the ingested lysergic acid, she had found herself in a weird version of Liverpool, and had initially believed it was all part of her 'trip'. Explosive rumblings could be heard and the police wore soldier's helmets. Sirens Suzi had only heard in war films and on television shows such as *Dad's Army* were echoing all about and the people – who wore very outdated clothing – were hurrying along, orderly but looking alert and worried. These people also seemed fascinated by Suzi's clothing, hairstyle and make-up, and one man asked her why she was dressed like a clown. Suzi swore at this man and he threatened to beat her with his belt, and went off to report her to a policeman, but Suzi ran off and suffered an intense anxiety attack. Her heart pounded and she thought she was going to suffocate because try as she might, it seemed that she could not get any air into her lungs. She went down the steps of a dark gloomy house and hid by one of those old doorways below street level of the type you see in Rodney Street and Abercromby Square, and there she crouched with her knees up to her chin and her hands covering her ears. She started to cry and when she closed her eyes she saw multicoloured geometrical shapes – shimmering diamonds and spinning triangles, and then time seemed to move forward a few hours, and Suzie felt large rough hands rubbing her breasts under her tee-shirt. She was sitting against the doorway, still below street level, and a silhouette of a man was hunched over her. The man was obviously trying to have his way with Suzi and she screamed, and suddenly the door she was leaning against began to shake. There came a rattling sound as if a key was being inserted in the lock of the door, and the man quickly stood up and turned, fastening his flies as he did, and he scrambled up the steps and Suzi could hear him running off. The door behind her opened a few inches, and an elderly woman looked through the gap. She said, 'Oh, why are you dressed like that, m'dear?' And then she opened the door fully and helped Suzi up off the floor. Suzi said a man had tried to rape her and the woman threw her hand to her mouth and seemed very shocked by the claim. 'Come in you poor dear,' she said, and led Suzi into a dark over-furnished room where a solitary candle was burning.

The old woman went upstairs with this candle and in the hallway she went to an old black telephone on a table and placed the candle down beside it. 'We must inform the police about this dreadful matter,' the frail old woman announced, and as she picked up the receiver, she turned and said to Suzi, 'What's your name, dear?'

'No, don't tell the police!' Suzi pleaded, recalling how the man she'd sworn at for calling her a clown had gone to report her to the police. How on earth would Suzi explain who she was and where she was from, anyway?

'Why on earth not?' the elderly woman asked, and she had suspicion in her faded eyes. 'You're not in trouble are you?'

Suzi ran blindly back down the steps into the pitch blackness, and somehow she located that door she had almost been raped at, and her hand found the key still in the lock, and she turned it and it clicked but that door would not budge. The old woman was descending the stairs to the room, and Suzi could see the glow of the candle getting brighter. She then spotted the brass bolt on the door and slid it back, She pushed, and then pulled the door open and the cold night air hit her. She fell over as she tried to leap up the steps two at a time, and she found herself on an unfamiliar street. There were glows from distant fires in the city centre which silhouetted the chimney pots and rooftops, and Suzi ran and ran, putting as much space between herself and the well-meaning old woman.

The LSD was playing its hallucinogenic tricks again, and the crust that normally separated Suzi's conscious from her unconscious was dissolving. She could see images from her childhood flashing before her as if someone was showing her the scenes on a flicker book, and at one point as the girl hurried along she had the terrifying sensation of the entire world and all of its weight and mass being pulled from under her feet, miles away from her, leaving her feeling suspended and weightless in space, but then she felt as if she had rejoined existence as she found herself stumbling to a pavement somewhere near Chinatown, possibly Berry Street, where she coughed and spluttered and spat because of the acrid smoke lacing the night air. She was on her hands and knees, when she began to experience a very unsettling feeling of being unreal. An elderly well-dressed man in a trilby crouched and asked her if she was alright. Suzi's father was an avid reader of *Lord of the Rings* and the picture on the back of that classic which showed the elderly author, J. R. Tolkien, was immediately recollected by Suzi, because this old gentleman looked exactly like him, and he had such a kind and friendly face.

The man said his name was Peter, and he helped Suzi up and took her to his home on what seems to have been Bold Place. He took great sympathy on Suzi, and let her stay at his little home, where the girl discovered she was in May 1941 – in the midst of the May Blitz. Not long after meeting the man - and the LSD had scrambled all track of time, so its impossible to say *when* this was - Suzi returned from an air-raid shelter with the old man and his sister to see St Luke's

Church ablaze, and the man's sister also seemed quite upset at the news of the death of some actress who had been killed locally by a bomb. After seeing the bodies of two people (one of them headless) and a dog (with its tongue hanging limp) at the site of a bombed house, Suzi suffered a panic attack and ran off, in search of the world she had come from in 1980, and during the attempted flight from an era where she simply didn't belong, Suzi recalled being chased by an abnormally tall ARP warden up Hardman Street. She then had that same frightening sensation of the entire world jolting away from her, and this time she became so dizzy she passed out, and after a strange dream of spiralling diamonds and triangles she found herself on the familiar doorstep of her home on Bedford Street South.

Suzi's Nan went cold when she heard this strange story, for she remembered seeing a so-called "clown girl" on a bomb site near Church Street, and how everyone was making fun of her because of her ridiculous appearance. Susan wondered if she had actually been looking at her future grand-daughter through some timeslip. Susan had occasionally mentioned the clown girl over the years to her daughter and the memory, from forty years back, was now a bit vague. Predictably, most dismissed Suzi's story and three-day absence as the result of some psychedelic trip, but the girl's grandmother recalled that a fairly famous actress had indeed died in the May Blitz, just as Suzi had claimed in her story. Mary Lawson, the 30-year-old stage and film actress, had been killed during an air raid on Bedford Street South on 4 May 1941. Suzi had never heard of this actress, and had not even known St Luke's had been bombed by the Luftwaffe in the Blitz.

Suzi later left the punk scene and today she has a great interest in the paranormal, and particularly in the area of timeslips.

In some of the following chapters you will find more strange stories which suggest that the time-barrier can occasionally be breached...

WILL PROUDLOVE

Many years ago, a man in his fifties with a friendly round face came to one of my booksignings at a tiny shop in Formby and told me the following story. At first I thought he was joking or being satirical, but he was deadly serious, and a few years later, quite a few other people mentioned the strange busker Rob had referred to in this strange tale. Here's the shape of it.

One muggy afternoon in the summer of 1975 Rob Reynolds, the multi instrumentalist one-man-band busker known as "The Undercover Orchestra" strolled into Frank Hessy's music shop on Stanley Street with Mazelle, an introverted marmoset monkey, perched on his shoulder. Rob had come in search of a gimmicky instrument to replace his worn-out wheezy concertina, and was pondering bagpipes, when he saw the answer to his dreams before him. He had to be a student; a man of about twenty sporting a fluffy insubstantial van dyke beard, and he was dressed like a motley jester of old with bells on his red and green hood, and what's more, he had a lute in his hands.

'Forsooth,' the oddball exclaimed to one of Hessy's assistants, 'tis a medieval lute, sirrah!'

'I doubt that, sir, no lutes that old have survived,' the assistant said with a smirk. He fitted the sheep-gut string to the antique-looking instrument and was about to tune it when the "jester" dismissed his efforts with a cry of: 'Go you hence!' and then he tossed a long-defunct silver groat coin at him before hurrying out of the shop, and the assistant caught the old English four-penny coin and growled: 'Hey! Pay with proper money!'

The garishly attired jongleur laughed and bolted out of the shop, and boy could he run. Rob dashed after him with poor Mazelle clinging to his bowler, and the one-man-band caught up with him at Whitechapel. Rob tried to engage in conversation with the outlandish musician but found it hard to understand him. He spoke another language, and one Rob had never heard before.'

'Cut bene winds you apple-john!' the lutenist suddenly cried at Rob, who returned a puzzled look. 'Plainesse, sirrah!' he went on, tuning the lute, 'Speak properly and truly!'

'That's rich coming from you,' Rob giggled, 'you talk double-dutch. Why the act?'

'By Cacodaemon!' the bizarre busker shrieked and made a fist and a gesture which suggested he'd like to punch Rob in the face, 'Verily thou art a dim onion-eyed jolthead! Tis no act! Should I converse with him instead?' the enigmatic entertainer pointed to Mazelle on Rob's shoulder, and the little monkey hid his shy face behind his tiny hand.

Rob had a weird feeling about this guy; he was either keeping the act up – or it wasn't an act at all and he was something truly weird and archaic. He stuck with the mysterious musician and somehow the two men partially overcame the language barrier by using short sentences and gesturing. The pied player's name was Will Proudlove, and he said, rather vaguely, that he had come here through the "Whirligig" because he was wanted for a murder he did not commit. He lived in an elaborate tree house no one could see in a 'special oak'.

'When were you born, Will?' Rob asked, suspiciously, and the answer shook him: April 1550.

'That's a long time ago,' Rob quickly calculated that it was in fact, 425 years ago, and he told Mr Proudlove this and raised his eyebrows as if he thought the poet-singer was going to tell him he was really 22 and from somewhere down south, but Will Proudlove returned a worried stare, and said: ''Pon my honour, what I have told you is true, Robert, but thou must keep it secret.'

'Fine, I won't breathe a word of it to anyone, and they'd lock me up if I did!' Rob replied with a shrug.

Will and Rob teamed up as an act called Now And Then, and busked all over the city, and each evening Will would sneak off to his home, but one foggy night Rob and his monkey followed the eccentric on a bike – as far as Calderstones. There, Will climbed the oldest tree in Liverpool: the 1,000-year-old Allerton Oak, and vanished completely in the ancient branches. Now Rob believed his musical friend's incredible claim, but knew no one would ever believe what he had just seen, and he had no wish to reveal Will Proudlove's secret anyway, nor did he quiz the timeslipped minstrel about the nature of the "Whirligig" or his other life in the Elizabethan era.

Now And Then busked outside the Augustus John pub on the University Campus near Brownlow Hill one day when Will fell madly in love with a passing willowy blonde lecturer named Magda, and one day he accosted her and performed a lute song he had written about her called 'Blonde Sunshine' but ironically, as flattered as Magda was for Will's strange song, she fell for Rob instead, and this caused some friction and Will almost challenged him to a "dagger duel". Magda wanted to know who Will was and where he was from and why he spoke in such an odd way, and eventually, with great reluctance, Rob let her in on the secret, and begged her to tell no one what he had told her but Magda laughed at the explanation and said it was ridiculous. Rob intended to go on the talent show *New Faces* with Will, but the troubadour fell seriously ill one day, and became so weak with a fever, he had to be helped up the Allerton Oak by Rob. Then Rob himself fell ill and a doctor diagnosed a form of TB he had not seen for many years, and he treated it successfully with a course of streptomycin. Rob went to Calderstones Park everyday on the lookout for his outlandish but lovable friend, and he even tried to climb the branches of the Allerton Oak, wondering if he could perhaps access the Whirligig and visit his absent friend's time, but nothing happened, and a park ranger chased Rob from the delicate old tree, warning him that the branches were prone to break because of their great age. Rob went into a depression for a while, and Magda began to visit the park with him when she could, and she saw how sad her lover was. 'Where can he be?' Rob asked her, and he actually had a tear in his eye, the first one he had ever shed for a man.

'Rob, I believe you now,' Magda told her boyfriend with a sincere look in her green eyes.

'You do?' Rob was taken aback by his girl's newfound faith.

She nodded and kissed him. 'I don't know how a person can come from some other time by climbing up or down a tree, but when you think of it, what do we really know about this universe?'

'That's so true.' Rob sighed and hugged her and he looked over her shoulder at the tree, and recalled a line from the song Will had sung in vain to Magda:

I love a girl not yet born, four centuries from now
See the sunshine of her hair, green eyes all aglow
Magda, will thou marry, a minstrel of long ago?

Will Proudlove was never seen again. In a bygone age that had no antibiotics, did he die from his illness or did the Whirligig – whatever it was – no longer allow him to venture into our time? We'll probably never know.

LOVE BEYOND DEATH

The relentless river of time eventually washes away everything, including our memories, and eventually our bodies and all of our belongings, and the only permanent thing in our life is, ironically, change, but in all of the years I have spent investigating ghosts and the supernatural, I would say the bond of love often remains, long after a person has physically left this life, and this is especially so with parents and grandparents. Why love outlasts life is unknown, but love is a powerful emotion, and perhaps, long after we have passed on, some imprint of it is left behind. Again and again I have noticed the post-death bond of love that exists between grandparent and grandchild, and how the love of Nan and Grand-dad transcends the grave itself, and this is the subject of the following true story.

In March 2010, a 19-year-old girl we shall call Natalie was deserted by her 22-year-old partner, Adam. Natalie was three months pregnant at the time and naturally heartbroken at Adam's departure. She was left alone in her flat in Huyton, and the teenaged mum-to-be soon lost her confidence. All of her friends were in relationships and many of them were married. Natalie tried to look for work but was turned down for every job she applied for, but still she visited the Job Centre almost every day, and one day as she returned from a job interview in Aintree, she saw her former partner Adam driving past in a new car with an unknown blonde and Natalie's heart broke in two. She came to a bus stop, and here she was counting change in her hand as she carried the baby of the man who had coldly driven past her as if she wasn't there. She felt so stupid; why had she ever believed he had loved her? By the time the bus came she was almost in tears. When she got home, Natalie texted her three closest friends, and not one replied, except for Keeley, and she responded two hours later. Natalie asked her if she wanted to come over 'for a gab' but Keeley said she wasn't well. Things picked up for a while when Natalie gave birth to her son David, because her mother bought the baby clothes and visited for the first few months, but after that Natalie's mother got a new job miles away and was always too tired to call around every day. Natalie's landlord then put the rent up and the girl had to move to an affordable one-bedroom flat in Kirkby, and as chance would have it, this flat was close to the place where the girl's Nan used to live ten years before. Her Nan had sadly passed away four years ago when Natalie was fifteen, and she had been close to her Nan and her grandmother had adored her. One wintry night in 2011, Natalie was sitting with the baby on her knee, rubbing his back to get his wind up, and she felt so low. She had only £3 left in the electric meter and sat in a semi-darkened living room in front of a miserable two-bar electric fire. She was not thinking of anything supernatural at the time – her mind was far too concerned with worldly affairs and she was occupied with finding ways to get out of the rut she believed she was in. Around 9pm, David, the baby, began to smile and looked at something above the electric fire. He made grabbing motions to whatever he could see, and this spooked Natalie a bit. 'What is it, babe?' she asked her son, and he giggled and said something that sounded like "nan".

At first, Natalie thought someone was shining a laser pointer through her window, because she saw a point of light out the corner of her eye, but then this light grew into what seemed like a huge luminous orb made of golden light, about five feet off the ground, and all of a sudden, in the centre of this ball of soft light, Natalie saw the face of her late Nan appear. The baby kicked his legs and laughed at this manifestation. Natalie was understandably a bit scared, but became more curious than frightened.

In her mind, the girl clearly heard a voice she had not heard since she was fifteen, and yet it was a voice she knew so well; she knew its cadence and timbre and right away it brought so many memories flooding back.

'Hiya Nat, don't be scared,' the voice in her head said.

'Nan, is that you?' the stunned girl gasped.

'Yes love,' came the reply, 'it's me but I can't stay long, but I had to come and see you because you look so down, and we're all worried about you over here, and little David.' And as this was communicated, Natalie saw the face smile and a tear seemed to roll from her Nan's left eye. Natalie could hardly talk because her throat had closed up with sorrow. She couldn't believe her Nan had come back to talk to her.

'I – I,' Natalie struggled to speak through her tears and her choked-up throat, 'I never thought I'd ever see you again, Nan.'

'Ah, don't be daft, love,' the girl's Nan said in a very reassuring voice, 'I'm with you everywhere you go, and your Auntie Lyn. Now, listen love, you can't be sitting in like this every night. I want you to start going out so you can meet someone to look after you. Start going out. I've got to go now Nat, give my love to your mum.'

And the golden light faded. David started crying. Natalie sobbed and rocked him, and then she got up and turned on the light and looked at the spot in mid-air where she had just seen her lovely Nan's face. 'Am I going mad? Or did I really see what I just saw? David saw her too'. Natalie had this argument with herself and then she calmed David down and picked up her mobile and was about to tell her mum what had just happened, but thought her mother would probably think she was losing the plot. On the following day, though, Natalie's mother called her, and Natalie decided to tell her what had happened.

'You saw your Nan in a light?' her mother sounded sceptical just posing that question; Natalie could plainly hear the cynicism in her voice.

'Mam, I know it sounds mad, but I swear on David's life – '

'Oh, don't say stupid things like that, Nat, God…' her mother replied.

Natalie butted in. 'That proves I'm not lying mum, I saw me Nan last night and she told me to start going out so that I'll meet someone.'

The voice of Nat's mum went up an octave. 'And who's gonna mind the baby if you start going out? I'm knackered working all the hours God sends. And where are you going to get money from to start going out on the town, eh? Come into the real world Nat.'

'I'm only telling you what me Nan said, Mam; you think I'm making this up!'

'Nat, you've been half asleep, and you've dreamt about your Nan because she used to live round there near Tower Hill – '

'Mam, can I just get a word in edgeways please? I've just remembered something. I am sure me Nan said she was with me everywhere I go – and so was Auntie Lyn. Has Auntie Lyn died?'

'What?' the girl's mother laughed. 'She'll outlive everyone. Course she's still alive, but as you know I haven't talked to my sister for years after what she did – '

'Mum, don't start going into all that; all I want to know is: is Auntie Lyn still alive?'

'Oh I'm going,' Natalie's mother announced grouchily, 'you're turning into one of those cranky mediums, you wanna get a grip!'

And she hung up. But an hour later Natalie's mobile rang, and her mum said: 'She's dead,' and her voice sounded flat and barely audible.

'Who's dead?' Natalie asked, and her mother told her as she cried. Her sister – Natalie's auntie – Lyn, had died from pneumonia after undergoing a heart operation three months back, but because of the long-lasting feud between Lyn and Natalie's mum, Lyn's husband had coldly kept the news of the death secret. Although this was tragic news, it seemed to vindicate what the ghost of Natalie's Nan had said, that she and Lyn were watching over Natalie.

Then something very bizarre took place. Natalie left her purse in a supermarket in Huyton one afternoon, and panicked once she realised it had been mislaid, but some kind soul posted the purse to her, and inside that purse was seventy pounds in crisp new notes. Natalie only had twelve quid in that purse when she lost it. She decided it was a sign, and took her Nan's advice. Natalie got her friend Keeley to mind the baby, and she went out for the night, and although it felt strange, being out alone, it was also a bit liberating to Natalie. She met a student named Ben in a pub in Mathew Street that night, and he was not like the usual predatory fellahs Natalie was accustomed to. Ben was very generous and caring and never laid a finger on Natalie or looked at her in a lewd way. He offered to pay for a hackney to take her home safely that night but she declined. She accepted his phone number, and they began seeing one another. Ben said he felt he had known Natalie all of his life, and she felt the same. Ben accepted David as if he was his own son, and he and Natalie are now engaged, and live together in Woolton, and Natalie believes this newfound happiness is all down to her beloved Nan.

BROOMSTICKS OVER

BIRKENHEAD

You may naturally associate the world of the occult - ghosts, vampires witches, doppelgangers and the sort – with ink-black wintry nights and leafless gnarled branches silhouetted against the waning skull of the moon, but some of the strangest and spookiest incidents I have researched have taken place in broad daylight at the height of summer. Meeting a phantom in the dead of night can be terrifying of course, but high noon courage can also desert you just as easily in the light of day in the midst of a heatwave, as it did for two painters one infernal June day in 1982. Insidious heat crept into the country at the end of May that year and bubbled road tar and inflamed tempers. A hosepipe ban was already being mooted by the authorities by early June, when a perspiring 17-year-old apprentice decorator named Dominic Bassett took off his paint-spattered teeshirt on the roof of an office building in one of the higher parts of Birkenhead, not that far from Bidston Hill. 'You get even hotter when you take clothes off in weather like this, you know?' the great master to the apprentice, 63-year-old Eric Hartigan, warned Dominic.

'How can you get *hotter* by taking your shirt off?' Dominic asked with an annoyed look, and Eric told him how the Arabs in the desert wore 'more clobber to keep the sun off' and then he started to go on about how the English conquered the world and built an Empire in India and other hot places by drinking piping-hot tea. 'You've heard of that old song about mad dogs and Englishmen going out in the midday sun, haven't you lad? That was the secret of the British Empire – overcoming heat by keeping cool and sippin' tea. The yanks drink coffee, see, and that's known to make you hotter and it also irritates the throat.'

Dominic raised a sarcastic eyebrow and wiped the sweat from his forehead with his crumpled up teeshirt. 'You haven't got heatstroke have ya, Eric?' he asked with a lopsided grin.

Eric ignored the playful insult and began to talk about the film *Laurence of Arabia* but something strange cut the chit-chat short. The sounds of distant shrieks – female shrieks – and girly laughter came from somewhere up in the burning blue sky. The painters both looked up and the ultraviolet stung their eyes.

'That came from up there!' Dominic placed his hand over his eyes as if he was saluting and saw only a gliding gull passing by high above.

Eric said the sound had come from the street but was known to 'bounce off hot air' like a mirror on days like this, but Dominic disregarded this pseudo-fact and kept watch on the acres of blue sky. Female screams pierced the air again, followed by melodic laughter – and this time it came from behind the painters. They both turned and looked out towards a Liverpool skyline ghosted by the haze of the heatwave and a light wind gently wafted up an aroma of tar and a scent of petrol fumes and Mersey salt, and there in the distance, some four hundred yards up in the Alice-blue sky were three coloured dots. They looked like three sprinkles off an ice cream at that range.

'Balloons,' Eric muttered, but the superior eyesight of youth could plainly see three people, and Dominic shook his head. 'Nah, its three girls!'

The hay fever began to water Dominic's eyes and he sniffled and rubbed them and looked again and the three girls moved off towards the north, until they were specks over the river. Dominic estimated the eerie flying people were heading towards Bootle. Then they were gone. Eric stuck to the balloons explanation but a sneezing Dominic knew what he had seen, but Eric then blamed the lad's hay fever, and said it was well known that allergies made some people see floaters – microscopic black spots that swum around in the liquid of the eyeball.

About ten minutes later the men had managed to resume painting. Eric climbed a ladder and then Dominic felt paint trickling onto his head. 'Eric!' he yelled, and stepped back and looked up - and he saw his workmate gazing at something in a daze with paint dripping off the bristles off his brush. This time the three levitating women were almost near enough to touch as they flew by, and Eric swore in shock.

'Jesus effing Christ! Look at that!' Eric cried out.

The first woman in the formation was a brunette of about thirty sitting side-saddle on a brush, and wore a flowing pinkish dress, and the young blonde lady flying behind her had her hand on the broom-mounted woman's shoulder, as if she was steadying her. The third figure flying closely behind the blonde one was much younger, possibly in her teens, and she was also blonde. All of these females were laughing and giggling and the brunette was screaming and shrieking with laughter as she almost fell off the broom. They were oblivious to the male observers as they flew in the direction of Bidston Hill.

'What are they?' Dominic came up the ladder in an

excited rush, and then he asked: '*How* are they doing it?'

Eric had gone a funny colour and one hand gripped the rung of the ladder and the other one was on his chest. He was gasping for breath.

'You alright Eric?' Dominic asked him, but obviously wasn't that interested in an answer because when Eric said, 'No, I'm having a turn,' the apprentice was still gazing at the three women flying through the summer sky.

'I wish I had a camera now, Eric! Eric?' Eric closed his eyes and almost let go of the ladder as he slipped into unconsciousness, and Dominic somehow managed to ease the painter onto a ledge, and then he went down the ladder and called an ambulance.

Eric was taken to hospital but discharged the same day and taken home. Years later I gave an account of this incident on the Billy Butler Show and was inundated with calls and emails from people of all ages and all walks of life who recalled the 'witch scare' that summer in 1982. The witches – sometimes numbering five or more – were allegedly seen skimming over treetops in Birkenhead Park, and one woman swore she saw two witches on broomsticks land near the windmill on Bidston Hill one moonlit night that year as she walked her dog.

Just who these modern witches were and what coven they belonged to, I do not know, but I suspect someone out there reading this knows the truth.

The idea of someone flying through the air with a brush may seem ridiculous but there have been thousands of reports of levitation over the centuries, right up to modern times. Many years ago when I was a young altar boy, an old priest told me about a certain Father John, a well-known priest at several Catholic churches across Liverpool from the 1950 to the 1970s. Father John was a very simple and, some said, quite naïve man, and he often got into a state of spiritual bliss when he looked at the sun through the coloured stained-glass windows of a church, and sometimes, while he was in this state of mystical ecstasy, he was seen to rise into the air; in other words, he levitated. On one occasion Father John levitated from the pulpit after a particularly dramatic sermon one Sunday, and this amazing incident was witnessed by many churchgoers and entered into local legend. It was said that he taught children how to fly too, often holding their hands in the church garden, but there were complaints from the parents of the children and from other priests (but never from the excited children themselves). The church authorities therefore moved this priest to other parishes when the rumours about his levitation started to circulate. The priest angered the church fathers by telling the curious that anyone could be taught how to fly and that levitation was just a frame of mind, and he likened it to the feeling a child has when he or she first rides a bike without stabiliser wheels. In the end, Father John was unfairly seen as an embarrassment to the Church and he was transferred to a remote parish in Ireland. In these days of dwindling church attendances I imagine the places of worship would be packed if we had priests who could teach the congregation how to fly! Ironically there are an astounding 230 Catholic saints on record who were alleged to have the talent of levitation, and there are a lot of flying nuns on record too, the most well known being Arabian Carmelite, Sister Mary, who often used a branch (shades of the witch's broomstick and the Indian fakir's staff) to stabilise herself in flight.

THE BODY IN THE OVEN

In August 1948, The Right Honourable Sir Stafford Cripps, the prominent Labour politician, visited Liverpool to inspect the Dunlop rubber factory at Speke, and after the inspection he had luncheon with Lady Cripps at the world-famous Adelphi Hotel down in Lime Street. Behind the scenes, the chef and his assistant and all of the hotel kitchen staff were run off their feet that day because of the banquet that was put on for Sir Stafford, his entourage and the local bigwigs of local government, but at one point the frenetic activity in the kitchen came to an abrupt halt because of Hermann Grundgen, a German baker who was understood to have had been living in Britain since the 1920s. Hermann opened the huge door of the hotel's bread oven and looked in horror; before him he saw a pair of large bare feet! Someone was lying on the long tray where the bread and baked cakes should have been. It was obviously impossible but here it was, a body. Hermann slammed the steel door hard and gazed at Tommy Mercer, one of the kitchen dogsbodies who was charged with cleaning a huge tray in the big marble sink. 'What's up, Adolf?' Tommy asked, seeing that Hermann had suddenly gone very pale.

'Tommy, what do you see in here?' Hermann said, and he held his hand to his mouth as if he was about to throw up. 'Come and look, please.'

'I've got to do these, mate,' Tommy said, scouring the tray in hot water with wire wool. 'Why? What am I supposed to be looking at?'

Hermann opened the oven door again a few inches, and his eyes bulged and he slammed it shut again.

'What the bleedin' hell's wrong?' Tommy asked, leaving the sink and picking up a damp old towel to dry his reddened hands. 'Have you burnt the bread?'

Hermann waited till the humble kitchen worker came over, and then he opened the steel door – and Tommy Mercer gazed with a hybrid look of horror and confusion at the bare soles of someone's feet. He swore and then said, 'Get him out of there you stupid kraut!'

The German backed away, trembling, and said, 'No, no, I can't! Oh Got! Oh Got!'

'Who the friggin' hell is he? Have you killed someone?' Tommy grimaced and tried to grab the feet but they were hot, and he turned to Hermann, who had now almost backed into a pastry chef. 'Turn the bastard gas off you stupid German burke!'

Hermann shook his head and almost seemed delirious. His eyes rolled back into his head as if he was having some fit, and he staggered in a drunken manner towards a side door and pushed against it. He went through that door and was never seen again. Tommy panicked and went to see another kitchen worker named Johnson, and then the two men went to see the assistant chef, and when Tommy told him about the feet sticking out of the oven, he was shouted at and pushed aside, because his words were not taken serious. Tommy and his colleague went to see the hotel manager and told him about the body in the oven and he sensed that the men looked afraid and knew they were not the joking type, especially on such a busy and chaotic day as this with such a dignitary visiting. However, when the hotel manager got to the oven, he saw it contained nothing but overdone bread and scones, and he told Tommy and his workmate off. The mystery was never cleared up, but many years later, when the full horror of the Holocaust became more widely known, Tommy happened to see a shocking photograph of one of the 'ovens' in the crematoria in a well-known Nazi concentration camp, and in this photograph there are two members of staff posing besides the oven with its door open to reveal the feet of a Jewish victim who had been gassed, and this oven was capable of incinerating three people at once. Tommy felt physically ill when he saw the photograph, and he wondered if Hermann had in fact been a worker at one of these Nazi death camps who had perhaps put the bodies of gassed men, women and children into the infamous ovens. A search has been made for Hermann Grundgen but as so far been futile, so perhaps he was someone who had somehow fled to Britain after the war, and perhaps he had not lived here since the 1920s as he had claimed. Perhaps his conscience had somehow caught up with him, and he hallucinated the body in the oven, but if that was so, how did two other people share that hallucination?

WHO'S BEEN DOWN YOUR EAR?

Not far from Cooper's Building on Church Street in 1955, there was a suite of claustrophobic offices belonging to a certain unremarkable insurance firm, and in one of those stuffy rooms a fifty-year-old man named George Averly worked. George dealt with every aspect of life, fire, motor accident and general insurance, but of late he had noticed his hearing was getting a little fuzzy, and his boss had picked up on this and advised him to get a hearing aid. George thought he'd never have a chance with Betty Lewes, the blonde secretary (who was a dead ringer for the shapely actress Liz Fraser) if he took to wearing a hearing aid. Now, some strange things have happened in Liverpool café's over the years. For example, in September 1969, one Vladislaw Davydenko staggered into a café on Bold Street and asked for political asylum – and was later granted it. The Ukrainian had stowed away for a fortnight without food on a Russian ship and got off at the docks. He was subsequently allowed to stay here. In that same café in 1955, in the coffee lounge over lunch, George Averly mentioned his hearing problem to his cerebral work colleague Simon Peake, and received some unexpected advice from him: 'Ah, okay, well you've probably heard of the Bates Method of improving eyesight – but there's also a similar technique to increase hearing ability, and Siddhartha Gautama hit on this, basically through meditation and certain physical exercises.'

'Sid who?' George asked, cupping his hand around his ear. 'See what I mean? Only heard you mention his first name.'

Simon Peake sighed. 'Siddhartha Gautama – you know – Buddha?'

'Oh, *him*?' George joked.

Nightly visits to Simon's home for Yantric and audio-meditation lessons ensued, and eventually George could calm down and hear things tenfold, but George pushed the technique too far, and eavesdropped and pried away. He could often hear conversations several rooms away and sometimes opened his office windows and eavesdropped on street conversations that were taking place far below. His boss was very impressed with George's newfound acute hearing, but then *the voice* made its debut one day. 'George, don't be alarmed,' it said, and the insurance agent froze. 'No, you're not hearing things,' it said, 'so calm down. Now, do you want to be very rich?'

George looked about the office, and his palpitating heart sounded even louder than normal of course. No one was there. The disembodied voice said: 'That secretary Betty is waiting for you to sweep her off her feet, but you'll need money, George! Men are more cosmetically attractive when they have lots and lots of money.'

'Who *is* this?' George was now more intrigued than scared, and a reply came.

'Never mind who *I* am – who are *you*? A nobody who could become somebody.'

The voice seemed close to his left ear now, and it told him secrets - like what his boss called him behind his back, and the voice also planted seeds of greed and animosity in his mind. 'I will make you rich and so powerful,' the invisible speaker promised. 'Now,

George, this is just for starters: call the manager of your bank and tell him to wire a thousand a month or you'll tell his wife about his two mistresses in Rhyl and Chester! Tell him their names: Rita and Jean, and mention the clothes line he likes to get tied up with.'

'But that's - blackmail,' George gasped, and the voice laughed and said: 'The word isn't even mentioned in the Bible! He'd blackmail you George, he is a legal extortionist after all if you think about it.'

'Who the hell are you?' George asked.

'The voice of common sense, George,' It said to him, 'Now make that call and stop being a nobody.'

George knew the bank manager's telephone number by heart, and he had been turned down so many times for loans by the pompous ass. George found himself dialling the number when Betty the secretary came into the office, and her eyes bulged – then she screamed and pointed behind George. She was a bit psychic, and fully able to see the demonic figure, which vanished instantly.

George put the receiver down and gazed at her in a daze. 'Can you...*see* that bloody thing, Betty?'

'Yes,' Betty held her face between her hands and was still gazing in horror at the back of George Averly's chair. 'It's gone now – it was horrible. What was it?'

George got up off the chair and looked back, and then he turned to Betty and said, 'Come on, love, let me take you for a drink.'

'What? But we're working – ' Betty said, astonished and a bit nervous at the way George firmly held her hand now.

'Damn work, we won't be missed by any of this lot,' he assured the secretary, and Betty smirked and actually went with him out of the building.

With the help of Simon Peake and a priest, George ended up free of the strange being, but - heaven forbid – one day you might just find yourself in a quiet place, and *you* may hear a whispering voice when the mundane sounds of the day are absent…

MUM IN THE MIRROR

In the early 1970s a 39-year-old man we shall call George lived in the terraced house on Penny Lane he'd been born in. George had had a few ephemeral girlfriends over the years but now felt it was time to settle down with a woman and start a new family before it was too late. Around the time he started making plans to make a determined effort to find a wife, George received a visitor at his home one hot July morning. It was a man in a bowler hat and pinstriped suit who identified himself as a solicitor named James Throckmorton-Peacock, and he tapped his index finger on what looked like the traditional Budget briefcase used by the Chancellor of the Exchequer. 'Sir, I have something to tell you which will be to your advantage.'

'Oh, so it's not a summons or anything?' George asked, eyeing the case anxiously.

'No sir; may I come in?' Mr Throckmorton-Peacock asked.

'Yeah, er, hang on while I stick the dog in the yard,' George went and grabbed his little mongrel dog Billy by its collar and dragged him into the kitchen. He opened the door to the yard and launched the dog outside, then hurried back to the solicitor and invited him into the parlour. The solicitor asked for documented proof of identity and George gave him the rent book and his library card, then found his dog-eared birth certificate in a biscuit tin, and Mr Throckmorton-Peacock explained his visit. 'Your Uncle Magnus, er, Mr Magnus Helmsley, died six months ago in Miami, and left a million dollar trust fund and his mansion – '

'Sweet Jesus!' George felt faint and gripped the arm of the sofa he sat on, 'I've been left a fortune.'

'Well he left it to his cat, actually,' the solicitor said, and George recoiled in horror and said, 'What?'

'But, the cat has since expired, and so, according to a proviso in the will, you are the next in line to have the money, which in our currency amounts to one million, seven-hundred and fifty seven thousand pounds Sterling.'

With the new fortune, George had his teeth fixed, and spent hundreds on clothes, but had a huge fall-out with his brothers because he didn't share his wealth with them. He hit the pubs and clubs and a stunning woman in her mid-twenties named Deborah latched onto him, and it was love at first sight. After just a month of courting they were engaged, but George hadn't told her he was rich yet. He took Deborah to his mother's resting place at Allerton Cemetery and the girl put a bunch of roses on the grave. George had been ten when he lost his mum in the war, in 1942, and he still missed her. 'That was a lovely gesture, Deb, getting' roses for me Mam,' he said, and they kissed. That night as the couple lay in the dark in bed, sweltering because of the summer heat, something landed on them. Deborah screamed and George put the light on. It was a bunch of roses. 'They're like the ones you bought today, for me Mam,' George said, and his eyes looked up at the ceiling.

'Ooer,' was Deborah's reaction to this weird incident.

That morning as George was shaving in the bathroom, he saw a familiar face appear in the shaving mirror: it was his mum, looking exactly as he remembered her in the 1940s. 'Get shut of that girl, son, she's just after your money!' the ghost said, casually adjusting her earring as she gazed in the mirror. And then she was gone. George said nothing to Deborah about the ghost and her message, but that night his fiancée's screams startled him from his sleep. Deborah said she had seen an 'evil-looking' woman at the foot of the bed, glaring at her. The ghostly mother continued to visit each night and in the end, Deborah said she'd had enough and asked George to move house, but George wanted to stay put, and wondered if his mum's accusation about Deborah was true. He tested her by saying he had inherited a fortune but had given it away to an animal charity, and Deborah coldly left him. He later discovered one of his brothers had told Deborah about the inheritance. George later met a shy selfless girl named Ruth who worked in a local cake shop and ended up marrying her, and his mum must have approved of her because there were no further spooky goings-on at the house on Penny Lane.

LOOKING GLASS ALICE

For three years in a row the Fairhurst family of Liverpool enjoyed their annual fortnight's holiday in Blackpool, back in the days before cheap air travel enabled the working classes to sun themselves in Spain and other continental destinations. This was July 1953, and Mr and Mrs Fairhurst and their three children, 15-year-old Donald, 10-year-old Davy and 6-year-old Sue, were looking forward to staying in Mrs Bath's boarding house, where the food was home-baked and hospitality was laid on thick. But when the Fairhursts arrived at the boarding house they were shocked to find it had closed and they were saddened when they were told by a local man that Mrs Bath had recently passed away after a short illness. Mr Fred Fairhurst therefore took his wife Gertrude and the kids on a trek around the streets where they scanned windows advertising affordable lodgings, and as it was July, most of the boarding houses were already full, but Donald Fairhurst spotted a card in the window of a terraced house facing the seafront which read: Large Rooms to Let, Enquire within. And enquire Mr Fairhurst did. The fee wasn't as much as that charged by the late Mrs Bath, but that was because the landlady – a Mrs Rusk – didn't provide any meals, just tea. The house was also ancient and had a musky cell to it, and when Gertrude Fairhurst first set foot in the huge room, which was partitioned with several old Victorian screens, she remarked: 'Fred, there is something very wrong with this room. Let's go somewhere else.'

'I've paid her now,' her husband said, opening the dusty curtains. Beyond the grimy window panes there was a fine view of the sea.

The children badgered their parents immediately after laying down their little suitcases. 'Can we go on the donkey rides mum?' Sue asked, tugging the hem of her mother's dress. 'And then I'll build a sand castle,' she added and waved a little plastic bucket and spade at her smiling father.

'Nah, we're going the penny arcade first, aren't we dad?' Donald said with excitement in his big blue eyes.

'I want to go on the waltzes and the big dipper at the fair, Dad!' Davy pushed at Donald who shoved him back.

'Alright! Pack it in you lot,' said Mr Fairhurst with a smile. 'We're going to get some candy floss, pop and hot dogs and we're going to the beach first!'

When the family returned to the boarding house around five that afternoon they were exhausted from food, sun, sea air and the great times spent on the Golden Mile. They all washed and changed and rested for a while, then went out again around six for a meal at a restaurant near the Tower. They returned back home about 8pm, sapped, and little Susan was put to bed. By nine the other children were sound asleep. Fred and Gertie Fairhurst sat up in bed, talking of the day's highlights and planning where to go tomorrow, when they both saw some brief movement in the old gold-framed mirror on the wall facing. 'What was that?' Mrs Fairhurst said in a low voice, not wishing to wake the children.

'I think it was just a moth,' Fred told her, but seemed uneasy. The couple soon dozed off, but around 3am, Mrs Fairhurst opened her eyes. She couldn't sleep because of the heat. She got up, opened the window a few inches, admitting the cool sea air and blazing moonlight, and then she returned to the bed to lay on the blankets. Her eyes drifted to the mirror, and suddenly, she saw a woman with a very high, old-fashioned collar, peering from the side of it, actually *in* the mirror, as if the looking glass was a window which looked into some dark room. She had hair done up in a little bun and a pallid moonlit face that looked ghastly. Her bony fingers were curled around the side of the frame as she looked over at the sleeping children. This ghost then jumped out of the mirror, and Mrs Fairhurst saw that it had no legs, just a ragged dress of some sort. The thing ran rapidly and silently along the floor on its hands – towards Susan's bed.

Gertie Fairhurst let out a scream and she got up and switched on the light, and her husband and her children Donald and Davy woke up – and all of them saw the spinechilling legless ghost race along the floor on its hands and jump up into the mirror, where she vanished. Needless to say, the traumatised family soon left the boarding house and never returned. Years later, other people reported seeing the same phantom and that room became impossible to let because of its spooky reputation. The ghost is said to be that of "Looking Glass Alice", a woman who was supposedly sawn in half by accident (but probably on purpose) by her magician husband, an adulterous man known as Zirque, in the 1890s. Zirque's behaviour after the alleged gruesome mishap was rather strange, but some thought it was down to shock. As Alice lay bisected at the waist on the floor, with her blood and loose faeces and other bodily fluids oozing out onto the carpet, Zirque cruelly showed her what he had done by placing that gold-framed mirror in front of her as she lay dying, and the shock of seeing her horrific state in the mirror finished her off. In the world of the occult, mirrors are traditionally covered or reversed in rooms where someone is dying in case their departing spirit gets trapped in them, and this seems to have been the case with Looking-Glass Alice. The news of the accidental sawing in half of the magician's wife was hushed up for a while and then when it did get out it was said to have been eclipsed by the more sensational and romantic Toomey murder at Blackpool in the autumn of 1895.

A REAL ZOMBIE PLAGUE

I know from personal experience that the future can be seen in dreams, as I dreamt of things like the Toxteth Riots and other local and international events long before they took place. I think under certain psychological conditions, the mind, once it is set free from its day to day responsibilities - running and coordinating the body and so on – uses unknown senses (mostly during sleep) to gather information from the past and future, and in some cases these manifest as prophetic dreams. As an example of this curious power of the dreaming mind to peek into the future, I will lay before you the following story from a reader named Joan Cassy, who lives in the Formby area. When Joan was about fifteen she started to have the same nightmare over and over, and the dream would start where she was in some sort of park walking along on what seemed to be a late summer evening because it was warm and the sun, on the point of setting over the chimneypots, was casting long shadows on the grass. In the dreams, Joan knew somehow that she was being followed, but was always too afraid to slow down and look back. And then she would see the stretched shadow of a head and shoulders to her left – the shadow cast of her pursuer, and she would then heard a male voice calling to her: 'Come here you little bitch! Hey! Come here!'

Joan would run at this point and the shadow would start to gain on her. She always ran past a large branch which would have made a decent weapon to strike the pursuer with, and this scary dream would always end by the gates of the park with the feeling of two huge hands on her shoulders.

Sometimes a week would go by and the recurring nightmare wouldn't play in her sleeping mind, but sometimes Joan would have the dream night after night, and would always awake in tears. This was in 1970, and Joan tried to recall where the park in the dream was, but she had never seen a place like it. Eventually, after about a year, the recurring bad dream just disturbed her sleep every now and then, but as soon as she would dream she was walking through that park she would be filled with a horrifying feeling of déjà vu, for she knew what was coming.

Five years later, in 1975, at the age of twenty, Joan was a university student, and was sharing a flat in Aigburth with two other female students. One evening around 8pm, in the August of that year, Joan and her two friends went to a party on Princes Avenue in Toxteth. Joan hadn't been there long when she saw someone at the party she had had a blazing row with a few days before. It was another female student named Brenda, who had claimed that Joan had tried to steal her boyfriend off her. Joan knew there'd be trouble if she stayed and pretended to go to the toilet, but instead she sneaked out of the house and headed back to her flat in Aigburth – which necessitated taking a short cut through Sefton Park. The sun was just setting at the time and was throwing long shadows of trees and bushes across the grass, and all of a sudden, Joan felt a chill run down her spine, because she instantly remembered the dream which had haunted her for so long – and she looked around nervously. There wasn't a soul about and it had gone pretty quiet all round. All she could hear was herself panting as she hurried through the park.

And then she heard a familiar but terrifying voice shout: 'Come here you little bitch! Hey! Come here!'

'Oh God!' Joan yelped and tried to run off, but she could hear a gruff voice saying something unintelligible as the man behind her gave chase, and Joan looked down to her left – and saw the shadow of the chaser – his head and shoulders.

'Help!' she screamed, 'Murder! Help!'

'Shut up you fu –' the voice was saying, when Joan looked down, expecting to see the branch of a tree that was always there in the recurring dreams.

And there it was, a branch partly stripped of its smaller branches, perhaps by some minor vandal. It was about five feet long and pretty thick at one end, and looked a bit heavy too. But Joan stopped and bent down and picked it up. She turned and saw a male of about twenty to twenty-five with long sandy-brown hair and he wore spectacles. He was dressed in a denim jacket and black flared pants, and on his feet he wore dark brown boots of the type Joan had seen in the Army and Navy Stores on Ranelagh Street.

The spectacled attacker looked furious at the branch in Joan's hands as she stood there, ready to wallop him with it.

'You hit me with that you bitch and I'll slit your throat!' the unknown would-be assailant threatened, and he reached into a breast pocket in his denim jacket and produced a flick knife with an orange handle. He pressed the button in the handle and a knife blade, about five inches in length, shot out.

Joan swung the branch at the armed attacker and its

broadest end hit the man so hard, his glasses flew off and landed about six feet behind him. Joan had a strange reaction to fear sometimes, and this was involuntary laughter. When she had seen her aunt knocked down and killed in front of her when she was seven, the girl had burst into laughter, and this is not an uncommon abreaction to shock and fear in certain people. On this occasion, Joan started to laugh, but tears came flooding from her eyes as she did. The man seemed stunned by both the strike against his forehead and the way his intended victim was now giggling. He swore and lunged forward, but Joan thrust the end of the branch forward and a sharp part of it, where it had been torn from a tree, went into the man's left eye, and blood issued from that eye upon impact. The man screamed, and this made Joan laugh even louder, but she also wet her self, and then she began to cry – and laugh – alternately, as the man tried to run off with his hand over his damaged eye.

Joan chased him, and this time she lifted the branch, and brought it down on the back of his head, and he fell to his knees and then fell on his face, and his left leg began to kick, as if he was having a fit. Joan struck his backside with the branch, and then, for some reason probably born out of intense fear of what the man would do to her if he recovered, Joan knelt down and bit the man's left ear – hard. He was obviously out cold because he didn't react or cry out, and Joan felt her teeth meet as she must have almost bit off a great part of his ear.

Then she hit him repeatedly with her little fists on his head as she saw blood pour from the partly severed ear, and she suddenly tasted the salty blood on her tongue and spat it at out on him. She got to her feet, and by now the nervous laughter had turned to loud sobbing, and she ran off, still spitting out the awful taste of the blood of a man who had probably intended to rape her. She got back to the flat and bolted the door, and then she gargled with water straight from the tap in the bathroom and brushed her teeth over and over to get the taste of blood from her mouth. The girl sat rocking back and forth by the window with the lights out, wondering if the attacker had followed her, and was only to glad when her two flatmates returned from the party at 1.40am. When she told them what had happened, they urged her to go to the police, but Joan believed she might have killed the man and started to cry again. On the following morning, Joan and her two friends, plus a male student friend named Jimmy, went to the lonely spot in Sefton Park, where Joan expected to see the body of her attacker, but there was no trace of him. Three days after this, the most extraordinary and chilling coincidence took place. Joan went down to collect the mail from the communal hall – and when she looked up, she saw the face of the attacker looking through the narrow windows of the front door. He had a bandage on his left ear and a plaster on his forehead, and a nasty gash under his eye. His eyes widened as he recognised Joan, and as she screamed, he fled from the front step of the house, and a resident, a man in his fifties named Mr Warner, came out a nearby flat and asked what was wrong, and Joan said: 'A man who attacked me in the park was just there! Looking through the window!'

'What?' Mr Warner went to open the door to see if

anyone was there but Joan cried 'No! Don't open the door, please!'

'I'm expecting a young man to move into my flat – I'm leaving you see. It wasn't him was it?' Warner asked. Then he said: 'Did he have glasses?'

'Yes!' Joan replied, and her hand covered her mouth as she gazed in horror at the door.

Warner squinted and recalled what he knew about the prospective tenant. 'He said his name was Smith, and he phoned me yesterday from a call box, so I don't have his number, and he said he was going to bring references with him, and a fortnight's rent as well.'

Joan lived in mortal fear of Mr Smith's return to the house but thankfully she never set eyes on him again, and Smith – if that was his real name – probably kept well out of her way.

Just why Joan had dreamt of the attack on a recurring basis some five years before is a mystery, but it's possible that something, somewhere was trying to prepare her for what could have turned out as a rape and even a murder, by showing her that branch lying on the ground as a potential weapon. That's a possibility, but some dreams of the future which people experience don't seem to allow you to change that future. In 2005, a Childwall woman named Fiona Godwin emailed me to tell how she had had a number of dystopian dreams about the future, and what's more, Mrs Godwin had written to me many years ago to tell me of two dreams that subsequently came true, so she has a good track record for predicting the future via her dreams as far as I can gauge. On the previous occasions she told me how she had seen the unmistakable aircraft Concorde on fire, and how she dreamt of three screaming children inside the supersonic jetliner before it exploded. I even mentioned this dream on air, and of course, a few years later, on 25 July 2000, a Concorde took off from Charles De Gaulle International Airport near Paris, bound for John F Kennedy International Airport, New York City, with 49 men, 47 women and *three children* on board, as well as nine crew members. The plane had been overloaded well above its maximum weight takeoff safety level – and no one had inspected the runway at the French airport prior to take off; had they done so they would have found a strip of titanium-alloy metal that had come off a Continental Airlines DC 10 earlier on, and this was the strip that hit one of the Concorde's tyres as it took off, and the results were nothing short of catastrophic. The tyre was ruptured by the strip and exploded, sending a chunk of tyre debris weighing almost ten pounds into the undercarriage at a speed of about 310 mph, and upon impact the shockwave ruptured a fuel tank in the plane at its weakest point. At this point, the airliner was unable to land again and so the pilot couldn't abort the flight because he would have needed at least three kilometres of runway, and Concorde only had two kilometres ahead of it. From that moment everyone on board was doomed, all because of a strip of metal which measured just 17 inches in length. People for miles around could see the distinctive triangular-shaped plane with a massive plume of flames trailing it, and the Concorde lost airspeed and altitude quickly as its wing disintegrated with the heat. It then crashed into the Hôtelissimo Les Relais Bleus Hotel close to the airport, killing four people there and critically injuring a fifth. Fiona Godwin went numb with shock when she saw the Newsflash about the Concorde crash on her TV. Her nightmare had become reality. Seventeen years before, Fiona had dreamt that two teenagers in the Whiston area named Stephen and Tom had been horrifically killed by a train as the two lads walked along a train line near Dragon Lane. Fiona was just fifteen at the time, and told her mother of the vivid and terrifying dream. Her mum said it was nothing but a nightmare. But on Monday, May 2 1983, Fiona's nightmare came true when the two teens, from Huyton and Mosscroft in Kirkby, walked along a train line after the motorcycle they'd been travelling on broke down. As in Fiona's graphic dream, there was a heavy rainfall at the time and the two lads didn't hear the train as it thundered towards them from behind, killing the instantly. Fiona has had two chilling dreams that have not come to pass yet, and hopefully they never will. The first one was reported to me in 2002. Fiona dozed off in her armchair one evening and had a strange dream about a massive crowd which had gathered on the plateau outside of St George's Hall on Lime Street. Fiona was trying to get through the crowd, and saw that the people were staging some sort of protest, but the protesters ranged in age from what looked like 12-year-olds to people of pensionable age, and she saw that many of them were toting placards which features some strange words and slogans, such as STOP RATIONING, FEED THE PEOPLE, and WE WANT FOOD NOT WAR. Some of the children holding these boards had shaven heads and looked very emaciated and a few looked as if they were seriously ill, with heavy dark circles around their bulging eyes. As Fiona fought to get through this vast mob, she heard something that sounded like machine-gun fire, and when she turned, she saw soldiers on top of armoured vehicles outside the Empire Theatre, and they were wearing gas masks of some sort, and they were also firing what must have been machine guns into the crowds. The multitudes on the plateau went into retreat from the gun fire and caused a massive crush which left Fiona immobile and fighting for oxygen. The screams were terrible as the gunfire got nearer, and then Fiona woke up in the armchair, immensely relieved that it had just been a dream, but that weird nightmare was replayed in her head twice that night when she went to bed, Fiona just knew these dreams were not the usual ones, but some sort of premonition of a future event. In recent years of course, we have seen the rise of the food bank here in the UK, where free food is meted out to the low paid and those on inadequate benefits. These food banks, which are undoubtedly the result of Draconian Government welfare reforms, are like something from a past Dickensian age, and its surreal seeing them in one of the richest and supposedly most civilized countries on earth. Perhaps Fiona's nightmare about the machine-gunning of people rallying to be fed is not too far away down the timeline. Another recurring nightmare Fiona has had seems to concern a shocking future plague which turns people in zombie-like beings, and this dream is striking because it is apparently in agreement with another reader who had a similar nightmare in Australia some years before. But first let us look at Fiona's recurring dream of an apocalyptic plague of some sort. One howling night in January 2010, Fiona Godwin got into bed and immediately fell fast asleep. Not long afterwards she found herself in the midst of a disturbing lucid dream. She was on Church Street, and as she walked toward the shopping arcade Keys Court, which leads to the Liverpool One complex, she noticed that several people passing by were pulling bizarre faces, and seemed to be subject to exaggerated facial tics. Two worried young ladies of about twenty-something were looking at a woman in her late forties who, Fiona felt, was their mother, and she was not only pulling a peculiar face, the woman's eyes were almost white, as if they had rolled back. But then Fiona noticed something else. When the woman opened her mouth and gave a bloodcurdling grin, her teeth were not horizontal, but tilted by about forty degrees, and the slanting upper and lower teeth looked ghastly. This woman, afflicted by some disfiguring condition, was leaning on the window of a well-known natural beauty and skin products store. Fiona hurried on, but as she got further into Liverpool One, she saw more and more of these people – children, teenagers, middle-aged men and women, and people in their seventies, all pulling the same creepy faces and exhibiting the same nervous tics. All of them had the white eyes and the teeth at tilted angles. Then Fiona bumped into a smartly-dressed man of about twenty-five with a smart buzz-cut hairstyle and tanned, healthy complexion – but his eyes were white, and Fiona could just see the bottoms of his irises. He opened his mouth and made awful guttural sounds as if he was finding it hard to speak, and when Fiona saw his mouth, she realised why he couldn't talk; the man's teeth were slowly turning, so the front teeth were moving backwards with a slow tilting motion as his bottom teeth seemed to become longer as they were pushed up from the gum-line. It was quite extraordinary yet frightening to watch, and Fiona could see some sort of whitish yellow pus rolling from the sides of the mouth onto the unfortunate young man's lips. The man grabbed Fiona by the lapel of her jacket, and would not let go as he made a choking sound. His teeth rolled further back, and Fiona, being unable to loosen the afflicted man's powerful grip, slipped out of her coat and ran off further into the shopping centre. All around her she noticed more and more of these people, all of them struck down by this strange illness or condition – or whatever it was. Some of the victims of what was perhaps some infection were attended by worried relatives, but some of the sufferers were wandering blindly along, some feeling their way along windows with their hands on the panes with those eerie white eyes. Fiona asked a man what was wrong with these people and he said, 'It's got to stop, but they won't do anything about it, and they keep saying its nothing to be worried about.'

'I don't understand,' Fiona said, 'are they ill?'

'The Government is trying to sweep it under the carpet but...' the man stopped talking, and suddenly, a look of absolute horror crossed his eyes. He moved his lips like someone trying to talk with a mouthful of food.

'Are you okay?' Fiona asked the man, but backed away slightly, for she had a growing suspicion that this man had now succumbed to the mysterious infection.

And sure enough, the man's eyes rolled back, presenting the whites of his eyeballs, and when he opened his mouth, Fiona could see his slightly off-white teeth tilting backwards and simultaneously sideways slightly, as if his teeth were turning on some skew-whiff axis. The motion must have pushed his tongue into a confined space, making routine speech impossible. The man seemed to freak out, and his hands shot towards a terrified Fiona, but she evaded their grasp and ran off in terror. She then woke up with a start and looked at the clock. She had only been asleep about fifteen minutes. She told her husband Gareth about the realistic nightmare and how she felt it was a portent of a plague of some sort, but Gareth mumbled, 'You and your dreams,' without even opening his eyes. It was hard to put into words but Fiona knew that this was a prophetic dream, because such nightmares had a distinct psychological 'flavour' or defined mood to them, and this really worried Fiona. She read a book and tried to forget about the upsetting sleep vision. Three nights later, there was a petrifying sequel to the nightmare. In the dream she was at the wheel of an unfamiliar car, and was coming down Brownlow Hill. The city centre was pure pandemonium and where Lewis's once existed there was some other store, and a single-decker bus was sticking out of a shattered and blackened shop-front window there. People were standing and lying all around, and all of them were pulling the same type of faces Fiona had seen in her last dream, and only then did she realise that she was dreaming and that this nightmare was some sort of continuation of the last one. Fiona wanted to wake up but didn't know how to, and she was travelling so fast, her thinking distance was non existent, and she tried to brake as she tackled the corner from Renshaw Street into Ranelagh Street by MacDonalds, but the side of the car not only sheared its sides on the curvature of the railings in that corner, she also ran over a few of the bodies lying there, and felt the bones crush beneath the wheels of the car. As she slowed down upon reaching that stretch of Ranelagh Street near to Central Station, Fiona saw to her horror that the road was blocked with buses which looked as if they had run into one another, and clouds of bluish smoke obscured her view of Hanover Street. She drove around the crashed buses and turned right onto Church Street, so she was now driving along a pedestrianized street. Here she was greeted by the same awful sight: people blundering into one another and walking blindly into the plate glass fronts of the shops. Fiona felt so afraid, not only because she could not wake up, but because of the zombie-like behaviour of the public. 'What has happened?' she asked herself over and over. She pulled up on Lord Street and found this street deserted. She looked at the strange car she had driven and shuddered at the splashes of blood around the tyres and front registration plate; the mingled blood from the people she had accidentally driven over. She felt sick and drained as she turned away. She walked along Lord Street towards Derby Square and she could hear what sounded like a distant tumult of voices. To her it sounded like the cheering crowd at a football match, heard from about a quarter of a mile away. When Fiona reached James Street, she could see the multicoloured specks of what seemed like thousands of people down at the Pier head, and they seemed to be fighting to get into the water. Fiona felt hypnotically drawn to the tumultuous crowds down there, and she walked trancelike in their direction, but upon reaching the Strand and Goree, she beheld a surreal and fearsome sight. To the left of the multitudes fighting to get into the river, Fiona could clearly see two enormous jet airliners lying embedded in the sandbanks of the Mersey. One was clearly an EasyJet Airbus type of plane in its orange and white livery, and the other plane, which lay with its tail fin slightly higher in the air than the other craft, could not be identified by Fiona. The planes looked as if they had just crashed into the Mersey but there was no sign of life anywhere near them. The spectacle was so dreamlike, especially with the crowds fighting and crushing into one another to get into the river. Fiona had the unaccountable feeling that water somehow inhibited the appalling 'plague'. She woke with a start and there was a sharp intake of breath as she found herself lying on her back. She shook Gareth awake and he was furious and threatened to divorce Fiona over her 'unreasonable behaviour'. She sobbed and curled up into a ball and only then did he have sympathy for his wife. He hadn't meant what he had said about divorce, he had just said that because he hadn't had much sleep. The same dreams presented themselves almost every night, and always, Fiona would wake up either in a sweat or with a pounding heart and an inability to breathe. After several months, the dreams eventually became less frequent and nowadays Fiona seems to have one of the distinctive recurring nightmares about once every six months. And now for an intriguing addendum to this account of futuristic nightmares; in 2003, an Australian woman named Meg, who is married to an expatriate Liverpool man named Owen, emailed me to tell me of a series of strange dreams she had been having which concerned both her hometown of Sydney and also Liverpool, and these realistic and terrifying nightmares concerned a breakdown of law and order because people were infected with a disease which disfigured their faces – *especially the mouth* – and left victims as sickening shells of their former selves. This was years before television series about zombies such as *The Walking Dead* had hit our screens and Meg certainly wasn't a horror buff, and she never watched any horror films at all. Unlike most nightmares, there seemed to be a coherent chronologically ordered background to the events Meg was dreaming of, and each time she'd have these graphic dreams they'd be a continuation of the previous nightmare. From what she could gather, something had landed on earth and caused a plague of some sort, and for some reason, the infection could only be cured or alleviated by immersing the head in water for as long as possible. In Meg's dreams, people were storming swimming pools and public baths, and jumping into rivers to try and cure themselves of this sinister infection, and many people were being crushed to death in the water as a result. In one harrowing dream, Meg managed to pull a little girl from a crush of people at the Entrance Ocean Baths in New South Wales, a swimming bath she had never seen before in her waking life, but one which she later recognised during a visit to a relative a few years later. In the dream, the little girl's mouth had become inflamed and her rows of teeth had become twisted somehow, and the effect of this twisted smile made the child look macabre and sinister.

Perhaps these dreams of an apparent global plague are just rooted in anxieties about modern health, for we live in a frightening world where the human race is constantly at war with deadly viruses, be they AIDS, HIV, SARS (Severe Acute Respiratory Syndrome), Avian Flu (H5N1), or the legion of "superbugs" that are resistant to the most powerful antibiotics. But I suspect that the lucid dreams of two women living thousands of miles apart, who do not know one another, may be stark warnings from a possible future, and the way the world is going - spending billions on military technology when it should be financing research into cures for cancer and other diseases - we may one day see the advent of a virus that will cause hell on earth, and I think this will be sooner rather than later. Incidentally, a controversial document leaked many years ago revealed that the authorities had purchased acres of land near Bootle, where, in the event of a plague, over 50,000 bodies will be interred. No doubt there are many more of these secret human-landfill sites in other parts of the country.

PATRIOTIC GHOSTS

Elise, a New Brighton lady in her seventies recently told me a fascinating story about her father George, a young Flying Officer who fought in the Battle of Britain and many other aerial skirmishes of WWII. In the autumn of 1940, Liverpudlian George – who was stationed at a base in one of the southern counties - was sitting, playing cards with a circle of other brave airmen in a so-called "dispersal hut" – from which the pilots were immediately dispatched at short notice to their Spitfires to fight the Luftwaffe. On this particular day, one of the pilots was talking about Bobbo, a friend who had crash-landed on farmland after being shot down "by the Hun". Bobbo had described his rapid fiery plummet to earth, and how he thought of his wife and children as he looked death in the face. Through some miracle, Bobbo pulled back on the controls and glided to an almost perfect landing in a field.

The telephone in the dispersal hut started to ring, and that was a signal for the airmen to scramble to their Spitfires. Within minutes, George was airborne, and for some reason, the face of his patriotic grandfather, Arthur, appeared before his eyes for a few seconds, but George dismissed this vision as a product of mental strain and anxiety. He thought of his wife back at home in Wallasey and even his old cat, Tomkins. He felt so sad as he flew to his destiny, and he was soon in the thick of it. Thousands of feet over Hampshire, a Messerschmitt zipped right into the gunsight and George fired. As the plane spiralled in a strange graceful path to earth trailing black oily smoke,

George wondered if the pilot had a wife and a cat waiting for *him* at home, but before he could start getting sentimental, three loud bangs shook the Spitfire and caused the left wing to burst into flames. He'd been hit. George felt time stand still as the plane went into a dive. He slid back the cockpit hood and the wind blasted his face as he tried to undo his harness, for he intended to bail out – but he couldn't get the harness off and realised his boot was jammed because of the fuselage damage. This was it – he'd either be burned to a crisp or die on impact, but shock affects people in some strange ways, and instead of feeling scared and having maudlin thoughts about his wife, George started to sing *There'll Always Be An England* as he was gripped by an odd mood of patriotic fervour – and suddenly, he saw a man appear next to him. He thought it was some hallucination because of the altitude. The man had a white beard, moustache and a head of wild white hair, flowing – as were the red white and blue robes he wore in the nightmarish descent. He also had the blue cross of St Andrew painted or tattooed upon his bare chest. He turned to George and in the pilot's mind he heard the words: "I am Albion! Britain shall *never* fall!' and the man reached into the cockpit and wrenched back the controls with something that would require superhuman strength. The Spitfire pulled up in the nick of time and skimmed over a field where it landed in a shallow lake. George lived to fight again and again, and he survived the war. He later discovered that Albion was the original ancient name for Britain, and to his dying day he believed that some ghostly personification of our nation, perhaps a Druid, or some ancient British warrior, saved his life that day.

I have had reports of other patriotic ghosts over the years. In December 1995, a 45-year-old long-distance lorry driver named Ken Jeffers set out from a depot in Liverpool one evening, bound for a factory in Ipswich, and this 244-mile journey usually took about four and a half to five hours. About fifty to sixty miles into the journey, Ken was ready to pull his eighteen-wheeler into a service station just beyond Penkridge, for he was feeling peckish and just fancied a steak and kidney pie. Something very strange took place at this point in the journey that baffles Ken to this day. The time was almost one in the morning, but the M6 was unbelievably quiet – almost deserted in fact, and one minute, Ken was at the wheel of his HGV, and then suddenly he was on the hard shoulder, and all about was deadly quiet. Not a single vehicle passed him on the motorway. He coughed, because he thought his ears had been blocked by wax or something, but he could clearly hear the cough. He could not remember how he had arrived at this stretch of the southbound M6 and wondered where the familiar service station was. To his left he could see the full moon in a cloudless sky, and below it in a field covered with frost, there stood a group of silhouetted men, some of them were almost naked, and they looked very eerie just standing there in the moonlight. Ken knew he should have driven on down the motorway, but he had an unaccountable urge to leave the vehicle, and he obeyed this strange longing. He gently closed the cab door and hopped down onto the floor and then he began to make his way to the figures in the field, because he now had a mounting feeling of some nostalgic belonging to them, as if they were old friends. One of the figures in the centre of the group was still in silhouette because the moon was shining down on him from behind, but Ken could make out the hood that the man wore, and he could also see that he held something like a long stick or perhaps a staff of some sort. This man raised his hand as if to acknowledge Ken's approach, and the HGV driver felt this was a greeting. He walked right up to the man and the peculiar figures, and saw that the hooded man was not holding a staff at all, but a longbow. He talked in a language that seemed to be a mixture of English and some other vaguely familiar tongue that was almost like Cornish, with bits of Welsh in it. Ken then realised at this point that the man before him was none other than the legendary Robin Hood, and fabulous memories of an amazing kinship with Robin and his associates came flooding back to Ken, and these recollections made him feel so sad. By the time Robin had embraced him, Ken found himself almost moved to tears. The people with Robin were part of his famed band – known in later ballads as his "Merry Men" but the others with him – the ones who were almost naked – were members of the ancient Cornovii tribe – the mysterious and mystical Celtic People of the Horn, and they regarded Ken with grim painted faces. Robin spoke in a cryptic manner to Ken, and said things like: 'They are disturbing the rest of Arthur down in the south with their diggings and upheavals, and we had to kill some of them. Merlin stirs in his slumbers, and if he awakes, this land will tremble at his wrath.'

Robin then intimated that Ken should use his vehicle as a weapon to destroy the people disturbing the long sleep of Arthur, but Ken said he couldn't do that, because he had a wife and children in this life. 'We called upon you,' Robin told him, 'and we put our faith in you, and you have always shown allegiance to this land.'

'Robin, I love you as a brother,' Ken found himself saying, 'but I cannot wreak havoc this time, I am sorry.'

And all of a sudden, Robin nodded, and bowed his head, and smiled, and then he turned, and he and the uncanny painted men turned and walked off towards a wood, and Ken stood there, watching them leave with tears streaming from his eyes. He felt as if he had betrayed them, but then suddenly, all of the emotions seemed to evaporate and the long-distance lorry driver felt as if he had snapped out of some hypnotic spell. He was standing in the bitter cold in a lonely field in South Staffordshire, and he felt eyes on him. He hurried back to his vehicle and drove for miles until he came to a service station where he had a hot meal and sat collecting his thoughts. He naturally worried about the state of his mind; had all of these long hours of sleep-deprivation on the roads finally taken their toll? He had been lousy at history in school, so how would he have known who the Cornovii tribe were, and how did he feel so connected to Robin Hood? And what on earth was all that about Arthur's resting place being disturbed by digging? Well, later that morning, when Ken was back on the road, he switched on his radio and heard reports about the so-called "Battle of Newbury" waged by over 7,000 protesters who were actively opposing the planned clearance of 360 acres of land – a lot of it woodland – to create the Newbury

Bypass (officially known as the Winchester-Preston Trunk Road) which passes Newbury in Berkshire. The Thames Valley Police and the Hampshire Constabulary had to join forces to tackle the protesters, and over thirty million pounds had to be spent on additional security guards and specialised security fencing to keep the protesters at bay. The protesters were finally defeated and the road was completed by November 1998 at a cost of £104 million. Some believed the bypass was a necessity, but others saw it as another assault on rural England. A number of ancient graves were allegedly disturbed during the construction of the Newbury Bypass, including a mass grave containing the bodies of Roundhead and Cavalier soldiers from a Civil War Battle, and there were reports during this period of phantom voices that were heard to sing unknown songs in the area. There were also outbreaks of poltergeist activity in some places where the excavations were carried out for the bypass, and something overturned a bulldozer and also shook a portakabin with several terrified guards inside. The guards also said their walkie-talkies would often go dead for no reason.

Ken wondered if this massive excavation project had disturbed the 'sleep' of King Arthur, who, according to an ancient tradition, is said to be sleeping in a form of suspended animation beneath the earth, awaiting the time when his country needs him.

Before I end this chapter on patriotic ghosts, Ken's experience of reliving some previous life reminds me of a certain well-known radio DJ we shall call Ian (not his real name) who once told me of a group of similar experiences he had of reincarnation when he was in his teens. When Ian was ten years old, he went down the subway on Lime Street with a can of aerosol paint and began to spray all sorts of graffiti and rude phallic sketches on the walls, and all of a sudden, he found himself in a cave of some sort, and he was drawing a picture of a stag on the wall with some sort of stick made of some black substance. As he sketched the antlers of the stag, Ian felt as if he was some Stone Age boy, but then he found himself back in the subway under Lime Street with the aerosol can in his hand. Years later, Ian opened a book at school and saw photographs of the famous Palaeolithic paintings of animals and people found on the walls of the Lascaux Caves in southwestern France. These images were painted around 17,300 years ago, yet Ian felt as if he knew the paintings well, and one of them instantly caught his eye: the one of a stag with its spreading black antlers, sketched by an ancient Stone Age artist using mineral pigments. Some of the images were also engraved into the cave walls. Ian had other flashback to his previous life. On one occasion he was walking home from a football match with a crowd of supporters, and they all started to get a bit rowdy and started pounding on windows and doors of the street they were passing through, as well as running over parked cars. As all of this rowdiness was going on, Ian found himself with a huge tribe of wild-looking men with long hair, going on the rampage through some village. Some of the wild men grabbed women, picked them up, threw them over their shoulders and ran off with them, and then the scene reverted to the modern day again. Eventually, as Ian left his teens, these bizarre flashbacks became less frequent, and then ceased all together. Perhaps Ian was somehow tapping into racial memory – also known as genetic memory. This hypothetical memory is a record of all the previous memories, ideas and feeling of our ancestors that is somehow accessed in certain states of consciousness. Alternatively, perhaps Ian had been reincarnated several times and was recalling memories from past lives he had led.

THE WHEEL OF DEATH

In the mid-1960s a convoy of coloured trucks and cars snaked into Speke and a fairground appeared overnight near to the ponds on Clough Road. Young and old were drawn by the Waltzes, the sweet aroma of pink beehive candyfloss, the red and white striped barberpole helter-skelter, the caterpillar rides, the big dipper and the high striker, where you tested your strength by smashing a hammer down on a lever mechanism which propelled a puck up a tower to hopefully strike the bell at the top. And then there were the dozens of stalls where you could win goldfish in clear plastic bags if you landed a hoop on a certain peg or shot the heart out of a playing card with a magazine of pellets fired in machine-gun succession from an air rifle. In this fairground there was even something for the romantic – The Wheel of Love and Fortune – a huge wooden wheel about twelve feet in diameter that was spun by a woman dressed as cupid if you laid a shilling in her palm. That wheel would tell you the star sign of your future husband or wife as well as the colour of their hair and eyes. Cupid spun the wheel and the indicator arrow would settle on one of the 12 signs of the Zodiac and light up its corresponding coloured lightbulb. Cupid would even yell out the first name of your future partner – the one you were fated to marry.

A 12-year-old boy named Phillip who came to the fair that summer fell in love with cupid, even though she was twice his age. He would stand there at the Wheel for ages, watching Cupid spinning it. He waited there one day till it got dark and his mother and sisters all the way over in Halewood went out looking for him after he failed to return by 8pm. Phillip saw something very strange at the Speke fairground that evening. The Wheel of Love and Fortune changed after dark, and his crush Cupid, was replaced by a man dressed in a skeleton suit. Now the attraction was called The Wheel of Death, and a gaggle of curious and morbidly bemused people gathered around it and a few offered the operator of the Wheel – Mr Death – a shilling to see how they would meet their end – in the coming month. The Wheel was divided into many sections, some said 32, others thought they recalled 33 or more, and each section labelled the many ways to die, from hanging to heart attack, from cancer to coma, and so on, and once you paid your shilling, Mr Death would grip the Wheel and send it spinning, and the arrow in the middle of the device would also spin. Wherever that arrow rested, a lighbulb would go on, indicating the macabre word next to it. One of the first to volunteer was a young man of about eighteen who had been skitting at Mr Death with a bunch of friends. Mr Death had a well-spoken and slightly effeminate voice, and the gang of youths thought he sounded 'queer' and told him so. This *was* the mid-1960s and people routinely used such homophobic words without even a second thought. One of the gang therefore offered Mr Death a shilling, and the plan was to give the masked fairground worker a good hiding later on and snatch his takings.

'What is your name, sir?' Death asked the mocking young man who was giggling with his friends.

'Harry!' the young man replied, and his four friends

burst out laughing.

Death held his gloved hand out, and Harry placed the shilling piece in that black leather love.

Death gave a little bow, then put the shilling in his belted purse and placed his gloved hand on the rough-wooded red and yellow wheel. He shouted: 'We come into this world but one way, from the pomegranate womb of a mother, and we slip out of that womb or are prised out through a Caesarean cut, but there are countless ways to die, and in the Devil's name I ask, how will Harry leave this world? Will he be crushed, torn or smothered, murdered or choked, or will he die old in his bed? Will he die in a war, or will he be hanged? There is only one who can say! Will he be fried, or commit suicide or will cancer eat him away?'

This spiel made Harry feel cold, and it was that shuddering coldness people describe when they say someone has just walked over their grave. He wanted his shilling back, for he knew this was a bad idea, but Death had already spun the wheel, and before a mesmerised crowd of about fifty people he watched the great wheel turn with a click-clacking sound, and the red arrow radiating from a double-faced woman – the Goddess of Life and Death who looks into the past with one pair of eyes and into the future with the eyes on her second face – and that arrow moved in the opposite direction to the clockwise turning wheel. That wheel did not just come to a gentle halt like a roulette wheel, it suddenly and inexplicably stopped dead with a resounding click, And the arrow locked onto the slot marked 'FIRE' and the bulb burnt beside it.

'Death by fire within a month!' yelled Death in a

happy sort of voice as if he was announcing a forthcoming wedding. 'Blackened bones and melted flesh, a terrible way to meet your death!' he pointed to Harry, who suddenly shouted: 'It's a swindle! I want me money back you stupid blouse!'

A lad of about fifteen snatched his younger brother's shilling from his hand and said he wanted to know how he'd die, but the lad's girlfriend screamed, 'No Johnny! No!'

Johnny had had a row with his 13-year-old girlfriend Maureen, and was feeling sorry for himself. He was always threatening to kill himself (but not for one moment intending to) and this was a great way to get back at her for looking at another boy. 'Before you ask me name is Johnny, and I want to know how I will die!'

Death took the shilling from him and Maureen seized Death's arm, and was about to plead with him to stop, but when her small white soft hands touched the rough black cloth of his costume, she felt ice cold and in her mind's eye she was besieged with a crowd of horrific crying and screaming faces; some were disfigured and some had no eyes, and when she later recalled the most horrific of these faces to her mother, Maureen's meagre powers of description could only compare the poor child to having a head like a broken blackcurrant pie with a face for a crust; a broken crust dripping dark red matter. Maureen felt as if these children had all died cruel and unimaginable agonising deaths over many years, and that Mr Death had somehow had a hand in their fate. And so, that evening, Maureen recoiled in horror from Mr Death, and noticed that his eyes seemed dark and cold behind the skull mask. He spun the Wheel of Death, and now there were almost a hundred people watching, and the red arrow pointing from the Death Goddess in the hub of the wheel flew counter-clockwise as the wheel rumbled in the other direction. Johnny felt his bowels give way as if he was about to defecate on the spot, and he shook his head and shouted: 'No, wait! I changed me mind, I changed me mind!'

The wheel stopped dead and then came the click as the bulb burned bright next to the yellow labelled sign which read: BEHEADING.

Maureen hugged a sobbing Johnny and Death stunned everyone by pointing to Johnny's little brother, Mick. 'Death by beheading within a month to you!' he pointed to the bewildered-looking child, who stood there as every face turned towards him. Then Death mused: 'Head on the ground, the only sound is the trickle of blood from the neck. A rolling head, and he is dead, a quick way to meet your death!'

Maureen released a terrible scream that made the entire crowd of ghouls jump and set the little boy Mick crying. 'No! He's only six!'

'I thought you were supposed to be telling me when *I* die, not him!' Johnny cried, and he crouched to pick up his hysterical brother.

'You gave me *his* money, didn't you?' Death said coldly, and Johnny recalled that this was so – he had snatched the prized shilling from Mick, the one he had refused to part with all day, given to the boy by his Auntie Mary.

'I'm reporting you to the police, mate!' someone in the crowd shouted, and then Harry, who would supposedly die by fire, chipped in: 'And he's a nancy boy as well! We'll be back tomorrow mate and we'll turn you over!' Harry threatened, and spat at the Wheel operator.

As unbelievable as it seems, people queued up to have their grim fortunes foretold, and people were told they would die in comas, in car crashes and that they would be drowned. They would die in their sleep within weeks, and some would succumb to tuberculosis, pneumonia and heart attack. The black-horoscope operator, the tricksy Mr Death - whoever he was behind that skeleton suit and skull mask - must have raked in a fortune. By day, the Wheel always changed to the romantic one operated by the curvaceous Cupid so beloved by Phillip, but once twilight gathered over the skies of Speke, the Wheel of Death and its infamous operator seemed to just appear out of nowhere. Word got round about the deplorable way a mere boy of six had been terrified by talk of decapitation, and plans were made to have the macabre attraction closed down and the operator fined, but before these plans could gain momentum, something very eerie took place. Little Mick, the boy who had been doomed to decapitation by the Wheel, was playing by a certain road in Liverpool the following day, and a boy challenged him to a game of Dare. The dare was to lay on the pavement with your head sticking out over the kerb, and you were to keep it there till a car came close to hitting you. And Mick was sadly naïve to the dangers of this dare and obviously lacked worldly experience to know that this game was exceedingly dangerous. He and three slightly older boys lay on the pavement with their chins just over the edge of the kerbstone and waited for a vehicle to approach, but a car didn't come down the road, a bus did. And when it was within about twenty feet, the older boys slid away, but, Mick had noticed a penny someone had dropped in the gutter and suddenly there was a muffled thump and an spray of pinkish blood, followed by screams from witnesses that seemed to go on without end.

And what of Harry, who would meet a death by fire, according to the ominous wheel? Sure enough, he siphoned petrol from his uncle's car into an empty milk bottle and went to a piece of secluded wasteland with his friends and set about pouring the petrol all over a massive wigwam of wood and old carpets obtained from the local back alleyways. A policeman in the distance spotted the mound of bonfire wood and shouted a warning, and Harry's friends fled. Harry threw the empty milk bottle down, took out his box of Swan Vesta matches and as the copper hurried over the wasteland towards him, he took out a single match and struck it. He threw it onto the wood from what he imagined was a safe distance of about five feet. Harry did not know how petrol behaved. When you pour it onto wood or anything you wish to burn, some of it trickles down onto the ground and spreads out into a very fine layer of evaporating gas which can crawl up your trousers without you even knowing it, and this form of partially evaporated petrol, mingled with the air, is the most explosive. And so, the bonfire ignited with a 'whumph!' sound, and a barely visible disc of blue flame expanded from the base of the bonfire, and it went up the teenager's trousers and within moments he was not only on fire, he was almost impossible to extinguish. His first reaction was to pat himself with his palms but that just made the flames spread more rapidly about his person. He fell to the floor, in shock, with his nylon jacket melting into his skin, and he let out screams many will remember till the day they die. The policeman took off his jacket and threw it over Harry but it was no use, the boy was as good as dead from shock alone, and had he lived he would have met an agonising end from septicaemia – a form of blood-poisoning many blaze victims die of when they are rescued from the flames. A crowd of people circled the burning body and saw how the flames had burnt his hair to a blackened and red raw scalp, and the boy's mouth remained open in a heart rendering expression of the extreme agony he had died from. Straight away, people recalled the chilling prophecy of the Wheel of Death. Other deaths linked to that wheel were reported over the coming days, and a mob of concerned locals led by a certain reverend went to the fairground to confront the shocking and tasteless fairground operator to have the Wheel of Death shut down, but when they reached the fair near Clough Road, there was no sign of Mr Death or his terrifying wheel, and the fairground boss said he had never heard of anyone operating such an appalling and outrageous moneymaking device on his patch. Where the Wheel of Death had stood there was only a small square of grass. If you ask some people over the age of fifty if they recall the sinister Wheel, you may hear of firsthand accounts of this fairground shocker. It was seen at a fair in Newsham Park as late as 1970 and I have talked to people who recall seeing it and other similar novelties with as much bad taste in Wavertree Park and the outskirts of St Helens. Just how Mr

Death was able to divine the many ways a person could die is unknown, but then I suspect that Mr Death was not just an ordinary person…

Printed in Great Britain
by Amazon